There's a Business in

EVERY WOMAN

There's a Business in

EVERY WOMAN

Ann M. Holmes

A 7-Step Guide to Discovering,
Starting, and Building the
Business of Your Dreams

BALLANTINE BOOKS   NEW YORK

Published in the United States by Ballantine Books,
an imprint of The Random House Publishing Group,
a division of Random House, Inc., New York.

BALLANTINE and colophon are registered trademarks
of Random House, Inc.

Grateful acknowledgment to the Center for Women's Business Research
for permission to reprint five of the graphs in this book.

LIBRARY OF CONGRESS CATALOGING-IN-PUBLICATION DATA

Holmes, Ann M.
There's a business in every woman : a 7-step guide to discovering, starting,
and building the business of your dreams / Ann M. Holmes.
p.   cm.
Includes bibliographical references and index.
ISBN-13: 978-1-4000-6488-5
1. New business enterprises—United States—Case studies.   2. Women-
owned business enterprises—United States—Management—Case studies.
3. Entrepreneurship—United States—Case studies.   4. Businesswomen—
United States—Case studies.   I. Title.
HD62.5.H642 2007
658.1'1082—dc22   2006042950

Printed in the United States of America on acid-free paper

www.ballantinebooks.com

9 8 7 6 5 4 3 2 1

First Edition

Book design by Jo Anne Metsch

To my husband, Tom
His encouragement and support made this book possible.

And for my nieces,
Meghan Carroll, Erica Holmes, and Caitlin Holmes

They inspire me to inspire them.

CONTENTS

Is There a Business in You?

Yes! There are millions of American women who started and are running their own companies. How does it happen? Could you become one too? This book is for all of those women, like me and the women I interviewed, who never dreamed of becoming the CEO of their own company. We never went to business school and for the most part none of us had any professional financial services experience either. We started our companies for a variety of reasons: Some of us found ourselves saying, "I can do that, and I can do it better!" In other instances, we felt we needed more flexibility in our schedules. Still others of us sought extra cash or wanted a way to fill our free time.

We learned the most important lesson early on, though: Once you have your own business, whether you're running your enterprise off your dining room table, out of your basement or garage, or from professional office space, there are a crucial set of steps to follow that can help you make smart business decisions all along the way. In hindsight most of us wish we had known the necessary steps to operating a solid, stable business—even a small one—and what can go wrong when you don't follow them. That's what this book is all about. In it, more than eighty women entrepreneurs share their start-up stories, telling you what steps they mastered and where they tripped in the process of turning their little business idea into serious money. These entrepreneurs also talk candidly about the challenges unique to women entrepreneurs: understanding the importance of and obtaining professional financing, from bank loans (even if you don't need one), to accessing venture capital; balancing business and babies; appreciating the value of a good mentor and networking successfully (like the "old boys" do); and learning how to build and position your company successfully in the marketplace, so that if and when the time comes, you're prepared and ready for the deal of a lifetime. By reading these inspiring, exciting, and sometimes turbulent stories, you'll learn how to transform your fledgling company—or even your pipe dream—into a profit machine that rewards you financially, and allows you to achieve your personal and professional goals. And who knows, maybe one day you'll do as some of us did: We found the business within—and became millionaires along the way!

—*Ann M. Holmes*

There's a Business in
EVERY WOMAN

CHAPTER 1

How Do You Know if There's a Business in You?

How do you know if you have a business in you? And how do you find it? Interestingly, after talking to many women from around the country, it's clear to me that businesswomen are born every day in every type of business; only the particular circumstances that led each woman to start her own firm varies. In the United States alone, approximately 11 million women own or are equal partners in their own companies, contributing nearly $2.5 trillion annually to the American economy and providing jobs for more than 19 million people (see figure 1). Despite this financial heft, most of us started out as ordinary "working Jills"—teachers, nurses, meeting planners—when we decided to try it on our own. In the beginning, many of us ran our budding enterprises from home before going out to compete in the business world. Whether or not you know it, you have a business in you—if any of the following sentiments sound familiar to you:

- I can make that product better than the people who make it now
- I don't see what I need on the market, so I'll create it
- I know how to save my husband's company
- The family firm needs my help
- Forget corporate life. I want a day job I love!
- Now that I've been laid off, I'd better get a new job fast
- My clients are encouraging me to go out on my own
- I need more flexibility in my schedule and a solid income
- To support my family, I have to make more money
- I'll let my husband stay home with the kids
- I need something to do to keep boredom away

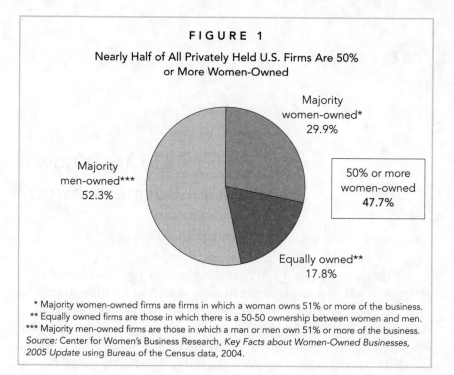

FIGURE 1

Nearly Half of All Privately Held U.S. Firms Are 50%
or More Women-Owned

Majority
women-owned*
29.9%

Majority
men-owned***
52.3%

50% or more
women-owned
47.7%

Equally owned**
17.8%

* Majority women-owned firms are firms in which a woman owns 51% or more of the business.
** Equally owned firms are those in which there is a 50-50 ownership between women and men.
*** Majority men-owned firms are those in which a man or men own 51% or more of the business.
Source: Center for Women's Business Research, *Key Facts about Women-Owned Businesses,
2005 Update* using Bureau of the Census data, 2004.

Going Out on My Own

My own career as an entrepreneur began inadvertently. After working for
nearly a year for a political science journal where I learned basic editorial
work, I realized that I was itching to try something else. I began my job
search by registering with a New York editorial and publishing placement
agency, which lined up my first interview at a major publishing house. Despite my excitement, I failed to get a job offer by misspelling the word "em-
barrassed," an embarrassing mistake I never made again. Next, the agency
sent me out to a small medical communications company. I had no clue
what such companies do, nor was I confident that my college biology
course work would see me through an in-depth medical-editorial interview, but I went nevertheless. It was a buzzing office, filled with young, enthusiastic medical writers, staff physicians, and production workers, and
run by a managing editor who herself was barely thirty. I knew right away
that I wanted the job, and I was delighted when the offer came in.

After four years there I went to work as a managing editor at a New York
City medical magazine. From there, I moved to a managerial position in

another, larger medical communications company. Another four years passed, and I decided that I now knew enough to run such a company on my own. For me, the advantages to starting my own firm seemed clear: more control over my own schedule and the opportunity to earn a lot more money. I resigned my management post and joined forces with two partners to start my first medical communications company, TransMedica, Inc., in May 1981. We sold our company to CBS, Inc., in 1984, for millions.

This turn of events was about as unplanned a professional course as one could imagine. I certainly never set out to start, build, and sell medical communications companies. I simply stumbled into a field of business I had never even heard of before my job interview. Despite the random nature of this chance, and notwithstanding my lack of a graduate medical or business degree, I managed to start and sell my first medical communications company with nine years' experience, and to sell it within three years. I went on to start three more companies in the same field, and sold two of them.

Is my story unique? Not really. What I discovered when I set out to write this book was that there are millions of women out there who have career paths and success stories similar to mine, and no doubt many more entrepreneurial women are waiting in the wings, dreaming about the day they will launch their new ventures. As such, I thought it worthwhile to draw upon my professional experiences starting and selling companies, as well as the experiences of successful women business owners around the country, and put together a book for women entrepreneurs to help them navigate the steps to business success.

The Story of Finding the Business Within

A job finding jobs for others. Suzanne Collins, for instance, never thought much about starting her own company. Burned out from selling cosmetics for Estée Lauder and other beauty companies, Suzanne had no idea what to do next. A colleague working in the professional recruitment industry put Suzanne in touch with a headhunting firm, which hired her for its Dallas office. Soon she was placed in charge of a new venture, a human resources consulting group to be test-marketed in Dallas. Her boss gave her a corner of the office, a desk, and some rudimentary office supplies, and told her to get started. That experience taught Suzanne that she could run her own business. With these scant resources, she built an internal staff as well as a database of clients. "One day," Suzanne says, "I simply woke up and realized: I may as well try this on my own. I can pay myself the same measly salary, and get the same uncomfortable chair, and do it on my own." With that, at thirty years of age, Suzanne opened CareerLink in February 2000. Today, Dallas-based CareerLink does more than $5 million in annual revenue and has twenty full-time employees.

Car-accident karma. Judy Wicks's path was even more serendipitous than Suzanne's. After college, Judy married her childhood sweetheart and moved to Alaska with him to be a VISTA (Volunteers in Service to America) volunteer. When their tour of duty was up, they went to visit friends in Philadelphia, where they noticed a lack of good stores for students. With $3,000, they opened the Free People Store, living in the back of the shop to hold expenses down. (The store later grew into the national retail chain Urban Outfitters.)

But Judy soon realized that she had to leave her husband, whom she had known since she was ten years old. She loaded up her car and began driving away. A half a block later, Judy got into a car accident. She wasn't hurt, but the car was useless. Another driver stopped to ask her if she wanted a ride. What she really needed, she told the stranger, was a job, as she was now homeless, carless, and nearly penniless. The man told her that the restaurant where he worked was looking for another waitress. "So when anyone asks me how I got into the restaurant business, I always say by accident," Judy says.

In her new job Judy went from waitress to general manager, ultimately running the restaurant for ten years. Then she left and started White Dog Café, a small muffin and coffee takeout shop on the first floor of her house in Philadelphia. Judy's new business provided her with an income, and let her spend time with her then two- and four-year-old children. Today, Judy owns five houses: three for White Dog and two for her second venture, the Black Cat Gift Shop. The two companies now employ more than 100 people, serve 200 customers in the restaurant daily, and gross north of $5 million a year.

Inventing an industry. At the age of twenty-five, Angela Drummond turned an office job into her own business in a new market. Trained in fashion merchandising, the Virginia native decided to stay close to home after college rather than move to New York, as she had planned. She began a career in consulting in the Washington, D.C., suburbs, where she first heard about collaborative meeting software. An innovation at the time, the early 1990s, such software allowed people to hold meetings on-line, cutting down on travel and allowing greater project collaboration. Angela and two female colleagues saw this technology's promise, and after testing the software on a consulting project for the U.S. Army, they saw that it worked well as a way to foster consensus on tough internal issues, such as those among different ranks of soldiers. The three women built a case for starting a new company based on the collaboration software and presented it to their firm's management. But the bosses dismissed the idea: "No, girls, there's no market there." Angela and her colleagues looked at each other and said, "They're crazy! We can do this!"

Rather than give up on their idea, the women began meeting at night and on weekends to plan for their new business providing the software and consulting services. They incorporated in August 1992 as Structured Solutions, Inc., and landed their first government contract, with the Department of Defense, three months later. After twelve years in business, Angela is still president and CEO of the company, now called SiloSmashers.

Creating the Product You Need

From the Post-it note to the all-inclusive diaper bag, all of us have at one point thought that we could have invented a useful product ourselves. We all dream of being entrepreneurs. Many women, frustrated at not finding something that fits their needs, come up with their own solution, and then turn their idea into a profitable business. If you have an idea but think you can never turn it into a successful business, consider how these women spun an inspiration into a company.

A runner's best friend. Hinda Miller's story typifies how some women can see a market need and from there create a booming business, one that was never on their radar screens when they first went to work. A costume designer by training, Hinda was living in Vermont, where she designed costumes for the University of Vermont's Champlain Shakespeare Festival. This was during the late 1970s, as the jogging craze was sweeping the country. One day, she and two women friends, back from a jog, wondered aloud why a better bra wasn't available for women runners. From South Carolina, where she had moved to teach costume design for two years, Hinda and her partner, Lisa Lindahl, developed a prototype running bra

from a pair of men's jockstraps sewn together, and lined up a manufacturer. (A third partner left after the design stage and wound up designing
costumes for the Muppets!)

In 1978, Hinda, then twenty-eight, and Lisa, twenty-nine, went to their
first trade show, the National Sporting Goods Association Show in
Chicago, to exhibit their new product. They pinned up the JogBra on a
piece of canvas that they draped and secured across a coat rack, along with
an article that had recently appeared in the *New York Post*, picturing a
Playboy bunny wearing a JogBra.

In the company's early years, the pair tried to move from such improvi-
sations to a more rigorous and formal business structure. Hinda borrowed
$30,000 from her father to start the company, SLS, Inc., which later be-
came Jogbra, Inc., and then JBI, Inc. She and Lisa secured loans from the
Small Business Administration. They also agreed that product design and
manufacturing was Hinda's bailiwick while Lisa would cover sales. Overall, they developed eight different JogBra styles. Playtex bought the company for millions, after Hinda and Lisa were in business twelve years.

Hinda didn't set out to make a product, build an empire, or earn millions. What she did do was zero in on a market niche, centered around
one of her passions—jogging—and develop a product that would make
jogging more comfortable and enjoyable for women.

A shooting epiphany. When Doreen Marks was a high school junior in
1985, her father took her on a hunting trip one Saturday afternoon in upstate New York. Doreen started out trailing after her father in the damp,
snowy woods, and it wasn't long before she took a tumble, plunging her
firearm into the snow and mud. Her father hadn't brought any gun-
cleaning equipment, and when she returned to the hunting camp, she
found no supplies for getting the dirt off her gun.

At home, she looked around for her grandfather's old World War II gun
accessories, focusing in on a chain with a weight on the end. She took this
tool along on her next hunting trip, packed in a shoe-polish tin, and used
it to clean her gun in the field.

Doreen continued to tinker with different parts and she soon came up
with a new concept for a field cleaning system. By the time her father went
to the Shot Show, the industry's largest trade show, a short time later,
Doreen convinced him to take a booth for her so she could test-market her
eight prototypes. He got a ten- by ten-foot booth, and Doreen's mother
agreed to go along and staff the booth with her daughter. But the show's or-
ganizers stopped Doreen at the door, telling her that no one under eigh-

teen could enter. Undeterred, Doreen went back outside, put on too much makeup, and smiled her way back into the show.

The kits attracted the attention of several large distributors from around the state, who placed orders for the product. By the end of the show, her father told her, "You've got to start making and selling those things." Doreen hired four high school friends to make the kits at her parents' kitchen table. Even after she graduated early from high school and started college, she spent her nights attending class and her days running the business, which she named OTIS Technology, a family name that coincidentally stands for Outstanding Technology, Innovation, and Service. With help from the Small Business Administration she secured a patent for her kit. By 1990, Doreen moved the company out of the kitchen and into a horse barn on her parents' property.

Today, thirty-nine-year-old Doreen is raising two teenagers while running OTIS, where she remains president and CEO. OTIS has more than sixty full-time employees, 150 sales representatives nationwide, distributors in several countries, and more than thirty patents. In 2005 the Small Business Administration recognized Doreen as one of its five top U.S. women small business owners.

Helping Your Husband, Boosting Your Own Career

Sometimes the catalyst that turns women into CEOs is a crisis involving their husbands' jobs. Frequently it is the wife, not the beleaguered husband, who has the spark to start a company using her own marketing and administrative skills coupled with her husband's expertise to create a new business.

Building a modular business. When Wayne Lawrence arrived one morning at a construction company he owned with a partner to find the doors padlocked, his thirty-seven-year-old wife, Gail Warrior, faced a family dilemma that would reshape her professional life. An accountant by training, Gail had been at Mobil for eight years while Wayne worked in the construction industry, eventually launching his own firm, with a partner, to do underground jobs, such as laying fiber-optic cable. Gail had seen signs of trouble in the partnership, and she had tried unsuccessfully to persuade Wayne to abandon ship. But Wayne stuck with it until the day he found the company had gone under without his knowledge.

The couple was at a loss: Gail hated her Mobil job, Wayne wasn't sure what he should do next, and both were worried about paying their bills. Then Gail had an idea. They could start their own company using Wayne's sales skills and expertise with modular buildings and her own marketing and accounting skills. In early 1999, Gail and Wayne took 750 square feet of space, hired their first full-time employee, and formed The Warrior Group, with Gail as president and CEO. Today the DeSoto, Texas, company occupies a 10,000-square-foot modular building and generates more than $50 million in revenue with twenty-two employees. Unique among modular contractors, The Warrior Group is certified as both a minority-owned and woman-owned business. (These designations allow businesspeople to compete for contracts from the government or from companies that have diverse-supplier policies.)

A family company that both spouses enjoy. Beverly Gray dropped out of college after her sophomore year to keep her summer job at the long-distance provider MCI. In five years she doubled her salary; MCI was so impressed with her, they paid for her to take additional computer classes. But when she and her husband, Mike, decided to start a family, Beverly chose to quit her job. The couple cut back on expenses and refinanced their house so they could afford to live on Mike's salary from his job managing exhibits for clients.

But Mike's job became increasingly stressful, and he grew unhappy. One day in August 1992, Mike came home and announced to his wife that he had quit his job. He took on housepainting projects and other short-term gigs, but it was clear to both of them that he needed a new career. Then, a former client called to ask Mike to manage an exhibit. Mike's former employer got wind of it and didn't want Mike to do it. But Beverly and Mike discussed it, and in the end decided to start their own exhibit-management company. Beverly knew this meant that Mike would be traveling a good deal, but she felt that her corporate experience, coupled with her organizational and computer skills, would make theirs a good partnership.

Despite having fallen into entrepreneurship when she had planned to stay home with her two children, Beverly has become the driving force behind the Fairfax, Virginia–based Exhibit Edge, Inc. The couple's children will leave for college soon, but Beverly feels her career is just beginning. While Mike would be happy maintaining the company's revenue at its current $3 million level, Beverly says she's "gearing up to grow Exhibit Edge to a $10 million business within three years."

A Job That Gives You Your Soul Back

Many women dream of the perfect corporate job. For those who snag it, many later wish they could do something more independent, something that stirs their passion. Companies are born from this desire.

Staffing herself. Lynne Marie Finn's father always impressed upon her that a woman should be able to take care of herself financially. She always planned to become a doctor or a lawyer in order to be self-sufficient. Her first job after law school was as a litigator in a Buffalo, New York, firm, followed by a stint in the district attorney's office. As she rose higher in the legal ranks, her father tried to convince her to join a small group of companies he had started. Lynne was tired of litigation, and decided to join her father's company as legal counsel. She soon realized how much she liked working for one company and seeing it grow, rather than working as a hired gun for a long roster of clients.

As Lynne was working for her father, her mother used a small inheritance to buy one of the companies in the group, Superior Staffing Services, a clerical and administrative worker placement firm. She hired a female executive to run it for her, giving her a 5 percent stake in return. In 1987, after three years as the parent company's general counsel, Lynne herself became president of Superior Staffing. Under her leadership the company has grown from $2 million in annual revenue to many times that amount, with more than 150 full-time employees in twenty-five cities nationwide.

Business with a gourmet flair. Nancy Milby always loved cooking. But in her day job, she was a CPA, working at KPMG for seventeen years. Tapped to become chief financial officer of a small venture-capital-backed health care firm, Nancy helped the company grow from $1 million to $20 million in revenue. Then she asked the venture capitalists for a new challenge. They found her a new job restoring financial discipline to another small, growing company. There, Nancy realized what she needed: a position that not only let her enjoy the thrill of a start-up business, but also meshed with her own passions. Nancy concluded that life was too short for her to neglect pursuing her dream—in her case, cooking. She quit her financial job to start a culinary school in the resort town of Laguna Beach, California.

Rather than simply providing demonstration cooking classes, Nancy thought it would be more attractive to offer hands-on cooking experiences in a kitchen. She found a location overlooking the ocean and hired chefs to teach courses. Today Laguna Culinary Arts has eleven employees and thirty part-timers. The company offers professional chef training programs, caters corporate team-building exercises and incentive-rewards events, and teaches cooking to students. Overall, more than 8,000 students have taken classes. Revenue is more than $1 million per year, and Nancy, the CEO, is much happier now than she ever was in her two decades of working as an accountant.

A sweeter deal. In her twenty years in commercial banking, Joan Coukos kept with her the memory of her first job, as a banker to entrepreneurs. As a young M.B.A., she admired "the independence they had, pursuing their dreams. Even back then," she says, "I registered that I really wished I could do that someday, but I was never sure I would have the means, or the guts."

Instead, she followed a corporate path, moving around the world, working at four banks, and living through three layoffs. She spent time at Barclays, worked as a consultant to companies trying to do business in Russia, and moved to Moscow to work for Chase Manhattan. When her position was eliminated three years later, she landed at a German bank in Moscow. At the end of that job, she moved back to New York to take a private banking job at Chase. The new position didn't seem terribly exciting after her years in Moscow; she felt "like a cog in a wheel," she says, especially when, on her first day, the company issued her a cell phone, pager, and Palm Pilot. Within four months of her return to New York, Chase announced plans to merge with JP Morgan. As a new hire, and a fairly expensive and senior staffer, Joan knew she was vulnerable to another layoff.

She took off on vacation to Brussels in December 2000 as Chase began laying off workers in New York. On her first day touring the city, Joan visited an antiques market and came upon a stall of silvery metal chocolate molds. Intrigued, she couldn't put the 100-year-old molds down. She had to learn how to make chocolates. As she ran her fingers over the molds, she imagined herself running her own store. Perhaps she could be a high-quality chocolatier. A friend snapped her photo next to the stall, marking what became a new chapter in her life.

Although Joan managed to hold on to her banking job for another ten months, she began making chocolates at home once a month. A week after she was laid off, Enron declared bankruptcy, making her $18,000 investment in the energy company's stock worthless. Joan was sick of other people controlling her destiny. It was time to start her own company. After spending the following year doing research, taking courses on how to start a food business, and learning more about chocolate making, in November 2003 Joan launched her business, Chocolat Moderne, in New York City.

Lynne, Nancy, and Joan are the only women featured in this book who set out to earn formal degrees in business subjects and enter a specialized, professional field. But rather than stick with their planned paths in law, accounting, and finance, all three chose instead to leave the corporate world and risk entrepreneurship, making their education just another line on their resumes rather than a career qualifier. You don't need a business degree to run a business. Even with one, Joan is still growing her company the way all entrepreneurs must: by turning hard work into profit.

Life After Layoffs

When you work for someone else, getting laid off or fired is always a lurking threat, but it doesn't have to be the end of your career. Some women have turned their newfound unemployment into an opportunity to start something new.

Fired but fearless. When Sandy LeTourneau left Minnesota after a nasty divorce, she landed in Beaumont, Texas, where she stayed with friends until she could rebuild her life. A friend, Tom, got her an office job in the orthotics and prosthetics company where he worked. Although she was working as a secretary, Tom taught her about the business, a completely new field to her.

Then, one week in the spring of 1994, Tom's wife left him. That same week the company where Sandy and Tom worked was sold, and they both got pink slips. In the midst of a frantic job search, Sandy and Tom decided to gamble on their own ability to start a company doing what they had been doing all along. Tom had $5,000 in severance pay, and Sandy had an American Express card. With these meager assets, and no business expertise, they established LeTourneau Lifelike Orthotics & Prosthetics, Inc.

The new company quickly ran into trouble. In October, flooding hit the Houston area. Sandy and Tom—who later married—lost everything but a bed, a TV, a sofa, and a lawn chair. When Sandy put the sofa out in the sun to dry, scavengers stole it. After a summer with no furniture, working out of the trunks of their cars, Sandy and Tom rented an old house in the business district as their first office. The office was half-painted, with wiring dangling from the ceiling. Sandy cried a lot, but the company needed office space, and this space was what they could afford. At the same time, the new firm, held in Sandy's name, hit delays in Medicare processing that delayed their payments. They sank $450,000 into debt. "I was scared to death," Sandy says. What kept her going, she says, was her in-grained Minnesota work ethic: "If the cows come in to be milked, they just don't go away. Do you have a broken leg or a cold? It doesn't matter. You just have to go out to milk the cows."

Eventually things turned around for Sandy. The company now has several offices and more than $3 million in revenue.

A New Venture to Satisfy Old Clients

Sometimes you don't realize you want to start your own company until your clients ask you to go out on your own. This avenue of entrepreneur-ship comes with a ready-made roster of customers, but it has its own chal-lenges for women who have never run a business.

Research pays off. Jozi Legner began working for engineering firms when she was fifteen years old. She loved the deadline-driven research that civil engineering firms require. Her organizational skills and her ability to quickly ferret out what the engineers needed helped her build a reputa-tion as a reliable retriever of information. When an engineering firm de-signs a wastewater treatment plant, for example, or works on plans for a new sewer line, the engineers need the parcel information about the tracts of land so that they can acquire easements from those who own nearby property.

Jozi was happy working in the wastewater storm drainage department of a midsize Louisville, Kentucky, engineering firm, when she realized that she was getting increasing numbers of research requests from other depart-ments within the company. When she answered their requests rapidly, her clients encouraged her to go out on her own and start a research-service company. She wondered, though, if she could handle the headaches of owning her own company. But then a thirty-eight-year-old colleague lost her battle with cancer, jolting Jozi into recognizing how short life can be. She also realized that although entrepreneurship can be stressful, her cur-rent job was just as taxing.

Finally, in 1999, Jozi took her clients' advice. At the age of thirty-four, she and a partner ten years her junior, civil engineer Matthew Linville, in-corporated as J.Y. Legner Associates, Inc., a Minority Business Enter-prise/Women Business Enterprise (MBE/WBE)–certified firm. Today their services include engineering support, human resources management, and staffing for engineering companies.

Garbage In, Profits Out

New to Sellersville, Pennsylvania, where she had moved to get married, Susan Daywitt took a job selling advertising space for Yellow Pages in 1984. When it became obvious that she hated the job, her largest advertiser, a waste management company, tried to poach her. In 1987 she finally took the company's owner up on his offer, accepting a sales job with him. She worked there for three years until, dissatisfied again, she struck a deal with her boss to work part-time while she spent more time with her young child. She also set to work on her own business, which she ran out of her house and her car. The start-up, an independent waste contractor, handled small projects for larger companies, including her former employer. Then, in October 1992, Susan met Porter Bush, who worked for the fast-food chain Boston Market. He asked if she would like to handle all of the company's trash and recycling business nationwide. It was an enormous jump in scale for Susan, who went from minor contracts at four locations to a master contract for 1,200 restaurants. "Whether it was California or Ohio or Pennsylvania, I became responsible for getting a waste hauler to provide services," she says. Within a year Susan took on a partner and incorporated her company as Environmental Waste Consultants, Inc. She never planned a career in waste management, though it's now her passion.

A Company, an Income, and a Schedule of Your Own

Starting a business is often a way for a woman to right her family's finances, or to support her own desire for a flexible schedule.

Selling to salespeople. Despite a lack of typing or spelling skills, when Nancy Lauterbach moved home to Kansas City in 1978 after a divorce, she found an entry-level secretarial job at trucking giant Yellow Freight. A few months later she flew back to Texas to visit friends and sat next to another local secretary on the flight. After returning to Kansas, Nancy got a call from her seatmate, who was moving away and wanted Nancy's help in finding a replacement. The woman's boss, Dick Gardner, quickly talked

Nancy into working for him at his firm, National Association of Sales Education, for less pay and fewer benefits than her Yellow job. "I went ahead and took the job, but it was a gutsy move," Nancy says, "I had two young children and my financial future was far from certain." Dick's seven salespeople worked from his small home office, located in his basement, traveling the country organizing sales training events featuring motivational speakers and selling the events to real estate offices, car dealerships, and insurance firms. Nancy quickly found herself lining up speakers and organizing motivational sales programs as well. One of her first programs, in Kansas City, attracted 1,200 attendees. Nancy mastered the business, moved to another company for a few years, and gained more experience, and in 1988 she launched her own firm, Five Star Speakers and Trainers, LLC.

Creating beauty from desperation. Venezuela native Elena Caldera moved to the Washington, D.C., area in 1983, starting college and then working at Cartier, where she learned the jewelry business. When her husband moved the family to Boca Raton, Florida, Elena quit her job to raise her two small children. The family did well as her husband's company prospered, with an expensive house, a housekeeper, and two Mercedes-Benz cars in the driveway.

But suddenly the company began to fail. As her husband struggled to resolve his business issues, Elena had to let her housekeeper go, sell their high-end home and cars, and pull her children out of college. From the small house they rented, Elena drew on her past for resources, summoning up her skills from her Cartier days to start her own jewelry company. In December 2002, she borrowed $2,000 from her mother in Venezuela, the most her pride would permit, and used $1,000 to pay outstanding household bills. The rest she took to Miami to buy precious stones. What was left over didn't go far toward producing a jewelry line, but she was in business. Soon a close friend came to her, pledged his support, and invested $10,000 in the new company. She named it ME, after herself and her daughter Melissa.

Drumming up business for her jewelry became a group effort. Melissa, who had returned to college, worked part-time as a hostess in a large steak house where she wore her mother's designs. Elena pitched local magazines for publicity for her jewelry. She and Melissa lined up trunk shows in South Florida's ritzy gated communities and she flew to a major jewelry show in New York. Finally, Elena secured an appointment at Swarovski, the oldest manufacturer of man-made crystals in the world. She showed their reps her designs and asked for their business. They agreed to work with her, adding a prestigious brand to her line.

Today, the company, inspired by Elena's memories of her entry-level job at Cartier, continues to grow, and the family is back to financial health. One day, Elena hopes, Melissa will take over the business.

Designing a new job. Melissa Epstein's graphic design job at ad agency J. Walter Thompson in Chicago wasn't making her happy as an artist. She also needed more flexibility in her schedule, a difficult perk to find in a corporate job. At a loss for what to do, the young mother of two decided to stay home with her kids while her husband worked. But her instincts as an artist never left her. For her daughter's second birthday, Melissa made thirty party invitations by hand and sent them out. The response was immediate. Other parents called to inquire if they could commission customized invitations for their own children's parties.

Sensing a business idea, Melissa took her first order in September 2001. She turned her basement into a studio for her new venture, I Made This!, which specializes in invitations, holiday cards, and gift bags. When she needs extra hands, she calls on a squadron of other young mothers to pitch in. Running her own business allows her to make her own money and fulfills her desire to make art while her children are just upstairs.

The CEO and Her Stay-at-home Husband

One-third of married working women earn more than their husbands. Many of these run their own companies. Among them is Deborah Millhouse, a recruiting-firm CEO whose husband, Brian, is a full-time father.

Modern role reversal. Deborah spent only one year at college before family finances forced her to get a job instead. She ran a lighting store and helped grow a party-rentals firm before deciding that the scheduling demands of retail jobs were not conducive to raising a family. Thinking that real estate would be a better field, she went to work for a developer. She quickly became the company president's top aide. She enjoyed the work, which also allowed her the time to complete her college degree on the side.

Then her husband began searching for a new job as well. He came home with two offers: one in California, where they lived, and one in Charlotte, North Carolina. "Where is Charlotte?" Deborah asked him. "Do they have a mall there?" Her boss tried to convince her not to move. "You're a general contractor in California, and California sets the economies of the world," he told her. "Atlanta sets the economies for the South, and you're not even going there." But Deborah wanted to make the move with her husband, and six months later she joined him in Charlotte.

Her new home proved a poor choice for career prospects. Interviews with local building contractors turned up no offers, until one finally said, "You'll never have the job you probably should have because you're female, but you can be a secretary." As she could type fewer than thirty words a minute, secretarial work was out of the question. For a while she did some contract work, until she met a corporate recruiter who sold her on headhunting work and hired her for the firm. After three years there, Deborah moved to a competitor, CEO, Inc., in 1996, shortly before her second child was born. CEO's owner wanted out, and he agreed to sell Deborah the business over five years.

Just as her career was taking off, Deborah was also reevaluating her family life. Her husband's job took him out of town five days a week. One day their young son, Benjamin, shrank back from his father when he came home from a trip. Startled, Brian began thinking about getting a job that didn't require travel. The couple discussed what they wanted for their family, and both agreed that money wasn't as important to them as seeing their children grow up. A few days later Deborah made an offhand comment: "If we wait until you get to a certain level, I'll be one hundred before I can stay home with the kids." It was two weeks before Brian came home and asked her if she was serious. He said he was thinking of quitting his job to stay home full-time while she continued to run her company.

At first Deborah was concerned about what Brian's family, a traditional Midwestern clan, would think of this liberated arrangement. But Brian didn't care. She also made it clear that if he stopped working, he would also be responsible for running the house. She would not "be one of those women who brings home the bacon, fries it up in the pan, looks like Betty Crocker and gets it all done," she says. They traded their expensive lifestyle for a better quality of life. Brian took over at home. This division of labor has worked for the last ten years as Deborah's firm continues to grow.

Not Ready to Retire

From boredom to business. When Susan Schadt, a petite, charming Memphis native, moved to Southern California more than a decade ago, she and her husband, Chuck, planned to enjoy their retirement playing golf and socializing. But Susan quickly tired of her easy life. As Chuck was golfing one day in 1992, Susan browsed aimlessly through a flea market. She came upon a stall selling beeswax, with some women rolling candles. Susan watched and thought she could make much nicer candles than the ones they were selling. Susan bought up the beeswax planks, loaded them into her car, and hid them away at home. At first she planned to make candles just to decorate her home. But she quickly graduated to a professional's tools, with mixing wax, wicks, and a paper cutter for cutting the wax spread out across the kitchen table. The scope of the project expanded beyond her own interior design needs, and Susan Schadt, Inc., was born.

Susan was afraid to tell Chuck in case the fledgling business failed. While he was busy, she ferried her custom-designed candles around to local retailers. By the end of the first day she had sold out of all of her inventory. Susan didn't know whether to attribute her sales run to beginner's luck or the start of a thriving business, but she continued to make candles and take orders. A few months later, in December 1992, Chuck answered the doorbell to a man bearing Susan's new business logo, and a bill. The company was no longer a secret.

From the kitchen, Susan moved her work space into a guest bedroom, where she put her first few employees. Next the company took over the garage, where they worked late every night filling orders. After a year and a half, with revenue pushing $1 million, Susan took office space in nearby Del Mar. But the flush of having proven her product a hit was finished for her. When she and Chuck decided to move back to Memphis, Susan simply wanted to close the company, considering her project a success.

A homemaker's new home. Susie Clendenen and her husband, Bob, planned a lifestyle similar to Susan and Chuck's for their retirement. With their three children grown and Bob retired from his corporate job, they settled in to their oceanfront house in Rhode Island. Susie began by doing a major home renovation. But when that job was finished, she wasn't happy. She needed something else to do, a bigger project. At a dinner party the following week Susie found herself seated next to a Realtor, whom she asked about a large home for sale in a nearby town. The Wakefield, Rhode Island, house, which had been the summer home of the Welch's grape juice family in the nineteenth century, would be perfect for a bed-and-breakfast, Susie thought. She and Bob drove over to look at the colonial revival house and she outlined her idea for making it over into a small hotel. "I was comfortable with my homemaking skills and simply viewed converting the old home into a B&B as my final exam on domestic talents. While raising three children and moving around the country several times to accommodate Bob's career, I learned a lot about operating a home efficiently," she says. Susie could easily position and market the historic B&B as a sanctuary to corporate executives and their wives, a market she knew intimately. As the couple decided to scale down their living space, opening a B&B also solved the problem of what to do with their collection of antiques and family heirloom furniture.

Susie and Bob bought the building and reopened it as Silver Lake Cottage in September 2001. They live in an apartment on the third floor, with their furniture scattered throughout the hotel. In addition to accommodating overnight guests, they also host weddings and private parties on their landscaped grounds, and donate the use of the house for nonprofit fundraisers four times a year. Now Susie, sixty-five, is finally happy: "I am finally doing what I want to do," she says.

Every entrepreneur you read about in this chapter followed a unique path into the role of CEO. What follows are the details of how some of these women built highly successful businesses, step by careful step, while others endured some minor to serious setbacks, ones you should avoid. The steps outlined here are the building blocks to a sound company, one that can provide you with a financially rewarding future and fulfillment of your professional goals.

What It Takes to Turn an Idea into a Successful Business

Some entrepreneurs find out by trial and error that even when you excel at something, say making chocolates, it takes a lot more than mastering one skill or developing one product to succeed in business. Having a viable idea for a business and being good at bringing it to fruition is just the starting point. But what else goes into making your product the best? Why are some businesswomen successful, while others act like they are driving a bumper car around and around in circles, with no clear vision or goal in view? Thriving entrepreneurs have several traits common to all successful business owners. These are the characteristics you'll need to execute the seven steps to building a successful business. You may find out—as some of the women in this book did—that you don't possess all of these traits. That's okay, as long as you know where you fall short and fill in the gaps with a partner, a senior staffer, or a professional adviser who can complement your strengths.

Passion. The fuel that ignites a start-up company is the founder's passion. Your enthusiasm can help inspire your team to reach your company's goals. It can also work as an elixir to help employees ride out some very tough times. Beverly Gray calls passion "the fire in your belly," a powerful energy that flows through your operations. When you're in an office where there's passion in the leadership, that passion permeates everything.

Passion can be singular and quiet or contagious and ebullient. As the sole owner of my medical communications company, I ran the firm with robust exuberance for my business. I loved the business I was in, and I wanted every employee who walked through our office doors to embrace it with the same passion and gusto I had for it. But I was always struck by the passion my editorial director had for her work, which manifested itself as a thoughtful and focused resolve to turn out the best product, always. Our passions ran on equally important, parallel courses: Hers was a cool but relentless exactitude, while mine turned me into a cheerleader for the company and our ideas. I often would come up with an idea, and then race through to the global concept, sketching out in verbal brushstrokes a medical education program from beginning to end. She, on the other hand, would assiduously set about constructing the framework for the program, in exquisite block-by-block, line-by-line format. No piece of data went unquestioned, no reference went unchecked. My passion stemmed from the idea, the vision, and the thrill. I was aware that I occasionally created roller-coaster rides, but I always knew where we were going.

Adaptability. Sooner or later every businesswoman hits a wall. Successful businesswomen adapt quickly to setbacks and turn them into business opportunities where possible. Sandy LeTourneau turned an unexpected layoff into an opening to start her company. She also weathered a devastating flood and an onslaught of debt to bring her company to success within three years. Doreen Marks overcame her first business impediment when she had to charm her way into a gun show. As a sixteen-year-old, she also managed to juggle the demands of school and her company. Doreen went on to grow a profitable business that she still runs today.

Vision. Ideas for a new business are not hard to conceive. But translating those ideas into a viable enterprise that creates and sells a product is another matter. Both Hinda Miller and her partner Lisa Landahl temporarily lost sight of their vision for their sports bra company until a client's rebuke helped put them back on track (see chapter 2).

From the moment Angela Drummond learned about collaborative

meeting software technology, on the other hand, her vision crystallized. She believed an entire business could be built around this model. When her managers said no, Angela was undeterred, launching her own company and proving its market potential. Similarly, Gail Warrior sized up her husband's strong sales skills and knowledge of the modular construction market, then realized his shortcomings in running the financial side of a business could be counteracted by her strengths. She envisioned them both in the same business, and put a plan together to execute that vision, creating a multimillion-dollar firm in just five years.

Energy. Working for someone else can be a full-time job, but owning your own business takes even more time. You need boundless energy and devotion to make it work. Take Nancy Milby, the accountant turned culinary entrepreneur. Friends wondered whether her business idea was worth all the time it would take her. After all, they reasoned, owning a culinary business of any kind is extremely labor-intensive, likely consuming more hours per week than her old accounting job. But although she now puts in twelve-hour days, Nancy loves what she does and doesn't mind the hours.

Stamina. Energy will help you get your company up and running, but stamina is what's needed to keep it afloat. Joan Coukos calls on her reserves to persevere when she finds herself standing over chocolate batches late at night, trying to improve her mix. Judy Wicks, at fifty-eight, has a thriving business and a capable, supportive staff, but she logs long hours overseeing her restaurant, gift shop, newsletter, and community activities. Without endurance, no business can keep running.

Resourcefulness. Success also depends on drawing on all of your resources, including those you didn't know you had. These resources include not only money and formal training, but also friends, family, untapped contacts, and long-forgotten skills. Elena Caldera dug into her personal store of ingenuity when her husband's business collapsed, leaving her family in financial danger. She harkened back to her days working at Cartier, selling jewelry. Then she called on her connections, asking her family for start-up money, calling everyone she knew to set up jewelry shows, and going door-to-door for publicity. Entrepreneurship requires putting aside your pride and asking for help wherever you can get it.

If you have, or can hire, all these traits, you can run your own company. All that's needed to build and sustain a successful business is to follow the next steps carefully.

PART I

A 7-Step Guide to
Discovering, Starting, and
Building the Business
of Your Dreams

M

en have been doing it successfully for centuries: starting and building companies, and then *selling* them for handsome profits, that is. The good news is that more and more women are catching on; today, nearly half of all privately owned U.S. companies are majority or 50 percent owned by women. According to the Center for Women's Business Research, a Washington, D.C.–based organization that tracks women business owners, the number of women-owned firms increased by 11 percent nationwide between 1997 and 2002, or 1.5 times the rate of all firms. And the number of privately held companies owned by women of color grew by nearly 55 percent between 1997 and 2004. Furthermore, women-owned firms are as creditworthy and financially solid as the typical U.S. firm and in fact are more likely to stay in business than the average U.S. company (1). Women entrepreneurs have made tremendous progress, but many are still missing out on the opportunity to sell their companies, possibly for millions. Why?

Too many women today simply don't think that they can sell their companies. They think that others who achieve a high level of business and financial success have something special going for them that they themselves do not—that they're all computer whiz kids who created and sold hot dotcom companies in the Internet heyday, or that they have highly specialized job training that puts them in a class by themselves, or that they're all armed with M.B.A.'s. But nothing could be further from the truth (see box 1). In fact, only two women I interviewed who sold their companies successfully started technology-based companies (see their stories in chapter 10). Neither one had a degree in computer science or business. The others began as a grade school teacher, a nurse, a secretary, or an editorial assistant, or another non-high-tech job. In addition, even when women business owners are aware of exit possibilities, such as a sale or merger, they generally lack the professional network or the financial skills to put in place a successful business deal, and net millions.

Finally, women are still catching up to men when it comes to negotiating deals. Women business owners need to stretch their thinking and enhance their vision if they want to play the business game to the max.

BOX 1: IS YOUR PERCEPTION PART OF THE PROBLEM?

Too many businesswomen owners think of their firms as small and unattractive to anyone but them, more akin to mutts than to purebreds. How do you see your company? Is your view accurate? If any part of this story sounds familiar to you, take another look at your business now. You may be able to turn your small firm into a successful exit vehicle for yourself someday, too.

The office space for my second company, AM Medica Communications, was located in midtown Manhattan in a landmark building. All back-office space, with a few windowed offices overlooking the rooftops of neighboring buildings, it was far from glamorous. Almost all of our office furniture was secondhand. We paid close attention to holding expenses down, and worked hard to keep our sales and job deliveries up. I began with eight employees, and in our first year, sales topped $5 million. The company was under way and growing, but I didn't think it was worth much to anyone but me.

Two years into the business, a competitor approached me to discuss the possibility of his purchasing AM Medica. We actually went as far as a sales contract: He offered me $2 million in cash for my firm. I decided to turn it down because I did not want to commute to New Jersey twice a week to help run his office. But the proposal opened my eyes, and I became focused on building my business to enable a successful exit.

A few years later, my accountant and I reviewed my company's performance in detail, beginning with year one. I had always been careful about building up cash reserves. As a single woman and the sole owner of my business, I was keenly aware that I needed to keep substantial sums in the bank. If I became ill, funds had to be available to meet payroll and expenses for several months. However, I did not realize how well my company was performing year after year until I had that meeting with my accountant. For the first time I understood that while my office, with its industrial-gray carpets, used furnishings, and aging copy machines, might not look like the home of a robust, thriving company, we had sizzle where it mattered: in the earnings. A few years later, I sold my company for millions more than the initial $2 million offer.

According to the three successful women angel investors who wrote *The Old Girls' Network*, for women starting as well as building their own businesses, "marketplace inequality" remains very much in place. As these authors point out, women today are still programmed to think that they simply aren't entitled to succeed or win.

Men business owners don't make concrete plans for selling their businesses with any greater frequency than women; the difference is they think about it a lot more often. Men business owners whom I know often say things like "I'd love to score a touchdown," or "hit it out of the park," while women more often say "as long as my luck continues, I'm fine," or "I've just got to keep growing my business smoothly and, I hope, successfully." Women still have a way to go in everything from becoming fluent in business language to becoming comfortable with money. In *The Old Girls' Network* the author-investors write that

> We would argue that collectively women are far less powerful than men, a situation that stems in part from how we deal with money, how we earn money, and how we think about money. We see the disparity in all aspects of life, but especially in business (2).

Similarly, Dr. Lois Frankel points out in her book, *Nice Girls Don't Get the Corner Office*, that women in business still have some difficulty today talking about money because it smacks of being crass or impolite (3). In *Money, a Memoir*, Liz Perle wrote that her grandmother cautioned her: "You never talk about money. It's private" (4). Finally, in this climate of corporate greed and scandal, it becomes even more challenging for some women to overcome their uncomfortable feelings about making money. For them, thinking about an exit plan, and possibly reaping a significant sum for their business, is not something they've considered—yet.

Get Comfortable with Money

Women entrepreneurs need to learn that they can and should play in the Olympics of business: starting, building, and selling a company successfully. For the owner of a privately held company, getting out is the end point of the game. The company you start is an investment; after a marriage and children, it is likely the largest presence in your life, consuming substantial time, money, and emotional resources. As with any other investment, the goal is to get the best possible return. In the case of a company, the returns come mainly when you sell it. In terms of tapping professional financing strategies to grow the business, women rely more than their male counterparts on bootstrapping methods rather than institutional sources of capital (5). But even if your company is performing so well that you don't need a bank loan, it's still a good idea to get to know a professional banker and consider working with one on a business loan. Financing strategies may not only expedite your company's growth, but they can also introduce you and your business to investors who orchestrate exit-oriented transactions. Lastly, women are also less likely than men to indicate that someone close to them was an entrepreneur, 43 percent versus 59 percent (6). But these role models create invaluable networks. As a result of these handicaps, women have less experience with business ownership than their male counterparts.

The more business ownership experience you have, the greater the chances are that you'll become aware of how business deals, including the successful sale of your business, get done. Once I had the experience of selling my first company behind me, from day one in my second company I dreamed about the possibility of selling again. When that time came, I was both familiar and comfortable with the deal process, knowing that as a woman business owner I would have to negotiate effectively—and hard—to get my price. For many women business owners, though, that comfort level simply isn't in place yet. And after the last few years of sensational business imbroglios, it is not especially surprising to discover that many people, including women entrepreneurs, think that building a successful company the right way and selling it for a substantial sum of money are mutually exclusive concepts. But they are not. Furthermore, women would do themselves a terrific service if they struck the phrase "making money" from their business language and replace it with what we're really doing: earning money. Anytime I hear "Is that company making money?" I picture an imaginary flock of elves tiptoeing into an office, furiously printing greenbacks, leaving them in a huge heap on the owner's desk, and then vanishing. A company does not make money; a company earns money. The owner and the employees work tirelessly for years, and whatever profits the company shows at year-end are well earned.

Finally, keep in mind that money is the cornerstone of the for-profit business game. If you want your company to stay competitive—and potentially attractive to a corporate buyer—then you have to show increased earnings for several consecutive years. Do it well, do it ethically, and be proud of your accomplishment.

Even Sole Proprietors Need the Seven Steps

Whether you work alone making custom T-shirts or glazed pottery, unless you have an inheritance or an earning husband who will take care of you for life, you need the seven steps to help you navigate the business world. Here's why: A recent study from the U.S. Small Business Administration showed that growth rates of women sole proprietors among business owners was more than double that of men. The women, however, trailed men significantly in their total sales and earnings. For example, in 2000, women in retail and wholesale trade had just one-fourth the sales of men, while in finance, real estate, and insurance, women had one-third the sales of men. Furthermore, women's salaries weren't even half of men's; on average, men earned $43,002 in wages and $7,863 in business income, while women earned $21,830 in wages and $3,905 from their businesses. The study also revealed that in 2000, nearly 15 percent of women ran their businesses as head of households with dependents, while only 5.5 percent of men fell into this category. The study did not draw conclusions as to why women sole proprietors lagged behind men in earnings, except to say that more women than men were unmarried, and they therefore might have less family support while pursuing their work.

But many women, including me, would also say that there are other factors at work. Many women still don't have solid professional networks, a banking relationship, a mentor, or the knowledge to build a stable and successful sole proprietorship as a budding enterprise. The Seven Steps are for all these women, too.

How the Seven Steps Were Born

Fortunately, I learned from my first business partner that selling a company we had started and built successfully was a worthy business goal. Several other women entrepreneurs who shared their stories with me also understood that selling the companies they had created was a viable aspiration. And all of us learned—through trial and error—that several steps must be taken to build a successful business. After talking with them, along with business advisers, accountants, lawyers, and bankers, seven steps to building a successful business emerged (see figure 2). These are the key ingredients you need to put together to run a stellar business, one that might attract a serious buyer one day. And keep in mind, small businesses are bought and sold every year. Review the steps in the figure, and then go to Chapter 2, Step 1: Choose and Focus on Your Core Competencies.

Position for Payout: A Seven-Step Plan for Building a Successful Business that You Can Sell for Millions Someday

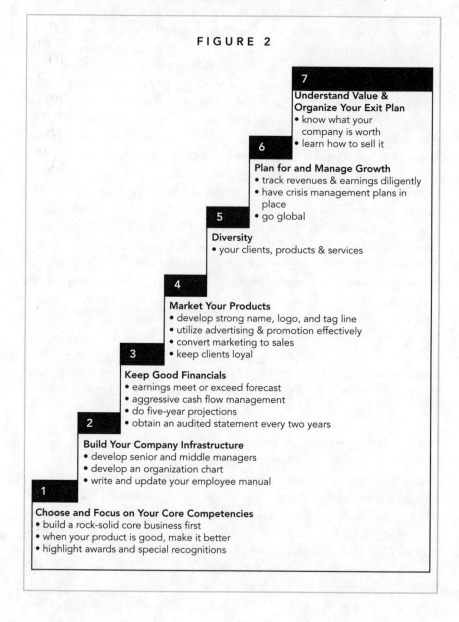

FIGURE 2

7

Understand Value & Organize Your Exit Plan
• know what your company is worth
• learn how to sell it

6

Plan for and Manage Growth
• track revenues & earnings diligently
• have crisis management plans in place
• go global

5

Diversity
• your clients, products & services

4

Market Your Products
• develop strong name, logo, and tag line
• utilize advertising & promotion effectively
• convert marketing to sales
• keep clients loyal

3

Keep Good Financials
• earnings meet or exceed forecast
• aggressive cash flow management
• do five-year projections
• obtain an audited statement every two years

2

Build Your Company Infrastructure
• develop senior and middle managers
• develop an organization chart
• write and update your employee manual

1

Choose and Focus on Your Core Competencies
• build a rock-solid core business first
• when your product is good, make it better
• highlight awards and special recognitions

CHAPTER 2

Step 1: Choose and Focus on Your Core Competencies

Every woman who starts her own business knows she is good at something: crafting handmade party invitations, preparing deluxe chocolates, creating computer software solutions, or finding temporary office workers. Early success reinforces this knowledge. When the first repeat client comes back, or the product sells, it is gratifying to know that you must be doing something well. But as any successful entrepreneur will tell you, being good is just the baseline. Now the race is on to perform. Only by becoming the best in her field can an entrepreneur enjoy long-term success with her company. Focusing on your core competency is the first step.

The Coca-Cola Company, for example, produces nearly four hundred beverage brands, everything from an African juice drink called Vita to Samurai, a beverage only available in Asia. But the first product the company made more than one hundred years ago, combining syrup with carbonated water to create Coca-Cola, remains the company's core competency. Similarly, FedEx began operating in 1973 focusing on shipping overnight envelopes and small packages in the United States. Today, the company provides international package delivery and freight-shipping services. Every successful company—Coca-Cola, FedEx, General Electric, Pfizer—began with a core product or service. Select your core product or service, then figure out how to make it better than it is now. Next, try to make it better than what your competitors are selling. Once your company has established a reputation for good work, you just need to maintain it.

FROM COSTUMES TO CASH

Wendy Goldstein has been sewing since the fourth grade. At Ohio State University, where she sewed costumes for campus plays, she tried to craft her own major in costuming in order to launch a career in fashion merchandising and costume design. The school wouldn't allow it. "They told me I would never make a living at it," Wendy says. After graduation, she went to work for Lazarus, a local department store, and quickly rose to become the bath shop buyer for ten locations, managing a budget in excess of $1 million.

One day, on a lark, Wendy decided to bid to produce a cast of Nutcracker costumes for the store's annual holiday display. To her surprise, she won the contract. "It was my first big job," she said. "I had to call all of my friends who knew how to sew." Wendy designed the costumes, and her friends gathered in Wendy's basement to sew them. That job cemented the realization that her college professors had been wrong. She could make a living doing what she loved. Wendy had found her core competency.

After getting married, having a child, and going back for her master's in fashion merchandising, Wendy launched her company, Costume Specialists, Inc., from her basement. Within a few years, she took a small retail space for her Halloween costume rental business. Her husband managed the store while she produced custom work, such as theater costumes, in the back. Now, twenty-five years later, Wendy's multimillion-dollar company includes a retail operation housing 5,000 rental costumes and a division that provides life-size book-character costumes designed for marketing promotions. Sewing is still her passion, and she has made it the cornerstone of her success as well.

A DESIGNING WOMAN

Of course, most of us don't develop an interest as early as grade school and then go on to turn it into a dynamic business. Ellen Bates took a part-time sales job with an office-furniture company in Dover, New Hampshire, her hometown, while her son was small. Ellen knew little about office furniture; her previous work had been with a telephone company. But she gradually learned the business, keeping her part-time hours until her son started first grade. She loved the work, and as soon as he was in school, she went to work full-time. During the nine years she worked at the company, Ellen supplemented her sales skills by taking courses in space planning, design, and project management.

Then the firm was sold. Powerless to help, Ellen watched in horror as the new owner drove the company out of business. When she saw what had happened to the once-thriving firm, Ellen realized she would be better off working for herself. She recruited her sister and a former colleague, and in 1986 launched Office Interiors, Inc., headquartered in some spare office space a friend offered them in Dover. Drawing on her decade of experience in office-furniture sales, Ellen pitched her new company as a full-service interior design firm for businesses, including space planning, furniture allocation, and finish selection. Knowing the local customers and how to build her base of clients, she signed up several New Hampshire–based banks and nearby Tyco International, eCopy, Inc., and the state government, which became one of Ellen's major accounts. Ellen grew her revenue from $250,000 her first year to several millions of dollars today. She accomplished this feat by doing one thing, her core competency, well: designing office interiors in the New Hampshire market.

Building Up Your Core Competency

Being good at what you do requires more than coasting on existing skills. It's a measured, planned process of objectively evaluating your company's abilities and getting the best available advice to turn those abilities into marketable products (see table 1). A handmade party invitation is a cute gift for a friend, but turning that one craft project into a line of commercial goods takes talent, careful market research, and an understanding of customer demand. Start your competitive-intelligence campaign early on, reaching out to all the advisers you can access, getting to know your industry's landscape, and understanding what your customers want. As you improve your products, you will benefit from your increased knowledge of the marketplace.

Research. Stay abreast of what is happening in your industry. Allocate time each week to read trade magazines, or attend an industry function once a quarter. Join a professional society or two and volunteer to serve on committees. This is a good way to get acquainted with your competitors and to hear the latest about their plans, pricing issues, and industry trends. If you join trade groups that lobby for your industry's interests, you will also be aware of impending government regulations or new laws affecting your company. Understanding the competition can also help you in later stages of your business if you decide to pursue joint ventures or group bids with your rivals.

Get customer feedback. A customer survey is crucial. This survey can be as simple as a printed, stamped postcard packaged with new orders, or a short form tucked into your restaurant's guest-bill folios. Offer small incentives for customers to fill out the survey, such as a prize drawing, making sure the initiative will bring them back into your store. Identify weak spots in your business, and work on them until the customer surveys improve to perfection. These surveys will also let you know what your customers think you're doing well. If their thoughts consistently fail to match up with your own views on your core competency, consider rethinking your business. Perhaps you have been overlooking a strength, or focusing too hard on a product your customers don't really want.

Get employee feedback. Don't overlook your in-house team as a vital source of information that can help you build a better business. Typically, most employees have experience elsewhere in the same industry. Solicit their ideas regularly to help you build your company's core competency. Encourage them to speak up with suggestions on how you can change your processes or tweak your products. Publicly praise, and if possible reward, employees who come up with good ideas. This approach also helps to foster a spirit of openness and innovation in your company. Finally, another useful way to enlist your employees is to ask them to talk with their colleagues and friends for thoughts on the company's services and goods. They are more likely to get candid opinions from people they know well, and you will benefit from this frank advice from the market.

Look for competitions. Business is a race; if you want to know who's best, look to see who's finished first. Most industries have competitions and awards. For instance, a local magazine might rank area caterers annually. Governmental agencies that regulate certain industries often cite top performers. Make sure you know about such reviews, and do everything you can to secure a first-place spot in the lineup. Understand the judging criteria, be certain to get the entry materials in on time, and read the citations from previous years to see what helped the winners get ahead. When you succeed in getting a prize or a recognition, let everyone know. Issue a press release and send it to your local newspaper, touting your core competency. The paper is unlikely to write a story, but the next time they need an expert in your field, they may just call you for comment.

Create an in-house competition. Challenge your employees to come up with a winning idea to make your core product better. Hold a structured contest with inexpensive but coveted prizes, like a reserved parking spot in the office lot or a gift certificate to a good restaurant. You and your top managers can be the judges. Make it an annual event to ensure your company stays on top of its game. To encourage your staff to share their best ideas all year round, allow any idea that has been suggested or implemented by an employee during the previous year to be entered in the contest.

Don't let your customers drive the bus. Don't let a customer force you into a product line or a service that doesn't make long-term sense for your company. When you receive a query about a possible way to extend your product line or new area in which to pursue your business, check it against your business plan to verify that developing it will help you achieve your company's goals. Remember, it's your business; you are not a DJ manning a song-request line, and you don't have to play every tune people want to hear. If you like a customer's idea but aren't ready to execute it, shelve it until you and your team know you are ready. If you don't feel that the idea fits with your plans, tell the customer so candidly, and offer to help him find a company that can provide what he wants. Use your network of professional contacts, which will help you build relationships with different companies and may lead them to refer customers to you as well.

Get a professional critique. After a year in business, develop a formal relationship with a SCORE (Service Corps of Retired Executives) representative or a retired industry professional. Find an adviser who can come in and evaluate your core competencies, talking with you and your top managers about your company's strengths and weaknesses. Ideally, try to get your adviser to commit to meeting with you for at least three consecutive years to track your progress on improving your core competency. Drawing on your adviser's experience in the field, map out your plans for making the company better, and develop useful benchmarks to measure your advancement.

Table 1: Seven Tips to Building Up Your Core Competency

1. **Research.** Stay abreast of what is happening in your industry. Allocate a couple of hours each week to reading trade magazines, or attend an industry function once a quarter. If you don't, you may find that while you are good at your core competency, everyone else is better.

2. **Get customer feedback.** Develop a customer survey to determine what your customers think of your business. Identify weak spots, and work on them until the customer surveys come back giving you a top rating.

3. **Get employee feedback.** Don't overlook your in-house team as a vital source of information that can help you build a better business. Typically, most employees have experience elsewhere in the same industry. Solicit their ideas regularly to help you build your company's core competency.

4. **Look for competitions.** Business is a race; if you want to know who's best, look to see who's finished first. Most industries have competitions and awards. For instance, a local magazine might rank area caterers annually. Make sure you know about such reviews, and do everything you can to secure a first-place spot in the lineup.

5. **Create an in-house competition.** Challenge your employees to come up with a winning idea to make your core product better. Make it an annual event to ensure your company stays on top of its game.

6. **Don't let your customers drive the bus.** Don't let a customer force you into a product line or a service that you never intended to develop. Remember, it's your business. If you like a customer's idea but aren't ready to execute it, shelve it until you and your team believe you are ready.

7. **Get a professional critique.** After a year in business, set up an annual program with a SCORE (Service Corps of Retired Executives) representative or a retired industry professional who can come in and evaluate your core competencies, talking with you and your top managers about your company's strengths and weaknesses. Ideally, try to get your adviser to commit to meeting with you for at least three consecutive years, so both of you can track your progress.

Making Your Core Competency
Fund Your Dreams

Both Ellen, the office interior expert, and Wendy, the costume maker, morphed their skills and passions into million-dollar companies with full-time employees. But if you master Step One, focusing on and maximizing your core competency, you could sustain a small but profitable business that might be very compatible with your personal lifestyle and goals.

My Book Place. In Tequesta, Florida, Lois Yaffe's longtime dreams of owning a quiet bookstore have come true—and are paying off. A stay-at-home mother of two, Lois was captivated by a small bookstore she passed one day. "If I ever go into a business, that's what I'm going to do," she promised herself. But it wasn't until years later, when her youngest was headed to college, that Lois decided to fulfill her dream. In 1985, she wandered into a used-book shop and discovered that the owner wanted to sell out. Lois and her husband agreed they could afford to buy the store for her to run. To test it out, she worked in the shop for a few weeks while the owner was on vacation. But it took her six months to make up her mind to buy the place. "I was sure I could handle the products—books—because I was an avid reader and knew books and authors very well," she said, but "going to work after all those years" made her think twice.

Deciding that she was ready to make the commitment to the business, Lois bought the shop, called My Book Place. She kept the focus on used books, which she buys from customers for store credit and then resells. She later added some discounted new books. Although she has occasionally hired an employee, Lois is the sole proprietor and often the only worker in her nine hundred-square-foot shop, responsible for ordering, unpacking, selling, stocking, and bookkeeping. She uses a calculator for transactions. The store hasn't made Lois rich, but she has paid back her husband for his initial investment in the business and reimbursed herself for money she spent on renovation work. Lois doesn't need the money she makes from the store, but she loves her work. "My store is fun for me and my customers," says the sixty-nine-year-old Lois. "It's a wonderful, simple, rewarding business."

Hither Creek Gardener. Julie Wood, thirty-three, says the same thing about her small but lucrative landscape-design business in Nantucket, Massachusetts. Unlike Lois, she needs the income to help support her family. After college, Julie held odd jobs and internships in nurseries, plant stores, and landscape architecture studios. By 2001, she felt ready to launch her own business. The Massachusetts resort island where she lives is known for its beautiful gardens, and Julie gets most of her business through word of mouth. During the summer, she takes on a temporary worker or two. While her husband, recovering from a back injury, works part-time in architectural drafting, computer graphics, and design, Julie's landscaping business allows her to make money her family needs and to spend time with her young daughter, Caroline. Julie works only when Caroline is in day care four days a week, working longer hours when needed, leaving her husband with Caroline. To meet the extra demand from customers, she eventually plans to add more staff. She also recently obtained her real estate license, and now spends winters representing rentals and sale properties on the island. "For now this business fits my lifestyle needs very well," Julie says.

Lois's and Julie's businesses complement their personal lives and provide the income levels they want. If this is what you want out of your business, mastering your core competency can be the whole company, for a while, or it can be a foundation for a larger enterprise. Either way, even sole proprietors should learn steps 2 through 7. If you don't, you could find yourself in trouble sooner than you think (see page 128 and the Regrets box on page 167).

Is Your Core Competency What You Think It Is?

What a ridiculous question. You're an event planner, your company is called Party Tots, and you arrange children's birthday parties. That's clearly a focused business, isn't it? But despite starting with an idea and a business plan to back it up, some entrepreneurs still manage to get lost. What starts out straightforwardly can quickly become complicated when the businesswoman loses sight of what she does best.

SPORTS BRAS (AND SUNDRY)

In 1978 Hinda Miller's company got its first order for forty dozen bras. The company sparked to life as Hinda and her partner, Lisa, focused on sales and production. They obtained and repaid Small Business Administration (SBA) loans and found suitable space, moving from an old doctor's office to a small-business incubator for five years. Finally, they built their own building.

During this period a mail-order catalog that had placed a lot of orders with the company called and asked the partners to design a brief for male runners. Thinking, "Okay, we can do that," Hinda and Lisa came up with a design for a product called Max. Next, joggers asked for knit exercise clothes, and they responded by bringing out a line that met this request. Hinda and Lisa changed the company name from Jogbra to JBI, Inc., to expand beyond bras and leave them more room to launch new products. A clothing line for aerobic workouts followed, but never took off. By this point their company was zigzagging, simply fulfilling customer requests for different products.

As they drifted from a focus on bras for jogging and toward whatever sports clothing customers requested, Hinda and Lisa assumed they were in the athletic wear business and were building a multifeatured product line. But their major accounts didn't think so. "In the early years," Hinda said, "we weren't exactly sure what kind of company we were." Eventually, a few buyers took the partners aside to tell them that while their sports bras performed excellently, the ancillary lines were just a distraction from their core business. "That was some of the best feedback we got," Hinda said, "because they told us what kind of company we really were." Hinda and her partner decided to stop making knits for workouts and men's underwear and refocus on what they knew best: sports bras. Soon they came up with a new "sports top," a bra that runs down to the waistline. Because it built upon their core competency—rather than distracting them from it—the sports top was an immediate success.

It's logical when building a business to look for ways to create spin-off products or services, or to move into an adjacent industry (see step 5 for diversification tips). At first glance JBI's drift into running briefs for men and lightweight knitwear for joggers might seem reasonable, even inspired. But for Hinda and Lisa it could have been a disaster. At that point in their business, they weren't developing and following a product diversification plan. Instead, they were simply responding to buyer inquires for specific items, without regard for how these products fit into a long-term business strategy. This approach isn't diversification; it's chaos. Stick to your core competency, making those products the best they can be, and you will understand what kind of company you are running.

PUBLISHER . . . OR TEACHER?

Judy Galbraith's company grew out of a thesis and a lawsuit. A teacher with five years' experience, Judy went back to school for her master's degree in guidance and counseling with a special emphasis on working with gifted and talented children. She wrote a book called the *The Gifted Kids' Survival Guide* for her thesis. When the publishing company that had bought the manuscript didn't honor its contract with her, Judy sued for the rights to her book and a promised second volume. Rather than find another publisher, she decided to start her own company, which she named Free Spirit Publishing. "One day," she said, "I just had an epiphany and thought, 'I'm as smart as anybody else and I think I can run a business well, or certainly better than what I've seen so far, so why not just do it myself?' " She was struck by how many books existed to help adults with everything from finances to relationships, but nothing similar was on the market for children. "I just knew there was a need for 'self-help' books for kids," Judy said, so she started with a mail-order catalog, packing the books herself on a Ping-Pong table in her basement. To pay her rent while the company got off the ground, she took a part-time teaching job in the mornings, ran home, and worked until midnight on her business. Just twenty-nine years old at the time and through a divorce, Judy realized that juggling teaching and publishing wasn't working out for either job. After a year she found herself thinking, "You know, Judy, pick a profession here. Either it has to be education or it has to be book publishing, but pick one and give it your all." She chose the company, quit the teaching position, and moved Free Spirit to a warehouse-district office in downtown Minneapolis. Today, Judy has upward of twenty-five employees and annual revenues in the millions. Self-help children's books remain Free Spirit's forte.

THE CITY CENTER PERSONAL TRAINING & FITNESS CO. . . . OR IS IT?

When Kelly Morgan (the company and owner's name and location have been changed) opened the doors to her new company in Denver three years ago, she planned to provide a workout center with exercise machines, free weights, and a couple of personal trainers. She named her company accordingly. But before she knew it, between customer suggestions and her own ambitions, Kelly found herself listing a dozen available services, including massage therapy, dance and martial arts classes, acupuncture, yoga, nutrition and weight loss programs, and even specific exercise and training programs for different sports. On top of all of these offerings, Kelly was eager to woo working moms, so she set up a supervised children's activities area while mom trained.

Although fitness trends seem to be in her favor, Kelly's business is struggling to survive. Providing a broad range of services for a broad range of clients—from working mothers to athletes—under one roof in less than three years is a challenge, even for a well-capitalized and sophisticated businessperson. Kelly's helter-skelter approach is killing her business. In her enthusiasm to get clients, coupled with her sincere desire to please every client who walks through the door, Kelly has lost sight of her initial vision for a fitness center, and it happened within the first three months she was in business.

Instead of sticking to what she knows best—identifying and providing good equipment and trainers—Kelly had to hire a slew of independent contractors: a nutritionist, a professional sports trainer, a yoga guru, and others. Before she realized it, she was spending much of her time dealing with scheduling and hiring more part-time help. In a start-up business, you simply can't be all things to all people, or be good at everything. Kelly is rethinking her business now, with the goal of trimming back or eliminating several services altogether, so she can build up the company's reputation and expertise again in her core area, personal training and fitness.

So You're Good at Your Core Competency. Now Make It Better.

Improving upon a core competency is perhaps the easiest and the hardest task you will face as an entrepreneur. The success of your business depends on your consistent ability to improve your products. First, decide what differentiates what you sell from what everyone else sells. Then, determine how you can exploit that difference and widen the gap between you and your competitors. Build on the vision that led you to create your product in the first place. This is not a one-time event; it's a process that must be repeated continually if you want to stay ahead of the market.

Building Better Bras. After their JogBra sports bras took off, Hinda and Lisa looked at ways to improve their product. They hit another home run in 1986 with the first sports bra for larger-breasted women, which remains one of the bestselling athletic products today. Then they worked on making the bras fit customers better. They came up with a measurement metric they called the motion-control requirement system. Each bra came in eight different styles, corresponding to a matrix of breast size and exercise level. Customers raved about how well the bras fit when they could choose a style perfect for their bodies. By honing their core competency, Hinda and Lisa were able to attract the attention of underwear maker Playtex, which bought their company in 1990.

Costumes Never Looked So Good. In her early years running her company, Wendy Goldstein concentrated on Halloween costumes and theater work, producing costumes for her alma mater, Ohio State University, and the Columbus Opera. Wendy also did corporate and team mascot costume work, but those orders typically came in short bursts. Then, business picked up. In 1989 retailer Child's World placed an order for 176 Peter Panda costumes for delivery within two months. Scrambling to hire extra sewing help, Wendy finished the job on time. The panda job set her to thinking: Maybe other companies, such as Barnes & Noble, might want a custom character costume too. But without a steady stream of large orders, she would have to lay people off. After several years of running her business on a small scale, serving local clients, Wendy decided to go after bigger jobs. She moved the company to a larger facility and hired both a sewing staff and managers. The new strategy paid off with several big-ticket orders, leading in turn to more business as her reputation grew. Her company created costumes such as Winnie-the-Pooh to appear at Barnes & Noble's bookstore story hours and brought to life corporate mascots such as the Pillsbury Doughboy and The Michelin Man.

Rx for the Rx Bottle. Deborah Adler, then a design student at the School of Visual Arts in New York City, was casting about for a thesis idea when she zeroed in on her grandparents' medicine cabinet. She saw an opportunity to redesign the antiquated prescription bottle to make it safer for patients. Deborah's grandparents, Helen and Herman, had recently been prescribed the same medication, but Helen's dosage was considerably lower than her husband's. When she began to complain of dizziness and nausea, her family realized that she had mistakenly taken some of her husband's medication.

As a school project, Deborah reworked the bottle from the traditional round form to a semicircle. Next, Deborah tackled the prescription label. She researched what information was required on the label and then developed a clear, standardized format, with the drug name, dosage, and dosing schedule on the top of the label with a horizontal line across the label, separating this information from the secondary information below, such as the doctor's name, expiration date, and quantity prescribed. Deborah then color-coded the prescription label, using a different color for each family member's prescription. Finally, Deborah developed a paper card containing important drug information designed to fit into grooves on her new bottle. Deborah filed for a patent for her design, which was subsequently acquired by discount giant Target in August 2004. Target then teamed Deborah with an industrial designer, and they continued to hone the design.

Deborah's bottle design was subsequently modified (the odd-shaped semicircle cap made it too cumbersome to certify for child safety). Ultimately, a flatter, flasklike bottle that stands on its cap was created. Next, they switched the bottle's color from the usual amber to a cautionary red (also Target's brand color), and added brightly hued bands that slip easily over the lid, one color for each member of the family in order to minimize the confusion her grandmother had. (The bands replaced Deborah's initial idea for color-coded labels, which would have meant supplying Target pharmacists with color printers.) Finally, they refined the "patient information card," which contains important drug information such as side effects and warnings, and designed it to slip in behind the label on the bottle where the patient will see it, rather than having the pharmacist staple it to the pharmacy bag that usually ends up in the trash. In May 2005, Clear Rx debuted in Target pharmacies nationwide. Deborah's newly designed bottle appeared in a fall 2005 design exhibition at the Museum of Modern Art in New York and was recognized as one of *Time* magazine's inventions of the year. Deborah herself was featured in a Target TV commercial touting the new bottling system. Today, Deborah works as a graphic designer at Milton Glaser, Inc., in Manhattan.

How to Tell If You're Good at Your Core Competency

You need some measure of outside validation to tell you how the marketplace views your products (see table 2). One useful way to get a read on the industry's opinion of your company is through trade publications. If industry-focused newsletters and magazines write favorably about you, you'll know that both your competitors and your customers will read the good press. The same goes for trade awards that professional associations give out annually. You can influence your reputation within the industry to some degree by joining professional societies and meeting your peers. However, the market acts like a scale most of the time: If your products aren't exceptional, you won't get singled out for praise. If you do get recognized, the boost to your reputation will help you build a stable business.

Table 2: Tracking Your Company's Core Competencies

1. Maintain a file of complimentary e-mails and letters from satisfied customers and clients.

2. When you win a service renewal contract or an order for repeat business, keep a record of it in a file. Nothing says you're good better than a repeat order.

3. When a customer or client offers to refer you to someone else, ask him to write a letter or e-mail of introduction and copy your company on it.

4. Maintain a record of all articles, awards, and recognitions that appear in newspapers, radio, television, and magazines. If you're good at what you do, before you know it you'll be able to make your own DVD of your company's achievements.

5. Track the development and improvements upon your company's core products and services, and periodically communicate this information to your customers and clients. A newsletter or regular e-mail is a good way to reach them.

To keep track of how the outside world sees your company, start by maintaining a file of complimentary e-mails and letters from customers and clients. When you win a service renewal contract, or an order for repeat business, keep a record of it in a file. Nothing says you're good better than a repeat order. When a customer or client offers to refer you to someone else, ask him to write a letter or e-mail of introduction and copy your company on it.

Winning a big-name or large-dollar customer is also a huge coup. Ellen Bates won her own measure of recognition when Haworth, the largest manufacturer of office furnishings in the world, asked her to represent them exclusively in New Hampshire and Maine. Ellen keeps careful records of new wins and repeat business. It's important to tally these votes of confidence, along with those you get from peers and the media. These records confirm that your company has mastered its core competency.

If you maintain a record of all the articles, awards, and recognitions your company has received in newspapers, radio, television, and magazines, and if you're good at what you do, before you know it you'll be able to make a DVD of your company's achievements. Hinda Miller and Lisa

Lindahl knew they had hit the recognition jackpot when they learned that their innovative bra designs were going to be displayed at the Smithsonian Institution in Washington, D.C. Deborah Adler's prescription bottle design, Clear Rx, was recently exhibited at the Museum of Modern Art in New York City. But national acclaim isn't crucial. Wendy Goldstein and her business, for example, have been written up several times over the years by her local newspaper, *The Columbus Dispatch*. By 2002, when Wendy's company was shipping costumes to France, Germany, England, Japan, and Mexico, Costume Specialists received an Export Achievement Award from the U.S. Department of Commerce. In 2005, Women for Economic and Leadership Development in Columbus featured Wendy in its annual calendar showcasing successful Columbus businesswomen.

Track the development and improvements upon your company's core products and services, and periodically communicate this information to your customers. A newsletter or regular e-mail is a good way to reach them. Signage in your store, or an insert for your packaging, also allows you to tell them how your company is serving them better.

SUCCESS

In her first year as a special education teacher in a Los Angeles grade school, Marlene Canter found herself struggling to control her classroom because of discipline problems. When she couldn't find any useful materials to help her address the issue, she decided to solve the problem herself. She cofounded Canter & Associates to develop a program for teachers providing guidelines for coping with classroom discipline questions. Marlene began by writing a program and organizing a live workshop for hundreds of teachers. She videotaped the entire interactive workshop and edited it into an instructional video for teachers. Canter's first teacher-training video, *Assertive Discipline*, was a success. The company subsequently developed approximately fifty different teacher-training videos on different topics, using trained experts and teachers videotaped implementing the experts' approach in the classroom. Canter's company marketed the teaching videotapes directly to teachers. Marlene built a solid core business creating and selling instructional videotapes before she moved on to develop additional products.

REGRETS

Stephanie Durkin* is a dedicated high school history teacher and part-time librarian in Oklahoma City. She loves helping students with research projects, regardless of the topic. The more remote and challenging the topic, the more Stephanie lights up at the thought of guiding a student to the proper resources and helping him gather the information he needs.

Stephanie recently decided to develop a research service. She sought the advice of a group of seasoned businesswomen, many of whom had started, grown, and sold successful companies. These advisers suggested she not advertise at first and that she limit her purview to a few narrowly defined topics. Otherwise, they told her, she would be overwhelmed.

Despite having the foresight to ask for help, Stephanie decided not to follow the group's advice. With the goal of working part-time at her business, she decided to start by advertising locally. But she didn't anticipate the avalanche of responses. Customers sent her far afield and on tight deadlines, asking questions on topics as diverse as Islamic religious ritual objects and Paleolithic fossils. Soon Stephanie was utterly overwhelmed with inquiries. Within the first few weeks, customers were complaining about her slow service, and she had to deal with these angry calls rather than fulfilling more orders.

*The owner's name and location have been changed.

CHAPTER 3

Step 2: Build Your Company's Infrastructure

Picture the most cluttered clothing closet you have in your home or apartment. Now visualize it after a professional closet installation, complete with exact-height poles to hang dresses, skirts and jackets, custom-size cubicles for sweaters and shoes, hooks for belts, shelves to display hats and handbags, and built-in drawers for lingerie and jewelry. Open the closet door: Lights! You can see your wardrobe and accessories in an instant.

That's how organized your company should be if you want to run it smoothly and successfully long term. Whether you have three employees or thirty or 300, you need to put a solid framework in place, one that can grow with you and your vision of your company.

I. YOUR START-UP TEAM

The cornerstone of your infrastructure is the people and documents you need to start the company and the system you implement to track them. When it comes to finding professionals to work with you, hire the best, most compatible people you can find. They must share your vision for your business and complement your skills.

1. Get a Good Lawyer and a Sharp Accountant

A lawyer. Most of the women in this book used both a lawyer and a professional accountant to get their businesses off the ground. Fees for incorporation can range from $100 to upwards of $1,000, plus annual corporate taxes and the bill for a lawyer, if you hire one. But it's both possible and

easy for you to file the papers of incorporation yourself, without a professional. Mary Ann Pompea, who launched her own temporary-staffing
company, Hire Expectations, in Northville, Michigan, found that she
didn't need to hire someone to prepare the documents for her. She asked
advice from a friend who had his own company, then went on the Internet
and sent away for her corporate seal and articles of incorporation.

Incorporation papers, however, represent only the first of many reasons
why an entrepreneur needs an attorney. Questions requiring legal advice
crop up often as a business grows. It's worth your time to identify a lawyer
you like and respect. She should charge reasonable fees, and understand
both your industry and your company. You will likely be relying on this
person for advice as your company takes off.

A Cornerstone of Your Infrastructure: Your Legal Structure

When I started my second company, AM Medica Communications, in
1986, a lawyer who was also a former colleague became a passive minority
investor. I knew, from the experience of owning my first business, that AM
Medica would not need legal services too often, so I was content to rely on
this partner for occasional questions. A few years later, however, my partner left the company amicably, and I no longer had an on-call counsel. I
then hired a good lawyer with a small firm on an as-needed basis to deal
with whatever issues came up.

BOX 2: A CORNERSTONE OF YOUR INFRASTRUCTURE: YOUR LEGAL STRUCTURE

*There are four options. The one you choose is usually determined by liabil-
ity and tax issues.*

Sole Proprietorship
*If you are starting out as a sole business owner working from home with
one or two employees, you may opt for sole proprietorship.*

*Register with your state government to obtain a business license and
you're off. As long as you remain a solo business owner in a business at low*

risk for a lawsuit initiated by a customer or client, this status is fine. Keep in mind, though, that if you are sued, your business and personal assets are on the line. In addition, if your business ends up in debt, you are personally responsible for payment. Finally, depending on the type of business you are in, such as a hairdresser working on your own, you may need a particular license.

General Partnership

Get a good lawyer, and make sure separate counsel represents each partner. The articles of partnership spell out the following:

- partners' names; the business's location, and type of business
- each partner's responsibilities, and the decision-making process
- how disputes will be resolved
- amount of money and time each partner will contribute to the business
- duration of the partnership and what happens when a partner becomes disabled or dies
- methods to alter the partnership, such as buyout provisions, dissolution, or the addition of more partners
- when and how profits will be distributed and how profits may get reinvested in the company
- the accounting method the partnership will use

Like a sole proprietorship, partners may also be held personally liable, and each partner is taxed according to their percentage of the partnership income.

Corporations, Sub-S and C

A corporation is a distinct legal entity separate from you, the owner. If your company goes bankrupt, defaults on bank loans, or is sued, your losses cannot exceed what you invested in your company. (The exception to this rule is if you, as the business owner, also personally guaranteed payment of certain bills, such as utility bills.) In addition, a corporation needs a board of directors, officers, and bylaws. It also has to hold meetings and keep minutes. Failure to do so may result in the IRS stating that you've run the business as a partnership or as a sole proprietor, in which case you could be held personally liable for claims made against the company.

continued

Sub-S Corporation

A "sub-S" status means the corporation can have only a small number of stockholders (75) and one type of stock. It protects you personally from being liable in a lawsuit; rather, your corporation is liable. In a sub-S corporation the income is subject only to personal income tax. Shareholders report their share of the company's profits on their income tax returns. A sub-S corp does not pay a federal corporate income tax. As a corporation you'll also be able to raise money by selling stock in your firm, if you wish, and you can fully deduct employee disability and health insurance premiums.

C Corporation

Unlike a sub-S, in a C corporation profits are taxed at the corporate level, and the stockholders who receive dividends must also pay ordinary income tax on the dividends. Thus, C corporations are subject to double taxation. Larger companies are often C corporations. These corporations can issue different classes of stock, such as voting and nonvoting or common and preferred, rather than being limited to one type of stock, as is a sub-S. Finally, a C corporation generally can raise more money than a sub-S because it can issue common stock.

LLC

The limited liability company combines the advantages of a corporation and those of a partnership. The LLC also provides favorable tax status in that the income and losses of the firm flow through to members who pay tax once on their personal income tax form. The LLC, like a corporation, also provides protection from personal liability. In an LLC, members are governed by an operating agreement, which may be similar to a partnership agreement, or more complicated. Finally, the LLC does not have the formal requirements that a sub-S has, such as scheduling regular board meetings or keeping minutes. An LLC can also have more shareholders than a sub-S, and they don't have to be U.S. residents or citizens, as they do in a sub-S.

Several years later, I was having dinner with friends, and I realized that one of them, Bill, had been picking up increasing numbers of pharmaceutical clients in his law practice. When I saw Bill socially, we would talk about the pharmaceutical industry and discuss my business. Bill wasn't working for me, but he knew all about my company. When serious preliminary negotiations began to buy my company, I hired Bill, whose firm had since merged with ReedSmith, LLP, a top law firm, as my lead counsel. I felt very comfortable with him, his level of expertise in my industry, and his experience in dealmaking. (The lawyer who had managed small routine legal issues for me agreed that I should retain Bill, too.) All that was necessary was for me and my accountant to give him the details of our financials. Bill already understood how our business worked, who our key clients were, and what services we provided.

An accountant. A good accountant can help you to design the financial infrastructure that makes the best sense for your company, your customers, and your suppliers. Although your company may be small today, it could mushroom within a few years. By choosing an accountant who has the capacity to serve your company as it grows, you can save yourself the time and trouble of having to familiarize a new accountant with your business. But if you make a mistake in your choice, it could be a costly one.

Bad experiences. Lane Nemeth ran into this problem as her California educational-toy company, Discovery Toys, moved out of its start-up phase. The idea for the company was born soon after her daughter, Tara. In 1978, caring for her toddler and casting around for something to do with her newfound free time, Lane discovered how few learning-related toys were on the market. Spurred by a shortfall in her family's finances—her husband had recently lost his job—Lane decided to pursue the toy business. When her father shot down her idea for a retail toy store, telling her she had too much energy to be a shopkeeper, she decided to become a toy distributor. Her father suggested starting a direct-sales toy business using home-based parties, Tupperware-style. She borrowed $5,000 from her grandmother, ordered shipments of twenty different toys at a trade show, and rented the best space she could afford: 900 square feet of a warehouse with mice and no electrical wiring.

Despite the conditions, Lane loved her new business and it thrived. The company was a quick success with parents who wanted stimulating toys for their children. Lane however, made the serious error of hiring an accountant and a lawyer unable to handle her work. Her accountant was sloppy, delivering her financial statements months late and in an indecipherable format. Her lawyer lacked the expertise to write appropriate employee agreements, a problem that haunted her years later, when the original clauses regarding stock options sparked pitched battles between Lane and some of her staffers.

Joanne Piraino, who founded an Essington, Pennsylvania, promotional-products company, the Main Line Embroidery & Design Company, made a similar blunder two decades ago. "We made the mistake of getting accountants who really didn't know what they were doing," she says. A competent accountant is a basic requirement, but entrepreneurs need someone who will help spot red flags in your financial statements. An accountant who simply computes your payroll and corporate taxes, gets your signature, and mails the forms in may be doing his job adequately, but without explaining to you what the numbers say and preparing forecasts for you, he is of little use. As Joanne advises, entrepreneurs should hire an accountant who points out trends, pitfalls, or an unexpectedly successful product or service.

Good experiences. As with all aspects of a new business, it's often helpful to seek the advice of seasoned entrepreneurs when choosing the professionals who will help you run your company. Suzy Vasillov opened her own fine-housewares boutique, Keesal & Mathews, in Manhattan's chic Upper East Side neighborhood at the age of twenty-six, armed only with an art history degree, five years' retail experience, and an idea for an upscale shop. Before she opened the store, she consulted two uncles who had started their own companies. Both told her to find an accountant to serve her company as it grew. A friend recommended a young CPA just opening a practice. The two shared the experience of launching their companies at the same time, and the accountant became a useful sounding board for Suzy. Her strategy, which she followed as the store became successful, was to hire professionals who, like her, loved what they did and brought a vision to their work.

Changing accountants. Because you hire lawyers and accountants for a fixed assignment—such as preparing one year's worth of taxes or a particular supplier contract—rather than keeping them permanently on your payroll, you should find a new person if your relationship is not working out. Wendy Goldstein replaced her accountant several times as her business grew. Originally, Wendy's husband handled the company's finances. When they divorced, she had to find a new accountant, someone who hewed more closely to her style of management. "I needed someone that I could relate to," she says. "I didn't always make the wisest choices when I first started out, but I learned and I got better," she says.

Table 3: Checklist for Building the Best Start-up Team

For your lawyer and accountant:

- Are you familiar with our industry?
- Do you have clients in our industry? Which ones?
- Are you generally available on a day or two's notice?
- If an emergency occurs, can I reach you in the evenings and weekends?
- Will you be my contact, or will one or more people in your firm work on my business?
- What is your fee structure, and can you wait thirty to sixty days for payment?
- How long have you been in practice?
- Have you ever been sued?
- Do you have references?
- What is your specialty?

For your advisory board:

- Can I identify you as an adviser in our company's promotional materials?
- Are you available on a monthly basis for a meeting?
- Can you provide me with sales, vendor, and employee leads, or advise me on financing?
- How long are you willing to serve as an adviser?
- When your tenure as an adviser is up, can you recommend someone to replace you?

2. Boards of Directors and Boards of Advisers

If your business is set up as a corporation (see table 3), you'll need a board of directors. This group can consist of as few people as you, your lawyer, and any individual outside the company. These directors are legally required to meet on a quarterly basis to discuss the direction and the finances of the company, and to keep minutes of their meetings. Because directors can be held legally liable if someone sues the company, you will need to take out directors' and officers' insurance for everyone on your board.

As a new entrepreneur, you may also want to assemble a board of advisers. This group has no legal standing; its only role is to give you advice on whatever business decisions you need vetted. If your advisers have recognizable names within your industry or are associated with top companies, having them on your advisory board will give your business instant credibility when dealing with vendors, customers, and partners. Good advisers can help you recruit the best employees, give you sales leads, and point you toward reliable subcontractors. Your advisers will support you and suggest strategies as your business grows. The membership of this board can also be changed as the company's needs evolve.

Beyond the individuals you tap as your personal advisers, a wealth of free services exists for entrepreneurs. The first place to look is your local chamber of commerce. This group is designed to help business owners navigate the complexities of local government and to advocate for policies that favor small businesses. Your chamber can tell you about regulations you need to observe, as well as local events or shows at which small businesses will be featured. Several women have found other organizations to be similarly helpful as their companies grew. The Resource Guide that begins on page 243 provides additional information.

Joanne Piraino, the promotional-product provider, found both her local chamber of commerce and the Newtown Square Small and Professionals Business Association in Essington, Pennsylvania, where her company is based, to be helpful. These groups gave her referrals to both an attorney and an accountant as she was starting her business, as well as linking her to insurance companies with group rates aimed at entrepreneurs. After twenty-five years in business, Joanne still employs the first lawyer her local business association found for her. Doreen Marks had similar luck with her local SBA, as well as with SCORE, a group of retired businesspeople who volunteer their time to advise entrepreneurs. "Retired individuals are out there who can help you; they just have a wealth of knowledge that, as a start-up, you can't afford to pay for," she says.

In addition, businesswomen should make an effort to have their companies designated women-owned, says Lynne Marie Finn, an attorney and president of Superior Staffing Services, Inc., in Williamsville, New York. Lynne is an ambassador for the Women's Business Enterprise National Council (WBENC) and serves on the group's Leadership Forum and several committees. Local chapters can help women get this credential, ensuring them better access to business from the government and from large companies that must meet diversification requirements.

BOX 3: STEPS TO WBENC CERTIFICATION

The process:
Typically, the process for becoming certified as a woman-owned business takes sixty to ninety days. The application is available online at www .wbenc.org. When submitted, it is funneled to one of fourteen partner organizations, based on location, covering all fifty states. Criteria include:

- U.S. citizenship or resident alien status
- Proof that a woman manages, controls, and owns 51 percent of the company

Numerous documents must be submitted with the application, including a history of your business, a copy of the bank authorization signature card, financial statements, and three years' worth of income tax returns. Personnel, management, and other legal documents are also required, as is a sworn affidavit verifying your information. Any woman-owned business that meets these criteria may apply for certification.

What it provides:
WBENC says that more than 700 major corporations, as well as several federal and government agencies, accept WBENC certification. This designation allows your company to compete for contracts from the government or from companies that have diverse-supplier policies.

Fees:
The fees range from $250 to $350

Recertification:
This is an annual process, and a small fee applies.

Source: http://www.wbenc.org

3. The Perils and Perks of Partnerships

The upside of a partnership is the ability to split financial risk and sweat equity. In a good working relationship, partners know their respective strengths and weaknesses, observe each other's boundaries, and remain focused on the same business goals. Partnerships have been useful for many of the businesswomen profiled in this book. Conventional wisdom holds that families should not work together, but several of the entrepreneurs you've already met have successful partnerships with their husbands. Gail Warrior and Beverly Edge both run businesses with their husbands and both recommend this arrangement. In Wendy Goldstein's case, however, a lack of financial discussion led to her business's demise and her marriage failed as well.

Partnerships can be tricky. Hinda Miller recalls that she and her equal partner, Lisa Landahl, had "a difficult partnership because we were so different, but through that tension we found the middle path to be successful." They stayed partners until they sold their company. Angela Drummond started her company with a partner, then another partner came on board a year later. But five years after start-up, in 1997, Angela and one partner bought out the third, and in 2000, Angela bought out her remaining partner, leaving her the sole owner of her company. Angela says her partners wanted to pursue other ventures; the partners also differed on strategic direction. Angela saw that she could build the business into a serious company rather than it remaining a small, twenty-five-person consulting firm. Today, she has more than seventy-five employees.

A poisonous partnership can rapidly tank your business. Unlike your lawyer or CPA, who are hired guns, your partner is integral to your company. During the start-up phase, your partner may be half the company's staff. If you and your partner don't agree on either a professional or a personal level, and you can't work out your differences, the company will suffer.

Husbands as Business Partners

Although many professional advisers warn against husband-wife business alliances, I interviewed several women whose experiences were positive when working with their husbands. What they told me reveals why these unions work.

Perks. Defining who does what is critical in any partnership, whether with a spouse or a stranger. Gail Warrior and her husband agreed at the beginning that he would meet with clients, focus on business development, and handle sales, while she would manage the company, deal with public relations, and take care of the accounting. To mark this division of labor,

Gail took the chief executive title, while Wayne became vice president of business development. "I always tell people that Wayne is not allowed to do anything on my side but I can dabble in whatever he is doing," says Gail, whose marriage has lasted twelve years and now sustains a successful company.

Beverly Gray and her husband, Mike, who run Exhibit Edge in Fairfax, Virginia, have split their tasks in a similar fashion. Beverly supervises the employees and oversees accounting, while Mike is the company's traveling salesman. From her earliest days in the company, Beverly has appreciated Mike's in-depth understanding of the exhibit business. "My first emotion was one of 'Wow, Mike really knows his industry,'" she says.

Perils. Wendy Goldstein wasn't as lucky. Her company, Costume Specialists, began as a sole proprietorship in 1981 and was incorporated ten years later. In the beginning, her husband ran the costume rental store and managed the finances, while Wendy and their employees sewed. The couple put all their money into the business and borrowed from family as well. But by 1992, the company, of which Wendy was the official owner, was in trouble, with several liens and filings against it. The couple's marriage, meanwhile, was breaking up, due in part to the company's difficulties. While both spouses shared the dream of making the business a success, Wendy says that she and her husband, who came from an entrepreneurial family, did not communicate candidly about the company's finances. Wendy left financial management to her husband while she focused on sales and product development. By the time Wendy grasped the full financial picture the situation was dire. As part of the divorce settlement, Wendy assumed the company's debt and took full control of the business.

Colleagues as Business Partners

The reasons partnerships succeed or fail are as varied as the people and the businesses themselves. Successful partners share goals and have complementary skills, while failed partnerships often stem from clashes in personality and management styles. Interestingly, I have never come upon a partnership that failed because the business itself was failing. In all cases, the partners simply could not work together any longer.

Perks. When Jozi Legner decided to start her own engineering services firm, at age thirty-four, she had several points in her favor, including fifteen years' experience doing research for engineering firms, a reputation in her field, and the ability to have her company certified as woman- and minority-owned. But she lacked formal engineering training. Jozi recruited a young civil engineer, twenty-four-year-old Matt Linville, to be her partner. Both had a driving ambition and a desire to make the company succeed at whatever personal cost. To save money, they incorporated the company themselves, and they scaled back their living standards. Matt moved back in with his parents, and Jozi took a small efficiency apartment over her family's garage. They poured their savings and the business's first profits back into the company for the first few years. Eight years later, Matt is still vice president and treasurer of J.Y. Legner & Associates, while Jozi remains the president and CEO. "We have a terrific working relationship," Jozi says.

Working moms as partners. Shelley Rote and Maria Irwin own a meeting-planning and special events company, Signature Events, in New Orleans. Shelley had been an X-ray technician and had worked in her husband's auto-parts business before joining Signature, where she met Maria, who was also on staff. The two bought out the company's owners and became equal partners in the business, which organizes events based on New Orleans themes. Later, they added two minority-stake partners as well.

Shelley and Maria are ambitious, but they also share quality-of-life goals, which they discussed before starting their partnership. Shelley has three children and Maria has four. "We're sensitive to working mothers," Shelley says. "As long as people get their work done, it's okay if they work at home." In their nine-year partnership, Shelley and Maria have managed to remain friends while respecting each other's contributions to the company. Their partnership agreements take a more hard-nosed view, however, spelling out in careful detail the buyout provisions in the event one partner wants to leave the business. The company is well organized and the partnership functions at such a high level that Shelley thinks she could "probably go into a coma for six months and come out and everything would be exactly the way it should be."

Perils. If you're lucky, you may be able to struggle through with a partner or two until the business is sold, as Hinda Miller and her partner did. But more often than not, dysfunctional partnerships dissolve. Make sure that in taking out a partner, you don't torpedo your own company.

Litigation. Helga Grayson and Dyana King came perilously close to losing their firm when they found themselves in a nasty lawsuit with a third partner. They started Thinknicity, a San Francisco biotech and IT place-ment firm, in 1997. The company was incorporated as a limited liability company (see chapter 3, box 1), which requires an operating agreement, and the partners wrote it themselves, Helga said. But although all three wanted to see the company perform well, the problems surfaced quickly. Helga and Dyana wanted a nonhierarchical organization, but their part-ner disagreed. Employees complained that they did not want to report to the third partner, who was in charge of sales. As such, the contributions she could make diminished. "At that point," Helga said, "everything just fell apart because there wasn't any role for her in the company anymore."

Helga and Dyana knew they would have to talk to their third partner about developing an exit strategy for her. They hired an appraiser to deter-mine the company's value in order to set a fair buyout price. Regrettably, before the appraisal was completed, the third partner sued for dissolution of the company. A yearlong court battle followed. In California, corporate owners have the statutory right to avoid dissolution by paying the dissent-ing member out. But Helga and Dyana agree it was never about the money. Rather, they thought that the third partner simply wanted to see the entire company sold or destroyed.

Finally, Helga and Dyana won the right to arbitration. The morning the process was scheduled to begin, the third partner agreed to a settlement. Helga and Dyana had paid out approximately $300,000 in legal fees. Helga said that their lawyers told them they had never seen a case as nasty as this one in twenty-five years of practicing law. The situation was so bizarre, in fact, that representatives from Berkeley's Haas School of Busi-ness came to the court hearings to witness the circus.

Helga and Dyana always knew they could work together because they complement each other's strengths and respect each other. However, both ignored a visceral feeling from the beginning that their third partner would be difficult to handle in case of a disagreement. "We should have followed our gut," Helga says. "The most important lesson I have learned is to choose your partner very, very wisely."

Dissolution. When Susan Daywitt secured both the Boston Market and the Office Max accounts, her company, Environmental Waste Consul-tants, received an overture from a competitor who had the Eckerd Drug account. The women barely knew each other, and Susan did not have any background checks or legal searches performed on her new colleague when they began working together. But after a year, in 1993, Susan asked her attorney to draw up a formal partnership agreement. Susan moved from sales to operations, and her partner began dealing with most of the clients. "At the beginning," Susan says, "we had the same goals, the same dreams," but as time went on, personal styles collided and tensions rose. Within four years, the partners decided to split up. Susan then went back and carried out a background search on her partner, checking for legal or professional issues. To her horror, Susan learned enough to know she was definitely not professionally or personally compatible with the woman she had taken on as a business partner.

The partners went to court in a battle Susan described as "the worst divorce a person can go through." The litigation was so ugly that the court ordered them to dissolve the company and take whatever accounts they could win. Instead, most of the clients simply left to find another contractor. Fortunately, Susan retained her first client, Boston Market, as well as Taco Bell and Wendy's. She started another company, SLM Waste & Recycling Services, in 1998, working from her house with three employees. But her confidence was badly shaken. "It was absolutely awful," she says, "and I will never, ever get another partner, absolutely never again."

In the start-up years of your company, you should expect to spend as much time with your partner as with your spouse, if not more. Ask yourself: Do I really need a partner? Do I think my partner will be as valuable to me in five years as she appears to be now? Before you go into business with a partner, consider these options first:

- If you want a partner to help finance the business, consider alternative sources of funding (see chapter 4, step 3).
- If you want a partner to contribute complementary skills, think about hiring someone with those skills and offer profit-sharing rather than full-blown partnership, including generous bonus provisions if you sell the company.
- If you want a partner to help share the emotional load of running your business, hire professionals you can lean on. Suzy Vasillov and I both used accountants and lawyers as sounding boards and found that they were always available when we needed advice. My accountant also offered to work in my office rather than his own when I took vacation, to ensure things ran smoothly.

If you already have a partner and want to take steps to safeguard the partnership, or at least to ensure that if a breakup occurs it is smooth, swift, professional, and disrupts your company as little as possible, discuss options with your lawyer now. Review your partnership or operating agreement carefully. Be sure you understand your options in a separation. Consider the range of worst-case scenarios and research how your partnership documents would handle such cases. Finally, you can also sit down with your partner on a quarterly basis to discuss the macro strategy of the business and to talk about how the partnership is going. Hold the meeting in a formal setting. Get any issues on the table as soon as possible.

4. Grow Your Infrastructure with Good Employees

Your staff is the foundation of your infrastructure. Every entrepreneur needs a core of employees who know how to handle the company's operations while she develops new business. Finding and keeping these workers is one of a businesswoman's toughest challenges. Shelley Rote and Maria Irwin made an early decision to start as equal partners, and then provide equity to one or two key employees who proved their value over the years. Since Shelley and Maria bought Signature Events, they have reduced their stake, while two additional employees became minority partners. That's one way to keep the best players in the fold. In other instances, though, adversity points the way.

Dealing with 9/11. By 2001, Joanne Piraino had been running her promotional-products company successfully for years. Delta Air Lines, Avis Rent A Car, Disney, and several destination management companies were all her customers. But after the terrorist attacks dried up the country's travel and trade-show business, Joanne's company lost many of its orders. Disney pulled out, basically shutting down her Florida business. Just before Christmas, Joanne realized she had to do major layoffs. "It was horrible," she says. "It was really hard to make the choices." Still, Joanne understood that to hold on to her business, tough decisions had to be made, and she made them. The company kept the most able employees, those who had the most experience, good attitudes, and good attendance. She had to lay off the rest.

A dramatic downturn in business is far from the ideal way to determine who your MVPs are and how to keep them. But Joanne learned a valuable lesson about evaluating her employees regularly. She and her senior team now meet frequently to talk about efficiencies in her workforce, including the best ways to reward and retain the most productive employees.

Saving the family business. Debra Revzen's loyalty to her employees, and their reciprocal devotion to her, made running her business possible through difficult times. Debra's father had founded an envelope company in Minneapolis, from which he retired in the early 1980s, leaving a relative in charge. Debra had never worked in the business; she was working as a lawyer for a large Minneapolis firm when the 2001 terrorist attacks hit. She knew the family company was in a rough patch, but she was shocked when the relative in charge abruptly announced, just after the attacks, that he would be closing the company and laying off all thirty employees. When Debra found out, she felt responsible for the workers, many of whom her father had hired years earlier. She met with the general manager over the weekend, and he assured her that the business was viable. Although she knew nothing about the envelope industry, Debra was motivated to save the company by "the thought of thirty people being out of jobs in a worsening economy." She shifted her legal work to part-time, bought workman's compensation insurance, and reincorporated the company as Twin City Envelope, reopening it in October 2001 as president.

Her employees haven't forgotten the way she stepped in to save their jobs. When her general manager developed pancreatic cancer two years after the reincorporation, he insisted on coming to work for as long as he could to help her out. When, six months later, he died from the disease, his sister, also an employee, continued to work for the company, and two other employees stepped up to split the general manager's job. Since Twin City Envelope began, Debra has not lost a single key employee. Her winning strategy is "to make employees feel good about being here, and recognize them for their contributions and good work." For her dedication and business success, she was named 2004 Woman Entrepreneur of the Year by the *Twin Cities Business Journal*.

Give Employees Reasons to Stay

Finding good employees at any level is as much art as science. First, be thorough in reviewing résumés and check references carefully. Next, when hiring a middle- or senior-level manager, speak with someone who has worked directly with the individual in another company. If you can locate and talk to more than one person, it's worth the effort. Whatever you do, don't rely on headhunters to do this work for you. Remember, they don't know your corporate culture, your customers, or your staff.

I was lucky to be able to retain my top staffers when I was running my company. My three top sales directors stayed on although our industry was highly competitive and recruiters called them regularly. My editorial director, who joined at the company's founding, stayed on even after I sold the firm, and my operations manager worked with me for years. To give them an incentive to stay with my company, I offered good salaries and commission structures just above the industry norm for my sales directors. But money is never enough to keep top people. I knew retaining talented, level-headed employees was a must if I wanted to grow the company and sell it someday. It's important to give your key employees reasons to stay, not leave. Here are the ten guidelines I recommend to keep the best employees.

1. **Never lose sight of your most valuable assets: your key employees.** Many businesswomen own and operate service companies. Without our best workers, we are out of business. I wasn't the first to say this, but I never forgot it when I heard it: My company's assets go up and down in the elevator every day. So on a bad day think about this: If one of your valued employees quit, how good would your company be?

2. **Be available.** Anyone can get rattled, from the most seasoned sales director or manager to a young assistant. I encouraged junior staff to talk to their supervisors when they encountered problems. If a senior person wants to talk to you about issues in the company or in her job, make yourself available as soon as possible. Don't let problems fester.

3. **Show respect.** I insisted sales directors call me after each appointment, whether they made a simple sales call or went on a major client presentation. Not only was I was able to hear how the meeting went, but far more important, this practice told them that the most important thing going on in my day was to hear about how their day was going. Show your key employees that they are a priority to you.

4. **Don't bother an employee who is traveling on business.** Working in different locations with several clients is challenging. Often it involves stressful travel, late-night and weekend work, and time away from family. As such, all of us agreed on a house rule: Don't call anyone traveling on business to relay bad news. These problems were brought to me to resolve, or to decide whether or not someone had to be notified. Give your key personnel peace of mind on the road. They'll thank you for it.

5. **Set a clear tone, direction, and goals in a dynamic environment.** My commitment to having a stable, successful business was well known among clients and employees alike. I wanted my company to be the best, but I wanted us to have some fun at it too. I met with my senior managers in early January of each year, the only formal meeting I held annually. This meeting set the tone and established goals for the year. The senior managers in turn conveyed these messages to the rest of the staff. Solid, professional employees working in an entrepreneurial environment need to see and believe in your leadership. Their careers depend on your direction, so make sure you communicate your company's goals to your top employees regularly, and set up a feedback system to get their input on where the company is going.

6. **Check in often with senior managers.** A once-a-month meeting won't do the trick. I asked my senior staff to drop in daily, if only briefly. I genuinely liked to see my senior sales directors and managers and talk with them, and they knew it. Mutual regard goes a long way toward turning a valued employee into a trusted part of your company's infrastructure.

7. **Be flexible when possible.** When you spend time with your key employees you get to know them better, and, hopefully, you can intercept a problem before it spirals out of control. Does a top exec need to work at home one day a week? Get the question on the table and provide as much flexibility and consideration as you can. That's one way to help keep a star employee from leaving your firm.

8. **Take a walk.** If you want to know how things are going in your office, get up from your desk twice a day and walk around the floor. You may spot a worker using skills you didn't know about, or you may find a top manager unraveling at her desk. While it's not wise to solve every problem you encounter on these strolls, it is useful for you to see your team in action, and for them to see you engaged as well. Gauging the "room tone" in your office is a good way to measure morale as well.

9. **Recognize contributions and achievements.** Never forget to say thank you, great job, or well done. An unexpected bouquet of flowers, a bottle of wine, or permission to leave early on the eve of a long weekend goes a long way toward building employee loyalty.

10. **Admit when you are wrong.** Employers aren't infallible, and you're no
    exception. If you've made a mistake, even a minor one, address it, apol-
    ogize if necessary, and move on. Solid, capable employees want to work
    for someone they believe is even better than they are. You can't be that
    boss if you don't know how to admit an error, correct it, and keep going.

Organizing Your Employees

Once you have employees, even just a few, you need an organizational
chart. Without a formal map of the hierarchy, companies can fall into
management traps, such as having every employee report to the owner.
Avoid these headaches from the start. Your organizational chart should list
job titles, show reporting lines, and spell out divisions of labor. Finally,
whenever possible, avoid having your employees report to more than one
supervisor. It's tough for a midlevel manager to please two bosses.

When I started AM Medica, I began with eight employees, three of
whom reported directly to me: a sales director, an editorial director, and a
senior meeting planner. When I sold my company twelve years later, with
four times the number of employees, I had three sales directors reporting
to me, as well as the editorial director and a senior meeting planner, who
served as operations manager. Although our revenues and earnings more
than quintupled, in twelve years I increased only by two the total number
of employees reporting directly to me. You can't run a company effectively
if everyone needs you for daily direction.

Some women business owners don't like the formality of a full-fledged
human resources infrastructure because they have difficulty delegating.
Often, women prefer warm, nurturing relationships, including with their
employees. This tendency leads to a reluctance to have staffers report to
someone else. In addition, many women in business have significant
hands-on experience performing support functions. They've answered
phones, changed copier cartridges, and filled out FedEx forms. Because of
this background, they don't see the need to designate an employee to do
these tasks, even when their own time is required for high-level strategic
thinking at the company.

Learn to delegate so you can devote more of your time to growth strategies. As your company grows, create departments with directors, and have
the directors report to you. Listen to your management team if it recom-
mends combining two departments. We combined two departments at my

company: meeting-planning services and operations. Revise your organizational chart accordingly, and review and update it annually, or as employees come and go.

Job descriptions. The job description is a secret weapon of successful small companies. When an employee quits or is terminated in a smaller company, the replacement is often left floundering. Small firms don't have human resources departments to direct new employees, and it's often not feasible to get one employee to show a new employee the ropes. Here a job description comes in handy as a step-by-step guide to explain to newcomers how to do each job.

Job descriptions should always include essential general information such as how to use all of the phone system features properly, how to fill out the company expense account, how the company organizes and maintains its computer and hard copy files, how to request supplies, when to seek a supervisor's approval on travel and expenses, and, most important, how a specific job is executed in the company. Department heads should develop these job descriptions, and employees should contribute to updating them regularly. Detailed job descriptions save considerable time, especially when an employee is out suddenly due to illness or is on vacation. Another benefit is the built-in consistency throughout your business. In our company, for instance, all sales directors followed the same formats for proposals and budgets. All meeting planners followed the same rules for opening and closing out jobs and initiating final invoices. Even dress codes for business travel were included in job descriptions. Putting these requirements in writing will help streamline your operation and ensure consistency.

At Laguna Culinary Arts, Nancy Milby and her managers spent a great deal of time creating an instructor's handbook for chefs. This manual details everything from "where to find the bathroom key to how to lock up at the end of the night, and everything in between," Nancy says. The one-inch-thick handbook has saved Nancy and her staff hours of training time.

II. DOCUMENTING YOUR BUSINESS

The least glamorous and most tedious aspect of having your own company is the assembly and maintenance of critical business documents. But this drawer full of paper can save you from legal snafus and strategic sinkholes. Once you hire a good lawyer and accountant, they can help you identify the documents you need and facilitate obtaining licenses, insurance, and regulatory papers. But before that, the first big document, the business plan, is up to you.

1. Writing and Maintaining Your Business Plan

A good business plan is a blueprint for success. Write a thorough business plan and refer to it quarterly to help you think through your goals and how to reach them. Ideally, your business plan should be in place before you open your doors. (See Table 4: Your Full Life Cycle Business Plan Checklist.) It's possible, of course, to simply start a company without bothering to formalize your plans for it, but the smart businesswoman will go back later and write a plan. Without one, a company can easily veer off track.

Table 4: Your Full Life Cycle Business Plan Checklist

Elements:	*What to include:*
_____ Executive summary	Summarize your plan in 3 to 4 pages
_____ Mission statement	Describe company's goals and solutions
_____ Legal structure	How is your company registered?
_____ Company founder/location	Your name, address of company
_____ Board of directors, if needed	List names, titles, experience
_____ Description of business	What does your company do? Describe competitors, growth strategies
_____ Marketing plans	Define your market; how you'll reach customers; what methods of advertising you will use; how you will compete; how you will distinguish your products and/or services

_____ Applicable regulations	Licenses and/or permits
_____ Intellectual property, trademarks, and patents	How will you safeguard your ideas, products?
_____ Sales	Who sells; will you outsource?
_____ Financials	Spell out how you will finance your business; list investors; detail start-up costs; show cash flow statements for first year; forecasts for annual revenues and earnings by quarter for three years, and how you got to the numbers
_____ Organizational chart	Job titles, descriptions, and reporting lines
_____ Employees	Personnel you will need, skills
_____ Operations	Day-to-day office management
_____ Exit strategies	Options appropriate for your company

The commando strategy. Ghislaine Bérubé enjoys fiddling with oils, creams, and makeup. As a hobby, she created and trademarked Lobsterman's Balm, a unisex stick cream for hands and body, in her South Portland, Maine, basement five years ago. The cream was a hit with her family and friends, so she developed other products, including a lip balm and skin lotion.

Ghislaine's first foray into the commercial world was at a local crafts fair, which a friend suggested would be a perfect way to market her products. She ordered bottles and labels, arranged clip art, and put the packaging together herself. But, without having done any research, she didn't realize that the label ink ran easily. "No one told me about the mistakes I was making, so I just forged ahead," she says. Her husband paid all of the expenses. He also carried the goods to the fair. The event earned her $1,000, barely covering her outlay.

Ghislaine continued to flounder as she tried to turn her creams into a real business. A $3,000 set of professional bottle labels had to be scrapped after delivery, due to her own incorrect measurements. She bought a pricey color laser printer, and hired a professional design agency to build her a website. While the site has done well, a series of ads she placed in *The New Yorker* and *Yankee* magazine has not paid off in sales. Although Ghislaine puts in forty-hour weeks and hopes to turn a profit within three years, she has seen no sign, thus far, of making back the $100,000 that her husband invested in the business. Although she knows there are experts who could help her get the company off the ground, Ghislaine feels that she is "reinventing the wheel all the time."

Ghislaine's business is eating up all of her brainpower and creativity. Despite her efforts, she is still spending money without thinking strategicly rather than dealing with the boring but vital job of writing a business plan that will help her get assistance with production, marketing, and finance.

Going with a plan. Unlike Ghislaine's approach, the skin care business that Joanna Schmidt recently started demonstrates the value of starting with a business plan. A mother of two and a former New York City event planner, Joanna began researching cosmetic formulations after her family moved to Florida. She has developed several products, which she sells through her website, www.productbody.com. Like Ghislaine's business, Joanna's burgeoning company represents a considerable investment for her and her husband. She used her credit cards and some of her savings to start the company from her kitchen table, and she promotes the products herself. But Joanna took the time to write a business plan detailing her goals and strategy. After reviewing the plan with her husband, Joanna agreed that she would either turn a profit within two years or give up the business. She sticks to her small operating budget and seeks advice from professionals, including her accountant.

A good business plan will also serve as a sales tool for you if you ever seek professional financing. This document is the first thing a banker or investor will request when deciding whether to give you financial backing. Throughout the life of your company, a business plan will save you from making the type of scattershot mistakes Ghislaine is making by forcing you to think through your aims and identify the steps needed to accomplish them.

A teacher's lesson plan. In her first years teaching elementary school in Los Angeles, Jill Gaynor realized that some young children were falling behind, often in kindergarten. Jill moved on to get her master's degree, and in her last semester started training at the Kelter Center, an educational, remediation, and testing center. There she decided to team up with

Erin Smith to create educational programs for children, beginning with a trademarked pilot program for three- to six-year-olds called Bright Bee. Erin and Jill incorporated their company, Beyond Learning, and agreed to develop additional programs for different age groups. But before they got too far ahead, the pair spent months writing a detailed business plan. They addressed such issues as creating complimentary DVDs, packaging, production of the learning kit, financing, marketing, and distribution. Both partners are still working on the plan, holding off further product development until they both feel comfortable that they've researched every major aspect thoroughly. Jill and Erin are still teaching while they finalize their plans for Beyond Learning. When their business plan is complete, it will be a road map for their product development and distribution. It will also be suitable for use in raising money (see chapter 4, step 3: Keep Good Financials).

Don't forget the exit strategy. One of the most exciting aspects of thinking about your own business occurs at the drawing board stage, when you can also think about how and when you will exit. When you put your business plan together, think about the full life cycle of your business, from start-up to exit. Think about how, when, and to whom you would like to sell or give your company. Although nearly all of the businesswomen I speak to have a business plan in place, many often say that they have no

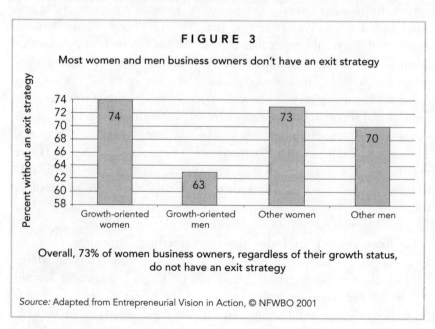

FIGURE 3

Most women and men business owners don't have an exit strategy

Overall, 73% of women business owners, regardless of their growth status, do not have an exit strategy

Source: Adapted from Entrepreneurial Vision in Action, © NFWBO 2001

plan for an exit (see figure 3). In fact, nearly 75 percent of U.S. women who own their own businesses today do not have an exit strategy of any kind in place (1). These are the same women who open a college savings plan when their children are born, and who wouldn't dream of attempting a road trip without a backseat laden with maps. Yet, when it comes to their businesses, which represent the fruit of their efforts for many years, many entrepreneurs don't think about what happens at the end. You'll learn more about the importance of exit plans in chapter 8, step 7: Understand Valuation and Organize An Exit Plan.

2. Paperwork

Depending on your industry and location, you will have to file different documents (see table 5 for a checklist). Check with your lawyer to see what's needed, and make sure your papers are in order. You need to register your company name, keep the corporate seal on file, and obtain an employer identification number. This number, issued by the Internal Revenue Service, allows you to pay your employees and your taxes.

Table 5: Document Checklist

Use the checklist of items below to ensure that you have the appropriate paperwork in place.

Licenses
_____ Business license
_____ License from the health department, if needed (for a spa, hair salon, catering business or other personal service company)
_____ Liquor license, if needed

Zones/permits/ordinances/signage
_____ Review this issue with your lawyer if you have a home business
_____ Meet state, city, and local fire codes
_____ Signage permits, if needed
_____ Mandatory postings, such as workmen's compensation, exit signs, location of fire extinguishers, stairwells; Heimlich maneuver, risk of alcohol-related birth defects (for restaurants)

Leases/contracts for your office
_____ Company cars

_____ Equipment (copiers, fax machines, printers)

Taxes
_____ Payroll taxes (federal, state, city, FICA, Medicare)
_____ Employer's federal quarterly tax returns
_____ Federal Unemployment (FUTA) taxes (employers pay FUTA taxes)
_____ Sales tax (if your business sells retail products)
_____ Resale tax (if your company buys products with the intent to resell them)

Insurance
_____ Life insurance for you and top employees, if needed
_____ Health insurance
_____ Health insurance for employees who are terminated (COBRA)
_____ Disability insurance
_____ General liability insurance
_____ Property insurance
_____ Auto insurance
_____ Workmen's compensation insurance
_____ Insurance for an at-home business
_____ Business interruption insurance (this policy provides compensation for lost earnings as well as operating expenses if your business cannot operate due to an insured disaster, such as a major fire). Check with your insurance agent. Business interruption insurance policies are usually added on to a property insurance policy.

In addition, review with your attorney the licenses, permits, leases, contracts, and insurance you should have in place, including looking at documentation that you may need at a later date. Finally, be sure you and your accountant discuss all of the necessary corporate and employment taxes and their due dates. Remember, you, and not your CPA, are ultimately responsible for these payments.

3. The Employee Manual

This thick volume lays out all of your policies, benefits, and requirements for your employees. Once you have ten to fifteen workers, several federal regulations governing employee relations suddenly apply to your company. As the company owner, it's your legal responsibility to comply with these rules, and you need to inform your staff of their responsibilities as well. Additionally, a thorough manual can free you and other staff from answering questions about vacation policies, health benefits, and so on. Let your employee manual be a comprehensive reference for your workforce. As you assemble your employee manual, be mindful of the following:

The Equal Employment Opportunity Commission (EEOC). This federal agency is responsible for judicial enforcement of the federal civil rights laws. These laws regulate hiring practices. Companies with ten or more employees are legally required to have an unequivocal policy of equal employment opportunity. Your company also needs a nonharassment policy, defining both verbal and physical conduct that's unacceptable, and a "protection against retaliation" clause.

The Fair Labor Standards Act of 1938. This federal law spells out minimum wages, child labor, and overtime pay. You must pay overtime to nonexempt employees, those who are paid by the hour and are generally nonprofessionals. In retail, for example, stock room personnel are usually nonexempt employees and therefore entitled to overtime pay, whereas a sales professional is an exempt employee—meaning exempt from the wage and hour laws—and does not get overtime.

The Family and Medical Leave Act of 1993. If you have fifty or more workers, this law says you must provide up to twelve weeks of unpaid leave for an employee who has worked a year or more during any twelve-month period for the following reasons:

- the birth of a baby
- the adoption of a child
- to get medical care for a serious condition
- to care for a sick child, spouse, or family member

As a practical matter, whether or not your company hits the threshold to qualify for this law, you'll win your employees' loyalty if you permit them a twelve-week unpaid leave for one of the reasons cited above.

The Americans with Disabilities Act of 1990. Employers may not discriminate against disabled persons and are legally obligated to provide them with equal opportunity. If necessary, an employer must restructure a job or change the layout of a workstation or office to accommodate the disabled employee. This federal law is applicable to your business if you have fifteen or more employees. Part-time workers count as employees, but independent contractors do not. The law also applies if you are a public facility, whether or not you have fifteen employees.

Consolidated Omnibus Budget Reconciliation Act (COBRA). Congress passed this health benefit act in 1986. This law allows employees who quit their jobs or are terminated for some reason other than "gross misconduct" to continue their health coverage at the company's group rates (but the employee pays for the health coverage himself). Employers must notify their health care plan administrators, and the employee then has sixty days to decide whether or not they wish to pay their health insurance premium and continue their coverage. For more information on COBRA, go to http://www.dol.gov/ebsa/faqs/faq_consumer_cobra.html.

The Occupational Safety and Health Administration (OSHA) Act. OSHA sets safety and health standards for Americans in the workplace. Overall, there are more than 2,000 OSHA inspectors in 200 offices scattered throughout the United States periodically checking in on companies to ensure that OSHA standards are met. Debra Revzen of Twin City Envelope found out the hard way that OSHA means business when agents dropped in on her company shortly after she took the helm and promptly fined her $600 because one fan did not have a grounded plug. "Then I became the safety director, too," she said.

Your company's employee manual should also cover pay procedures; vacation and sick day policies, absenteeism and lateness policies; reviews and salary increases; health benefits; employee conduct; complaint resolution procedures; computer, voice mail, and e-mail instructions; termination and resignation procedures; confidentiality of company information; and an at-will employee acknowledgement, among other items. Fortunately, much of what goes into an employee manual these days is standard. Your lawyer should have a boilerplate sample he can give you that you can easily customize for your firm. You and your attorney should review and update the manual annually.

Even if you have been running your business for several years without an employee manual, take the time to write one. Standardizing policies for all employees will eliminate confusion and make your life easier as the company grows.

Table 6: Rules and Regulations You Need to Know

_____ The Equal Employment Opportunity Commission (EEOC)
_____ The Fair Labor Standards Act of 1938
_____ The Family and Medical Leave Act of 1993
_____ The Occupational Safety and Health Administration (OSHA)
Act
_____ The Americans With Disabilities Act of 1990
_____ Consolidated Omnibus Budget Reconciliation Act (COBRA)

And ask:
_____ How does EEOC affect my hiring and firing practices?
_____ Does The American Disabilities Act apply to my company?
_____ How do I ensure that my company complies with COBRA?

III. YOUR IT SERVICES

Information technology—your computer and phone system—is often what connects your company to the outside world, as well as keeping the vital operations of the business running. Assess the state of your IT systems often, as well as your expansion plans. Without careful forethought, a spiraling problem can mean serious issues for your company.

Lane Nemeth knew the IT systems at Discovery Toys needed attention, but in 1983 she was busy dealing with operational issues, including bringing on a new chief financial officer. While this new executive organized the company's financial documents and procedures and helped her secure needed funding for the business, Christmas toy orders poured in from Lane's 5,000 sales reps across the country.

Then, the computer system crashed. Discovery missed every single one of its December deliveries. Scrambling to get the company back on its feet, Lane had to hire a new operations person and a dozen technical experts to rebuild the system. The techies brought mattresses into the offices and slept there often, littering the floor with pizza boxes. It took most of the following year to get the problems sorted out. Eventually, the company was back online with the software Lane needed to handle her booming toy orders, but the intervening year was an intensely trying period for Discovery.

Free Spirit Publishing ran into similar problems when moving its offices into a new building. Although Judy Galbraith had planned the move in meticulous detail, she and her managers had not considered worst-case scenarios. But once the movers arrived, everything went wrong. Free Spirit had checked the movers' references and found them satisfactory. But Judy didn't know that moving companies often have difficulty lining up workers for weekend moves. The moving company had simply grabbed a few extra hands from an unemployment line that morning, paying them cash. The replacement movers were so incompetent that Judy had to round up some of her own employees and move some of the boxes and furniture herself.

Next, she realized that her computer and phone system didn't work. This period was the "most exhausting and stressful time for me," Judy says, "because without our toll-free number working, we couldn't receive orders, and no orders, no business." The phone service provider missed its installation date to wire Judy's new office space. But the general contractor installed the Sheetrock without telling Judy the cable wasn't in yet. When Judy discovered the mistake, it was too late to fix it. The phone cables had to be run along the ceiling instead. Her only tech staffer was a freelance IT consultant, so her managers were left to figure out the tech problems as best they could. Next, carpeting and furniture went in, and the employees set up their computers simultaneously. "Things really slowed down then," Judy says, "because the union electricians wouldn't let the furniture installers connect the cables to power up the computers or the phones for my employees." Eventually everything got done, but the move took far longer than planned, and it cost Judy time and money. As employees handled the botched move, they fell behind in packing orders. Soon, book orders were backing up and customers were calling looking for shipments. Judy's staffers had to pack boxes on any surface they could find while dealing with irate customers. Free Spirit recovered, but Judy and her managers now think through all possible problems before she tackles any large change in her business.

Without operational phones, computers, and software you can be out of business. Even an hour can cost you dearly. Employees and customers get frustrated easily, and you'll spend weeks afterward on damage control. Provide as much backup for your programs as you can afford, and troubleshoot often. Don't ignore red flags or fail to call in experts who can help save you time and money in the long run. Also, if your system needs upgrades, do it earlier rather than later. You'll be far better off if you stay several steps ahead of a systems crash.

Once you have your start-up team, employees, key documents, and a functional IT system in place, you're on your way to creating a sound infrastructure, one that can grow with and support your company.

SUCCESS

Rose Saia hit Eastman Kodak's glass ceiling at the age of thirty-three, when she was a product director. After a brief stint at Novell, she cofounded Trilogy, a Concord, Massachusetts, software company, with two partners. All three had considerable corporate experience and knew the importance of a formal business plan, which they wrote right away. From the outset the partners agreed to pursue venture capital investments to help finance the company. To access the funding, they knew they would need to hire a strong management team, including a chief financial officer and a vice president of marketing. They would also need a detailed human resources organization. Rose and her partners "planned for a solid infrastructure" from the beginning, she says. The Trilogy team sold their company for approximately $4 million in December 2001 to Funk Software.

REGRETS

Harriette Waldron and Judy Kelly let their growing enterprises, Kelly/Waldron & Company, a firm that supplied marketing databases and sales force automation software to pharmaceutical companies, climb to more than a hundred employees before they put a formal, corporate-style infrastructure in place. They lacked both a human resources director and a full-fledged internal accounting department, although Judy says "the outside accounting company we used from day one organized our financials very well, so when a due diligence day came we wouldn't have any problems." Before they could put their otherwise very successful organization up for sale, they addressed their lack of a human resources director and their informal infrastructure. "We knew we had to have a number of line people established to be more valuable at sale," Harriet says. The partners realized they had to fix the shortcomings, and they did so within a few months, hiring a human resources director and then formalizing their infrastructure. But they also knew they were lucky that their personnel organization issues resolved quickly. When everything was in order, they sold their company.

CHAPTER 4

Step 3: Keep Good Financials

I s your company successful? If you have a growing roster of customers and a line of products that sell well, you might say yes. It's possible, however, that you're not seeing the whole picture. Outward signs of a prosperous business, such as repeat orders, rising revenue, and checkout-counter lines, don't always mean a company is financially healthy. True success can be found only in your financial statements. There you'll be able to see if you have enough cash to pay your workers, keep the electricity in your offices turned on, and take home some money for yourself at the end of the month. Your financial statements will also tell you how much money your company is making, and allow you to forecast your financial situation for future periods.

Without good financial statements, you are flying blind, unsure whether the cash that comes in will be enough to cover your bills. Just as every woman should know her own home mortgage rate and understand her brokerage statement, every woman business owner should know what's in her company's financials. You don't have to go to business school or get certified as a CPA; it's your accountant's job to do the math-heavy calculations for you. You just need to be able to take your company's financial temperature, and know when something is wrong.

Measuring Your Success

As a businesswoman, you may have already discovered how to make your company run. While starting up your company, you dealt with money issues: where to get money, what to spend it on, how to use it effectively. You may not know all of the accounting terminology for the business concepts you have already put into place in your company, but learning the business language will enable you to understand what your accountant, banker, and other professionals are saying. Two general, easy-to-read books that can introduce you to accounting are *Accounting for Dummies* by John A. Tracy and *Accounting Made Simple* by Joseph Peter Simini. And if you already know all the concepts between the covers of these two books, make sure your senior staff does as well.

Financial Language

Your accountant will prepare three main statements for you at the end of each three-month quarter and at year's end. These statements include the income statement, the balance sheet, and the statement of cash flows. All three link together, giving you a financial picture of your company. It is your responsibility to review these statements and query your accountant if the statements are unclear to you. A sample income statement, balance sheet, and cash flow statement are in the Appendix.

Income statement. In the business game, the income statement is the score card. This sheet presents your total revenue, or sales, and expenses, or costs, typically over a year. Because the income statement takes your revenue, subtracts your expenses, and shows you how much profit is left over at the end, you will often hear it called a profit and loss statement, or P&L for short. On the income statement, you will see how your company is doing over a period of time, typically one quarter or one year.

The income statement includes all the components of your revenue and your expenses. For revenue, the statement will record how much cash you received and how much credit you gave your customers. It will also show the value of returns or order cancellations, as well as discounts you gave. Under expenses, you will see the cost of goods sold, or how much you spent to create or buy the products you sell. If you manufacture goods, you'll see how much money went into direct costs, such as materials, salaries, labor, freight, and equipment repairs for your factory. The statement also details your overhead, or selling, general, and administrative (SG&A) expenses. These costs include salaries, rent, sales commissions, and advertising.

In addition, the income statement will show accounting costs that you don't actually pay in cash. These costs, called depreciation and amortization (D&A), equalize the difference between what you initially paid for equipment, computers, or company cars and what they're worth today. To figure these amounts, accountants rely on depreciation schedules, which allow for wear and tear on an asset over its estimated useful life. Accelerated depreciation is an accounting method that allows you to take a higher deduction in the first few years of an asset's life, whereas when straight-line depreciation is used, deductions are made in equal amounts over the life of the asset.

At the end of the income statement, when all the expenses are taken out of the revenue, you'll see how much money your company brought in before you paid taxes; this is called net income before taxes. After subtracting out your tax bill, the statement will show you how much money is left. This amount is your company's net income or profit, also called the bottom line because it's at or near the bottom of the statement. Profits are the goal of business; they're what you get to keep once you've paid your bills and employees. But they don't represent the whole story.

While the income statement represents the cumulative wrap-up of your company's financial condition over time, the balance sheet is frozen in time on a particular date, usually the end of the accounting quarter or the year.

Balance sheet. A major part of your company's financial picture is the balance sheet, a financial snapshot which details what you own and what you owe at one moment in time, usually at the end of the quarter. This conforms to the main equation that governs accounting:

$$\text{Assets} = \text{Liabilities} + \text{Shareholder's Equity}$$

Or, put the opposite way:

$$\text{Shareholder's Equity} = \text{Assets} - \text{Liabilities}$$

In other words, what you, the shareholder, own is all the assets of the company, minus all the liabilities. For instance, if your company owns a building and also owes a supplier $10,000, then your company's book value is the value of the building minus $10,000. This amount is called your firm's net worth. You've seen this concept applied to individuals: a family's net worth is the value of its house, cars, stock holdings, and bank accounts, minus what it owes on a mortgage, car loans, college loans, taxes, and credit card debt, for instance. Your company cannot have more liabilities than it has assets, or you, as the owner, will wind up with debts and no equity to show for it. Even if you've set up your company so that you can't legally be held liable personally for the firm's debts, ending up in bankruptcy court won't help your career as an entrepreneur.

The balance sheet reveals the value of all of your company's assets and liabilities. Assets include the value of your office furnishings and equipment, unencumbered cash in the bank, and your receivables, or money that your customers owe you. When you sell goods on credit, the customer's promise to pay you is an asset, known as accounts receivable. Liabilities include money you owe to your vendors, called accounts payable. All your borrowings are also listed, including notes, loans, and mortgages.

Statement of cash flows. This financial statement lets you see where your cash has gone. It's a record of all the cash that comes into and out of your company, divided into three ways of getting cash: operating activities, investing activities, and financing activities. Cash from operating activities comes in or goes out as a result of your regular operations. Inflows primarily come from selling your products, while outflows include salaries, vendors' bills, and tax payments. Cash from investing activities is money that comes in or out from investments you make, such as buying another company. Cash from financing activities comes from your borrowings and from money you lend to others. When a bank lends you money, depositing the loan check causes cash from financing activities to increase. Similarly, this segment of cash flow decreases when you make payments to satisfy your mortgages or loans or issue dividends to investors or yourself.

Managing cash flow is the key to keeping your business open. Though your company may be profitable, if the monthly expenses you have to pay, such as rent, salaries, and supply costs, exceed the amount of money (cash) your company is collecting from revenue and invoices, you will end up in a cash crunch, and you may have to borrow money to survive. (Revenue provided through credit is meaningless on the cash flow statement.) The best way to get around this problem is to be vigilant about collecting on your invoices as quickly as your terms of sale allow, and to keep your costs down as much as possible (see table 7).

Comparisons. It's worthwhile to compare each financial statement with the one you prepared in the previous quarter and in the prior year. You will be able to see how your revenue, profits, assets, and liabilities are trending, and which areas are growing the fastest. After you've had a chance to look at each statement and prepare questions for your accountant, sit down with him once a quarter and go over your financials. Ask him to point out potential problems and to highlight areas where you are doing well.

Table 7: Collecting Your Money:
Managing Accounts Receivable Effectively

- Be sure payment terms are clear in contracts and invoices.
- Close out the job or order and submit the final invoice as soon as possible. A final invoice should follow the completion of a job within thirty days.
- Review accounts receivable every week. Invoices thirty days or more overdue require diligent follow-up for payment. Some small business owners are reluctant to do this, believing that it makes them look bad. To the contrary, your customers look bad. They need to pay within the terms you set up before the sale, or make an alternative payment schedule in advance.
- Accounts forty-five days or more overdue need your personal attention. Make the call, or send the e-mail, and indicate you need a response.
- Establish an interest charge for late payments, print it clearly on your invoices, and enforce it.
- Don't ship more inventory to the delinquent customer until payments are current.
- Don't be afraid to drop a customer that consistently fails to pay on time. Cash flow is vital to a small business, and you can't afford not to get paid for services provided.

Understanding Your Financials

To make your financial statements speak to you about the condition of your company, you need to look at each component in relation to the others. This is accomplished by calculating various financial ratios. Some of the more useful ones include:

Working capital. The most basic gauge of your company's financial health, it sets up a relationship between what you owe immediately to creditors and what debtors owe to you in the short term. To calculate your working capital, add up all your current assets—your cash, inventory, and accounts receivable, as well as anything else owed to you within the next year—and subtract out your current liabilities, which consist of your accounts payable and any other debts due over the next year. What's left over is your working capital, the money you have available to run your business. Without adequate working capital, you will have trouble funding your operations.

Return on sales. In business the term "return" simply means profit. Business owners can tell how their company is doing by calculating returns on a variety of measures. When looking at return ratios, higher is always better. Return on sales is your net income before income taxes as a percentage of your annual sales, or your revenue minus your cost of goods sold (COGS) and minus your SG&A, or overhead expenses. This ratio represents the proportion of your net sales that falls to your bottom line and tells you how efficiently your company is operating. For instance, if your net income before taxes is $10,000, your revenue is $100,000, your SG&A (overhead) is $10,000 and your cost of goods sold is $80,000, your return on sales would be 10 percent, meaning that for every dollar you generate in net sales, you keep 10 cents in pretax profits. ($100,000 in revenue minus $80,000 in COGS minus $10,000 in SG&A leaves $10,000; that number divided by $100,000 equals 10 percent.)

Return on equity. This ratio describes how much profit you are getting for your ownership stake in the business. To derive it, divide your stockholder's equity, or net worth, into your net income. For instance, if your business has shareholder's equity of $500,000 and net income of $10,000 per year, your return on equity would be 2 percent.

Inventory turnover. This is the ratio of annual revenue to inventory and represents the speed with which you convert your inventory holdings into cash. When you buy goods for resale, you enter a race to sell them and collect the cash before you have to pay your suppliers. The longer those goods sit in your warehouse or store, the longer your cash is tied up, leaving it unavailable to pay off your debts or finance growth. It's important to keep your inventory turnover as high as possible.

Industry-specific ratios. Every industry also has ratios and metrics that are uniquely relevant to its needs. If you don't know which ones are used in your field, ask your accountant, or read published news stories about transactions that have been done involving your competitors to see which ratios are mentioned. One resource is First Research, at www.firstresearch.com, which sells profiles on 175 industries, including quarterly updates, trends, opportunities, and forecasts, for $99 each. You can also look at the annual reports of publicly traded companies in your industry.

You'll need to know how your company performs according to these benchmarks before you can sell it or do any major financing.

Keeping Your Financials

The key to understanding your company's financial situation is maintaining up-to-date records detailing every cent going into and coming out of your accounts. To do this, talk with your accountant about the type of accounting method you should use in your company. Small businesses usually rely on either the accrual method or the cash method (cash basis). In my service company, we used the accrual method. When we won a job contract from a client, we counted the money at the day of sale, even though it usually took us several days to submit the first invoice for work, and it typically took several more weeks for us to receive our first payment. With this method of accounting, expenses are also counted as soon as they occur. For example, if we ordered two hundred binders to use for the job, we counted the expense the day the binders arrived in our office, even if we didn't pay the supplier for thirty or more days. Accrual accounting is used frequently when businesses such as mine start work on a job or deliver the service or product before payment for it is made.

The cash method of accounting is often used by smaller businesses such as salons, flower shops, or clothing boutiques. When payment is made at the point of purchase, it is counted as income, whether it comes in the form of cash, check, or credit card. Similarly, expenses are counted when they are paid. Your accountant may advise you to use the cash basis method for tax purposes and the accrual method for financial reporting purposes, when you produce financial statements for your partners, investors, or the bank. It is legal and completely acceptable to keep two sets of books in this manner as long as the underlying expenses and revenues are the same.

At the beginning, you can keep records yourself. This accounting is most often done using software, often QuickBooks from Intuit, an easy-to-use program that works with nearly all computers. As soon as you make it past the early start-up stage and acquire more than a few customers or employees, you will want to track your finances using more sophisticated computer software and a professional accounting method. Ideally, you should buy a system that tracks not only your cash flow, sales, and expense histories, but also integrates your databases of employees, suppliers, and customers. The more integration your software provides, the better you will be able to see and understand your business. See table 8 for additional tips for good financial management.

Table 8: Five Tips for Effective Financial Management

- Keep your revenues growing, and continue to identify ways to reduce costs. If revenues flatten, begin to trim costs as soon as possible. A year-end financial review should never be a wake-up call.
- Call in key suppliers annually for competitive bids. Negotiate further with the vendors you select. Ask if they will give you an additional discount in return for bundled or bulk orders.
- Outsource: Do you need all the full-time people you have, or could you reduce overhead by hiring freelancers, part-timers, consultants, or an outsourcing firm?
- Insource: Are there services you outsource that might be more profitable if you did the work in-house?
- Space: If you have extra office space and you are reasonably certain you won't need it for growth over the next year, consider subletting it for a year, bearing in mind that you then take on the role of landlord.

Closely related to your financial statements are your payroll and tax filings, the preparation of which are labor-intensive tasks for anyone running a small business. One solution is PayCycle.com, a secure online program designed for small business owners that automates tax reporting and payroll. Employees are paid by direct deposit; check stubs can be printed from the website. The cost of the program varies from $14.99 to $42.99 per month, depending on the level of services ordered, but PayCycle offers a one-month free trial period and the following two months at $9.99 per month.

Ask your accountant which software to buy. Software vendors will also often set up booths at your industry's trade shows so that attendees can meet one of their sales reps and be given a walk-through of the product. Talk to competitors you know or those with whom you network about accounting systems as well, and do a thorough online search to understand what customers are saying about the software packages you are considering purchasing. Before you purchase or upgrade accounting software, it may be worthwhile to talk to your key clients and top suppliers to ensure compatibility with their systems.

Finally, when you select software, make sure you know what kind of service and maintenance contract you are buying. If you and your accountant are not tech-savvy and you don't have an information technology staffer, you might want to pay more for a full-service contract that obligates the software company to send someone right out to fix your problem. Although you don't need to do the nuts-and-bolts accounting personally, be sure you have a basic understanding of the program or system in use in your firm, and heed your bookkeeper's or accountant's advice if she tells you that your accounting system is no longer compatible with your customers' systems or is in need of an overhaul.

Writing a Financial Plan

The goal of keeping your financial statements in good order is to project outward and predict what your company's financial needs will be in the future. Once you establish patterns within your business, such as seasonality or ties to certain commodity prices, you will be able to estimate the company's sales, expenses, and profits going forward. To write a financial plan, prepare projections for the next three years for your company's revenue, cost of goods sold, and profit. Do this by observing the trends apparent in your financials and building in assumptions about the future, including such questions as whether the prices of the goods and input materials you buy will go up or down, whether your office rent will stay stable, and how many new employees you will have to add. When you do your projections, include a detailed analysis of how you intend to achieve them in your plan. You may need to cut costs, attract new customers, spend more on marketing, or hire more workers. Pay particular attention to your cash flow projections. Cash flow is the lifeline of the entrepreneur. If it looks from your projections as if you won't have enough cash to meet your expenses, come up with an emergency plan to correct this problem.

You will also want to set financial targets for your company and yourself in the plan. For example, discuss your total compensation goals with your accountant, as well as the amount of money (profits) you plan to retain in the company, for future growth plans. These will depend on the type of business you have, but may include ratios you want to achieve, such as re-

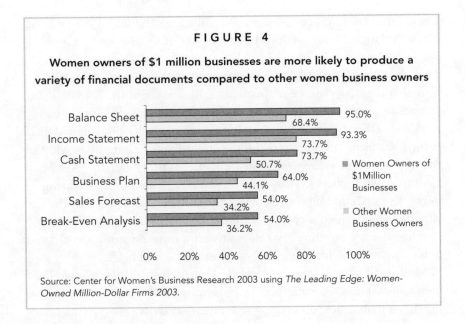

FIGURE 4

Women owners of $1 million businesses are more likely to produce a variety of financial documents compared to other women business owners

Balance Sheet — 95.0% / 68.4%
Income Statement — 93.3% / 73.7%
Cash Statement — 73.7% / 50.7%
Business Plan — 64.0% / 44.1%
Sales Forecast — 54.0% / 34.2%
Break-Even Analysis — 54.0% / 36.2%

■ Women Owners of $1Million Businesses

■ Other Women Business Owners

0% 20% 40% 60% 80% 100%

Source: Center for Women's Business Research 2003 using *The Leading Edge: Women-Owned Million-Dollar Firms 2003.*

turn on equity or profit levels. Your accountant can be a valuable resource to you as you write this plan.

To grow your company successfully and put it in a position to be sold, keeping your financial statements in superb order is a must. Figure 4 shows that the majority of women who successfully build their businesses to the $1 million level produce key financial documents for their firm. More than 90 percent produce an income statement and a balance sheet.

Financing Your Company

Your financing is your company's fuel; you can't run your operation without it. But whether you are looking for start-up money or money to grow your company, consider your options carefully and review your financing needs with your accountant to be sure you secure the right amounts. (Financing can be expensive, so don't pay for money you don't need.) Research available sources first, and determine what type of financing is best for your company. Whether you choose a bank, various agencies, a venture capitalist, an angel investor, or a private investor, financing will require a high level of professionalism on your part. Excellent communication with your financial partner is vital. As with any relationship, it takes time and effort to build trust and confidence. "No surprises" should be your mantra when working with any financial partner.

The "bootstrap" trap. A trap that many entrepreneurs fall into is to believe that their only source of financing is their savings, IRA, or 401(k) accounts; borrowing from family or friends; or taking out a home equity loan. More than half of the women I interviewed for this book started their companies using one or more of these "bootstrapping" methods. Most of them, such as Brenda Newberry, president and CEO of the Newberry Group, an IT services company in St. Charles, Missouri, specializing in network operations and cybersecurity, began their businesses from home. Brenda simply added a couple of phone lines, upgraded her copier, and purchased a fax machine. "When you start a business from scratch, you don't have a whole lot of resources to waste," she says.

Most small businesswomen start by asking their friends to invest in their companies. This tactic may bring you investors with your best interests at heart, but it obligates you to think about their needs in a way you might not were the investor simply a business associate. Brenda Loube and her friend and business partner Sheila Drohan started Corporate Fitness Works in 1988 in Montgomery Village, Maryland, providing fitness facilities and wellness programs for businesses, government agencies, retirement communities, hospitals, and hotels. To finance their venture, Brenda and Sheila approached Sheila's widowed mother, who took out a mortgage on her home to loan them the money. From the moment they received the money, Brenda says she had nightmares about what would happen if the company failed. "The greatest risk I've ever taken in my life was accepting that money," Brenda says. Although she and Sheila both knew they would succeed, Brenda found the obligation "scary" for her and she didn't rest easy until Corporate Fitness paid Sheila's mother back. Fortunately, they were able to pay her back earlier than they had agreed.

Before you take money from anyone whose relationship you value, think hard about what you're doing. Manhattan shopkeeper Suzy Vasillov became so enthusiastic about starting her company, Keesal & Mathews, that she raised more than $150,000 from family and friends in just a few weeks to get under way. Then her accountant asked her what her plan was if the business didn't pan out, an outcome she had not considered. "It was very fortunate for me that everything went well," she says, "because I didn't really consider the ramifications of failure." While you can also finance your company using your own consumer credit by charging company expenses on your credit cards, this alternative should be used as a last resort. The interest rates on credit cards are astronomically high, much higher than the rates you would pay on a business loan. If you think bootstrapping is your only financing option and you don't want to empty your savings account, consider a small home equity loan, ask your accountant for advice, or get direction from a women's business organization (see Resource Guide) to help you figure out the best way to get the money you need.

Your bank. As soon as you are able, establish a relationship with a specific bank and a particular bank officer in your area. Today, major banks actively court small businesses and women-owned businesses in particular. Take advantage of these programs, as they might help you get access to financing you might not otherwise receive (see the Resource Guide). Small-business financing includes asset-backed loans, in which the bank loans you money with collateral, such as substantial equipment or high-quality receivables, and lines of credit, in which you draw down the loan only as you need it. Be aware, though, that unless your equipment is worth a great deal—for instance, if you have a factory—you probably will not be able to use it to back a loan. If this is your first business loan, it's likely that you will have to guarantee it personally. Ask your accountant if you should prepare your personal financial records before the meeting with the bank. And make sure your personal credit rating is in good order. Finally, search the Internet to obtain more specific information on business loans from banks. As an entrepreneur, you will be the main reason why a bank will or won't give you a business loan, so know your personal credit score before you go in and be prepared to explain away any blots on your credit record. You can get your personal credit history and score for free or a very low price from the three major credit bureaus, Equifax, TransUnion, and Experian, all of which sell the reports on their websites.

Getting the bank loan. Processing a bank loan can be a relatively quick and easy process, or it can deteriorate into a stressful ordeal. How you present your business loan application, how much you want to borrow, and the financial health of your company will determine the outcome. Begin by putting together a brief, concise presentation. If you are meeting one-on-one with your banker, you may want to skip the formality of a Power-Point presentation in favor of talking through the key points. If you feel unsure about the process, ask your accountant to review your loan application and accompany you to the first meeting.

When Lane Nemeth needed a substantial infusion of cash for Discovery Toys, she relied on her CFO to manage the process. "I'll never forget how well Jim managed our relationship with the bank," Lane says. "We'd lost a lot of money but Jim told them that, explained what happened and what our plan was to fix the problem. The bankers' faces went pale, but that's when I realized Jim spoke 'bankese,' a foreign language to me. He knew what to say, when to say it, and how to interact with a team of professional bankers."

Any banker will request the following information:

- An updated copy of your business plan
- Financial statements
- Your proposed repayment plan (Discuss with your accountant in advance what a bank will expect.)
- What you will provide as collateral, such as real estate, substantial equipment, or high-quality receivables

Finally, the banker will ask you how you plan to use the borrowed money, who else is on your management team, who they can speak to if you are unavailable, and whether or not you have money invested in your business. Even with the paperwork in place, nailing the loan can be tricky. "We tried to get a loan from the bank, but I believe that to this day we didn't get it because we were women," says Brenda Loube. "We had three solvent, great-name corporate contracts, and no bank would loan us money."

Madolyn Johnson used $1,500 from her teacher's retirement fund to start her direct-sales home accessories company, Signature HomeStyles. But she quickly ran out of money and had to borrow $600 in baby-sitting money that she had paid a neighbor. Early on a friend advised Madolyn to get a good accountant. The one she found advised her to start building a relationship with a banker as soon as she could. Madolyn heeded the advice, took loans whether or not the company needed them to build up her credibility with the bank and her company's credit rating, and a few years later asked her banker to increase the company's line of credit. Her firm was growing and profitable. "The numbers were great," she said, but when she arrived at the bank visibly pregnant with her second child to secure the credit-line increase, her banker turned her down, telling her the bank was concerned about what would happen to the business after the child was born. Undeterred, Madolyn went to her local chamber of commerce for a recommendation on a new bank. She found a loan quickly.

When you're looking for money to fund or grow your company, don't take no for an answer. Listen carefully to what a banker says to you if he turns down your loan application, and address his questions. If your application is declined and it is not clear to you why, ask your lawyer and your accountant to review it, and either reapply or do what Madolyn did: Find a new banker.

Joanne Piraino got her first bank loan for her business "on a handshake, but that doesn't work now," she says. "Banks are much less personable and less open to taking risks; in fact, I think they want to be risk-free in most cases." But banks are there to lend money. Ideally, they are looking for clients like Phyllis LeBlanc, who turned a summer job making chocolates at Harbor Sweets, a chocolate-making company in Salem, Massachusetts, into a full-time career and then bought the company from the founder. When he confided to her that he wanted to leave the company, Phyllis sat down with him and his bank and orchestrated a $2.5 million leveraged buyout, using some of her own savings to buy a majority interest from the owner and other investors. Harbor Sweets paid back the loan in three years instead of five, making each payment on time. In an article in the *Boston Business Journal*, Phyllis's banker said she's done "a very good job since she's taken over." For her part, Phyllis says the bank was "great to work with, but we had, and have, an excellent track record."

While it is true that banks follow stricter regulations today, the banks that have specialized units committed to working with women business owners (see Resource Guide) work hard to get—and keep—your business. Even so, women owners of firms growing either the number of employees or their revenues by 30 percent a year still lag behind men when it comes to securing a commercial bank loan (39 percent versus 52 percent) (1) (see figure 5). But establishing a strong working relationship with one of these bankers can help you get additional funding when you need it. Also, these divisions are entrenched in the business community. Most organize special business events throughout the year to help their clients network. A good banker could be one of your best long-term resources ever.

The SBA and other agencies. Banks provide SBA loans to small businesses that have difficulty or are unable to secure a loan through traditional institutions. The SBA guarantees loan payments to the lender; generally, SBA loans range from microloans as small as a few hundred dollars up to $750,000, and are reserved for United States–based, for-profit companies. Applicants must have already used other methods of financing, including personal assets, and they must own a chunk of equity in the

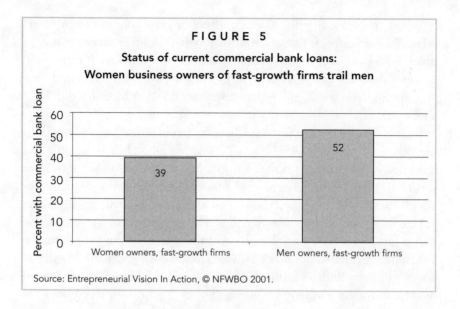

FIGURE 5

Status of current commercial bank loans:
Women business owners of fast-growth firms trail men

Source: Entrepreneurial Vision In Action, © NFWBO 2001.

firm. SBA loan programs change often, so you should contact your local SBA office (see Resource Guide). Finally, in certain industries, SBA loans are reserved for companies that fall below a certain threshold. A travel agency, for instance, would have to generate less than $3 million in commissions and income, while a retailer would have to make less than $6 million a year. (Thresholds are adjusted periodically by the SBA.) The agency also runs 650 Small Business Development Centers, most situated on university and college campuses, to provide training, educational support, and other resources to assist entrepreneurs in the start-up and early-growth phases of their businesses.

Several women in this book obtained SBA loans. Before Doreen Marks moved her company off the kitchen table and into an old barn on the property, she obtained an SBA loan for $87,000 to renovate the facility, turning the upstairs hay-bale storage area in the barn into offices and the downstairs stalls into a small manufacturing space. The SBA's Office of Women's Business Ownership is a good place to start if you are looking for a small business loan (http://www.sba.gov/onlinewbc/wbc.pdf). Their Women's Business Centers Program is a national network of more than one hundred resource centers that have been established to assist women in start-up and growing companies, with a mission of "leveling the playing field for women entrepreneurs who still face unique obstacles in the world of business." These offices also sponsor numerous local events, often attended or supported by local banks and businesses, so it's another good place to get exposure for yourself and your company.

Entrepreneurs can also apply to small business investment companies (SBICs) which help out small companies. SBICs provide loans of at least five years' duration as well as take equity stakes in companies, but under their charters they are not permitted to take control of the companies. Because they have federal licenses and a relationship with the SBA, they can offer favorable loan rates to women-owned and minority-owned businesses.

State governments also have divisions dedicated to loaning money or coordinating loans to small businesses, and city or county governments also sometimes have such agencies. Contact your local business women's organization or your local chamber of commerce to locate these services. On the local level, economic development zones or enterprise zones are often set up in underprivileged areas to encourage investment. In addition, governments and private groups sometimes have initiatives to encourage companies in a particular industry, such as biotechnology or light manufacturing, to set up shop in a certain area. Again, your local chamber of commerce, as well as locally based networking groups to which you belong, should be able to point you toward all of these types of financing.

You can also pursue loans from private nonprofit groups that target women entrepreneurs. Lila Valderrama, a thirty-year-old entrepreneur and cook, secured a microloan from Micro-Business USA to help her, her three sisters, and her mother open Lila's Bistro in Miami, Florida. The restaurant services the nearby downtown offices, delivering or catering business lunches and serving lunch in its own space as well. Lila began by taking a loan for $500, which the family paid back within six months. She then borrowed $1,500 to buy additional serving dishes.

Minority loans. Minority businesswomen have additional opportunities for financing. There are several government programs aimed at helping them that can be reached through the SBA. The Department of Commerce's Minority Business Development Agency funds Business Development Centers around the country that work with minority-owned entrepreneurial businesses. In addition, the National Bankers Association in Washington, D.C., represents minority-owned banks that loan to minority-owned businesses. The Minority and Women's Pre-Qualification Pilot Loan Program, at http://www.sba.gov/business_finances/prequal, also gives loans of less than $250,000 to minorities, based on character, credit history, and ex-

BOX 4: HELP TO HIT THE MILLION-DOLLAR MARK

Women-owned million-dollar firms are an important economic force in the U.S. economy. They also stimulate significant job growth (see figure 6). But reaching $1 million in revenues isn't easy. Lack of capital still holds many women entrepreneurs back, and without that bank loan, your company's growth can stagnate. The Resource Guide lists numerous organizations that can help you, from banks with divisions that specialize in loans to women's businesses to venture capitalists and SBA programs. Noteworthy is a new program, Make Mine a $Million Business, a collaborative effort of Nell Merlino, founder of Take Our Daughters to Work Day, and Susan Sobbott, president of OPEN, the American Express division that serves small businesses. The pair teamed up to help women entrepreneurs access money and mentors. Besides OPEN, the Women's Leadership Exchange and Count Me In for Women's Economic Independence participate in the program. WLE holds networking and educational conferences for women business owners throughout the country. Count Me In is a nonprofit group that helps women business owners access capital to build their firms.

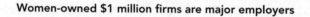

Women-owned $1 million firms are major employers

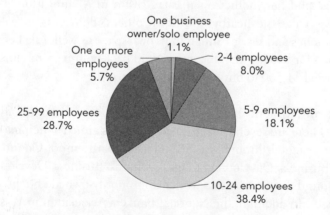

One business owner/solo employee 1.1%

One or more employees 5.7%

2-4 employees 8.0%

25-99 employees 28.7%

5-9 employees 18.1%

10-24 employees 38.4%

Source: Center for Women's Business Research 2003, using Dun & Bradstreet U.S. Marketing File (September 2004)

perience. Average annual sales for the preceding three years cannot exceed $5 million, and the firm must be 51 percent owned by a woman or a person of racial or ethnic minority.

Venture capital. In addition to loans, which are debts that you take on (debt financing), you can also finance your company by issuing equity (equity financing). This means that your ownership stake, once 100 percent, will be diluted, and another investor will own part of your company, take a role of some kind in setting the company's direction, and be entitled to some of your profits.

At a minimum, if a venture capital firm is investing in your company, the firm will usually secure the following, spelled out in a legally binding stock purchase agreement:

- The right to appoint a specified number of directors to your board
- Access to your quarterly financial statements and other specified documents
- Have the ability to register the firm's stock for sale in a public offering at your company's expense

As the company owner you will have to provide certain "representations and warranties" regarding your financial statements, liabilities, and level of compliance with all applicable laws and regulations, such as OSHA safety rules.

Most venture capital firms invest in ongoing companies that need capital for more rapid growth. Fewer are interested in funding a company that is still on the drawing board. Venture capital (V.C.) firms also do small buyouts whereby they control the company they invest in. Finally, V.C.'s also provide mezzanine financing, a combination of equity and debt financing used when companies are entering a rapid-expansion phase. This type of financing usually occurs once the company has passed the start-up phase and has a stable management team, a history of strong earnings, and a solid plan for expansion, such as an IPO or an acquisitions schedule.

If you want to secure venture capital to grow your company, start by identifying firms that have expertise in your industry. Because they are looking for rapid growth, venture capital firms usually specialize in industries such as software, biotechnology, health care, and education. Pick a firm that knows your field. Get recommendations from your accountant, lawyer, and local business contacts. Find out what type of deals the firm has done recently. Once you zero in on the firm you would like to approach, try to get someone to make a formal introduction for you. Most venture capitalists are flooded with funding requests, so getting their attention can take some effort. Once you know the firm you would like to target, do the following:

- **Prepare your presentation.** A presentation must include company history, financial information, and a pitch for the funds. Most firms are not interested in funding a company that doesn't have annual revenue growth potential of at least 30 percent or more. Venture capitalists want aggressive growth so they can cash out by selling your company or doing a public offering. An investment horizon of three to seven years is common for such firms.
- **Have a strong infrastructure, with solid managers.** Venture capitalists can recite the steps to a successful exit in their sleep. All of them want to see top professionals in place in the organization, in addition to you. Before they invest, it's likely they'll want to meet and talk with your key people, so make sure your staff is up to the task.
- **Demonstrate investment savvy.** Spend some time talking with your accountant and lawyer, as well as professionals in local business organizations, so you can learn the pros and cons of taking on a venture capitalist. For this new relationship to succeed, the V.C.'s want to know that you really know what the process means and the impact it will have on you and your business. Make sure you and the V.C. you select speak the same language, and make certain your views on growth and management are aligned.

Some women I knew who raise venture capital money failed to grasp beforehand that this new money comes with new management. Lane Nemeth, Discovery Toys' founder, says she would "never work with a venture capitalist again, as long as I live. I'd rather die than have another V.C. in my life." Lane feels that most V.C.'s are simply "money people." She found that her venture capital firm interfered in ways that did not help her manage the business, and came to believe that V.C.'s simply view entrepreneurs as expendable rubes who simply lucked out, rather than gifted businesspeople. Lane believes all would be served better if V.C.'s learned how to "prop up" entrepreneurs with professional management when they need it, rather than stepping in and trying to take over. When Discovery Toys hit $10 million in revenues, Lane's V.C.'s strongly encouraged her to hire a team of professional managers, forcing her to fire several people who had started with her, a gut-wrenching experience. Then the V.C.'s insisted she hire a professional CEO from the toy industry so she herself could focus on marketing and sales. When the CEO started, Lane let him run operations and "didn't pay attention to what was going on internally," she says. In October, returning from a round of selling trips, she saw the September financial statements, which featured a substantial loss for the first time in Discovery's history. "That was really, really scary," she said, because losses had always been limited to the first and second quarters. Her CEO told her not to worry about it; everything was "turning around." She closed her eyes and kept selling. "But I'll never forget November seventeenth," she said, "because that's when I saw the October financial statement showing that, to date, we'd lost $800,000. I knew we couldn't swing that loss, so I didn't bother consulting with the V.C.'s who recommended the CEO. I just fired him." Lane ultimately got everything resolved, but it remained the most stressful period in her business.

The benefits of venture capital. Janet Kraus and Kathy Sherbrooke*, cofounders of Circles, LLC, in Boston, are enjoying a different experience working with venture capitalists. After doing the research, Janet and Kathy decided to create their company, Circles, to provide round-the-clock concierge services to busy professionals who often find themselves running around in circles trying to get things done. They originally planned to market to individuals, providing services ranging from securing dinner reservations to picking up dry cleaning, but seeing the drawbacks, Circles decided to pitch largely Fortune 1000 clients. Once retained, the firm makes "Circles" services available to designated corporate employees as well as to their key customers, to build brand loyalty. Like most women entrepreneurs, Janet and Kathy started by exhausting $50,000 each of their own personal funds. When those funds dried up, they turned to family and friends, and ultimately raised another $505,000. The company was on its way, but it wasn't long before they knew they needed more cash. The partners went out to angel investors next, and brought in $1.1 million.

Although they were successful as a concierge company, Janet and Kathy recognized that they could move into a larger market by positioning themselves as a "loyalty management solutions" company. To do this would require more funding. Janet and Kathy met with advisers, put together their presentation, identified venture capitalists and set out to secure the additional financing. "But meeting after meeting," Janet says, "eyes glazed over." "I talked to about thirty V.C. firms before I realized that I was talking to all the wrong people," she says, "because V.C. tech-oriented compa-

*Both women have M.B.A.'s.

nies don't invest in business services." They finally found V.C.'s that make investments in service businesses. Once they located the right funds, it didn't take much more than a week to secure the financing. Circles raised approximately $25 million over eighteen months.

Janet and Kathy have been working successfully with their V.C. partners for more than five years. "The key," Janet says, "is to use the V.C.'s as strategic partners. We have five board meetings a year, and a planning session with them. They help us by making introductions for our firm, and we can discuss our ideas with them." Janet says that when there's a problem, she or Kathy alerts the V.C.'s, but always have a game plan defined to address the problem.

First, line up your ducks. From the V.C.'s perspective, women entrepreneurs should be sure to know what they're getting into before seeking venture funding. One Boston venture capitalist is often surprised to see entrepreneurs make classic mistakes. They often approach venture capitalists with tremendous enthusiasm, but the documents they need to secure financing just aren't there. "Have your business plan, a full set of financials, and a detailed timeline of when you need your funding and for what it's going to be used ready," this investor says. "I've been shocked more than once to discover that when we ask an entrepreneur presenting to us how the money will be used, they don't have a buttoned-down answer." Entrepreneurs looking for V.C. money need to give an enthusiastic but realistic presentation. Talk about market size, and how your company can climb into the top echelon with V.C. money; address competition squarely, and don't get defensive when challenged. After all, it's the V.C.'s job to be careful with the fund's money. Entrepreneurs should also realize that venture capitalists want to invest in high-growth companies that can be sold or taken public within a few years. Sometimes the entrepreneur's passion almost gets in the way; rapid growth in a short time period often means organizational changes, and the entrepreneurial owner may not be comfortable with that. Not every company should take V.C. money.

Keep in mind that venture capitalists generally want a substantial equity position in your company, something north of 20 percent. Gaining seats on your board is also a given, which means if things really don't work out, they can lobby to replace you as CEO. Lastly, remember that venture capitalists are working with other people's money, as the stewards of investor funds. It's their fiduciary responsibility to their own investors to help grow the companies they invest in and get them cashed out for a maximum price within a relatively short period of time. V.C.'s are accountable to their investors and must fulfill their fiduciary responsibilities to them. If you are uncomfortable with this level of outside control, seek funding else-where.

Angel investors. Another avenue of equity financing, angel investors differ from V.C.'s in that they use their own money to invest. They generally take a 10 percent to 30 percent equity position in a company and exercise less control over how you run your company. Angels are also more likely to spend time with you recommending how you can make service or product improvements. They genuinely enjoy the businesses they fund, seeking out companies where they believe they can make meaningful contributions instead of getting in your way. There are angel groups in most areas and industries, set up to hear presentations from entrepreneurs and invest small amounts of the group's money in return for an equity stake. Many angel investors prefer to invest in local or regional businesses, so to locate an angel investor group near you, either start with a Google search, or contact your local professional businesswomen's organization.

Strategic investors. These are individuals or corporate investors, both of whom may find your company's product or service attractive for investment purposes. Corporate investors provide funding when they see your product as a strategic fit with their business. Perhaps their distribution network is ideal for your product, or your infrastructure has the management depth they need.

Before you accept loans or equity investments, no matter how small, due diligence is mandatory. Meet with firms that specialize in your industry. Ask them if you can speak with a few executives of companies in which they have invested. Talk to colleagues in your local professional organizations to learn more about each firm, and seek advice from your professional advisory team before you make a final decision. If you decide to proceed, you and your attorney must look over the documents you are signing to make sure your obligations are clear and in line with your business plan and goals.

SUCCESS

Sharon Lobel was working for a packaging company twenty-five years ago when the owner tapped her to research and set up a new firm making tamper-evident bands for sealing packages. A year later he joined her, promising her a share in the company. But after another year or so passed and Sharon was still an employee, she decided to quit and start her own company. In 1986 she incorporated Seal-It, and worked from her basement in her home on New York's Long Island, selling heat-shrink bands used for tamper-evident packaging, shrink sleeves for promotional multipacks, and other shrink products. Sharon knew she would need deep pockets to push her company forward, but she didn't want to cede control in the process. Finally, in 1990, when she had four employees, Sharon was introduced to a strategic investor who took a minority stake in her firm. Everything "just clicked," she says, because "he's the money, and I'm the company." To fulfill Sharon's plans for growing Seal-It, the investor introduced her to a banker who handled his own significant line of credit. The money enabled her to relocate the company from her home to a small space in a warehouse. Sharon adhered to the company's growth plan, kept a careful eye on finances, and met regularly with her investing partner to discuss the company's performance. Problems were aired and addressed ASAP.

When her investor agreed to partner with her, revenue hovered at $2.5 million; today, with 260 employees, sales surpass $50 million.

REGRETS

Lila Valderrama and her sisters were eager to get started in their restaurant and catering business in Miami. But two years after start-up, none of them draws a salary. Lila says they don't have a formal business plan in place that indicates a timetable for giving the owners a salary. One of her sisters and her father are confident that the restaurant will make money one day, because customer response to Lila's Bistro has been good and the restaurant has had a favorable write-up. Lila also felt that it was good news that her bistro has survived for two years. But favorable restaurant reviews don't put money in your pocket. Lila says that "it is extremely hard and very stressful" to work very long days, so she doesn't have time to get advice from a women's business group or a financial adviser. The family has already discussed closing the bistro because running it is so difficult emotionally and financially. For now, they've concluded that they would rather succeed at this venture than have an easier life.

CHAPTER 5

Step 4: Market Your Products

O nce you've perfected the steps involved in setting up your business, you now have a product, or a service, that you can sell. Launch day, for me, was not the day I decided to start a company, but the day I announced to the world that I was open for business, ready to take orders, call on clients, and deliver goods. For your professional debut, it's crucial to do it right, with a memorable logo design, a sophisticated website, and a solid marketing plan.

Your Marketing Plan

A marketing plan covers the gamut, from product and service development to promoting your goods, pricing them competitively to sell, and delivery. Like your business plan and your employee manual, this plan should be a formal, written document. The act of setting down your marketing goals and strategies will help crystallize them for you and your staff. Begin by brainstorming with your key personnel and your start-up team and discuss the following:

- Your core product or service
- Your company's branding, including name, logo, and tagline
- Which advertising and promotional methods to use
- How to sell your product
- Distribution channels
- Pricing strategies

Your marketing plan should be specific. For example, at our annual "year beginning" meeting, I set as a goal that each sales director bring in either two new clients or two new contracts from an existing client. Don't set unrealistic goals that your team can't meet. That will only discourage your staff. Business takes place in a dynamic environment. Review and adapt your marketing plan accordingly. Quarterly or semi-annually should work.

Your Core Product

You've started a company because you know what you're good at, and now you want to sell your product or service to customers. But don't embark on an expensive promotional campaign without working out the kinks in your marketing strategy first. Melissa Epstein, for example, found the initial response to her daughter's custom-made birthday-party invitation to be very strong. Numerous mothers called Melissa to ask for their own handmade invitations. Although she was ready to go to work making the invitations, she paced herself because, she says, "I hadn't been using my computer for two years, and I wasn't up-to-date on the software."

Melissa fell back on her background in advertising and her skills as a graphic designer to see her through the early orders. Still, she says, it was a "bit of a struggle" to come up to speed quickly and fulfill the orders she received. To avoid letting her new business snowball out of control, she essentially used her first group of orders as a test market. Tinkering with paper selection, she settled on an expensive but effective type of photo paper that allowed her to use children's photos on the invitation covers. She then shopped for sturdy, elegant envelopes that would appeal to her customers. With all of these pieces in place, Melissa felt ready to take on more invitation orders. Try out your product or service with just a few customers first, so you know what works and what doesn't before large volumes of orders roll in.

Your Company Name, Logo, and Tagline

View these as the advance men for your company. A good name, logo, and tagline have staying power and will continue for years, even if you sell or leave your company. Naming a company sounds easy enough, but if you get this crucial step wrong, you'll discover there can be unfortunate consequences.

The name. A company name can simply describe what the company does. Wendy Goldstein's Costume Specialists, Inc., makes costumes, while Beverly Gray's Exhibit Edge, Inc., makes and manages exhibits. A name can also reflect an image you want to convey. Lynne Marie Finn's staffing company is called Superior Staffing Services, Inc., to invoke thoughts of high quality, while Lois Yaffe's bookstore, My Book Place, suggests a cozy space. Or select a name that means nothing, but with a cadence that sounds pleasing to you, such as Himanshu Bhatia's IT services company, Rose International, so named because Himanshu likes roses. Names based on location are popular, although they present a problem if you ever decide to move offices or expand beyond your local area. Imagine the disconnect if you name your company South Side Yoga and then open a location on the north side of town. You will lose your brand equity and confuse your customers.

You can also use your own name, as in The Warrior Group and J.Y. Legner & Associates. But naming the company after yourself has one major risk worth noting: it's literally your good name that gets damaged if things go wrong. Of course you can change your company name later, but you may lose some momentum in the process, and you'll end up spending money on new business cards, stationery, and corporate checks. It's easier to get it right the first time.

The logo. Ideally, your logo will grow into a symbol that helps your customers identify your company's products. The best way to come up with an appropriate and successful design is to hire a professional graphic designer who can hear what your company offers to clients and create a logo that conveys the image you want. Some designers may even do a logo for free if you agree to give them design work on other company projects, such as marketing brochures or sales presentations.

Just like a company name, the use of color and design in the logo can also convey what the company does. For example, when Paula Pillsbury opened a general contracting business in southern Massachusetts several years ago, targeting women who need small home-repair jobs done, she named her company The Pink Hammer. Her logo displayed her hammer, in pink, signifying that this was a woman's company doing contracting work for women.

The tagline. Coin a catchy phrase that captures what your company does, and your tagline could endure forever. Shelley Rote's Signature Events uses as its tagline, "A destination management company unlike any other," while Wendy Goldstein's costume business says, "We build character." Taken together, your company name, logo, and tagline should tell a potential customer who you are and what you do, at a glance. Print the tagline on all of your marketing materials so it becomes associated with the company (see table 9).

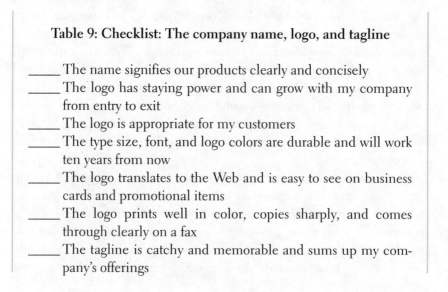

Table 9: Checklist: The company name, logo, and tagline

_____ The name signifies our products clearly and concisely
_____ The logo has staying power and can grow with my company from entry to exit
_____ The logo is appropriate for my customers
_____ The type size, font, and logo colors are durable and will work ten years from now
_____ The logo translates to the Web and is easy to see on business cards and promotional items
_____ The logo prints well in color, copies sharply, and comes through clearly on a fax
_____ The tagline is catchy and memorable and sums up my company's offerings

Branding your company and products. Your company's name, logo, and tagline are the starting point for establishing your brand. Branding is critical. It helps you create and nurture a company culture and build client loyalty. Develop a position for your brand based on competitive market research. In our company we incorporated our tagline, "Where experience and expertise add up to the best in medical communications," into virtually every proposal we submitted to clients. That tagline was how we wanted to be known, and how we worked to distinguish ourselves from "just another meeting-planning company." Because we pledged to deliver the best, we always requested postmortem meetings with clients after we organized a program for them, so they could tell us whether or not we lived up to our brand. Feedback is vital; it helps you continue to work on improving your brand. Finally, make sure that as you develop your brand position, you focus on advantages to your brand that have value to your customers, and that your brand message is clear and consistent. It doesn't do any good, for instance, to highlight that you offer gourmet catering services if the bulk of your customers use your services to order sandwich trays for in-office business lunches (see table 10).

Table 10: Five Tips to Successful Branding

An outstanding brand isn't made overnight. An innovative name (Viagra), creative packaging (Pez candy), or a clever tagline ("A diamond is forever") is just the beginning. A successful brand delivers on its promises, thereby generating revenues and client loyalty year after year.

1. Know what you do best and communicate your competitive advantage doing it.

2. Develop your brand message after you've studied your competition, so you can define your relationship with your clients.

3. Know your client base and their value to your business. Periodically evaluate who your strongest clients are. Will they continue to be strong? Are they loyal, or do they come and go?

4. Keep your brand message consistent. This begins by coordinating your company name, logo, and tagline, and continues with consistency in presentations and product delivery.

5. Deliver, and measure your results. Make sure you get feedback from your clients on your products and your level of service on a regular basis. Your goal should be to make your brand better.

Advertising and Promotion

Two key factors influence your advertising and promotional choices: your customer base and your budget. Start by thinking about your target audience first. Will you be working for large Fortune 1000 companies, or does your customer base consist of a consumer group, such as teachers or parents?

Customer base. Think about your customer base and determine what messages you want to convey before you develop your marketing materials. Doreen Marks, the founder of OTIS Technology, told me that her company customizes certain promotional materials according to the market segment for her gun-cleaning products. Wal-Mart and L.L. Bean, for example, don't need or want the amount of detailed information the army requires before placing a purchase order. But the company tagline, "Keep It Clean!" serves every client. Although you and your graphic designer might prefer to be represented by a modern-looking four-color brochure printed on heavy paper, this might not be the best way to connect with your target market.

Because Shelley Rote and Maria Irwin often find themselves managing multimillion-dollar budgets for megaclients such as Cisco Systems and Johnson & Johnson, their promotional materials must reflect an ability to serve large, sophisticated companies. To show how capable they are at packaging events, Shelley and Maria commissioned a CD and several full-color information sheets listing their company's services, including parties, tours, programs for spouses, team-building outings, and polo matches. The packet, wrapped with a yellow ribbon with the company name printed in contrasting letters, comes in a four-color pocket folder emblazoned with the slogan "All wrapped up just for you." Several clients have told Shelley and Maria that their promotional materials do a great job of showing off their expertise and excellence in event planning. Judy Galbraith's catalogs lack the gloss and sophistication found in Signature's brochures, but an independent book publisher promoting goods to parents, teachers, and teens doesn't need that either. Judy's practical catalogs display useful categories and recommendations from outside authorities like the New York Public Library, which recommended more than twenty of Free Spirit Publishing's titles on its lists of recommended books for teens, and "Quick Picks," a list of books recommended by teens compiled by the American Young Adult Library Services Association. Judy promotes her books by packing her four-color catalogs with detailed descriptions of her self-help books for kids, thereby hitting the perfect pitch for her target audience too.

Your promotional budget. Most women who start their own businesses can't splurge on an elaborate promotional or advertising budget. Remember, advertising doesn't have to be expensive to be effective. Also, keep in mind that for women who own their own businesses, there are a number of resources available that are free, or cost very little. Try these out first before you spend money you don't have.

Spend little, but gain a lot. One useful promotional tool is obtaining certification as a women-owned business. If you're a minority, you can get an additional level of certification. These designations allow you to compete for contracts from the government or from companies that have diverse-supplier policies. Companies with MBE (minority business enterprise) or WBE (women business enterprise) certificates are eligible for the Small Business Administration's 8(a) business-development program, which helps small, disadvantaged businesses access the huge federal procurement market. Jozi Legner's website touts her company's WBE and MBE certifications, a qualification she used to become one of the first suppliers under LG&E Energy's diversity program in 2001. Don't expect to rest on your certifications, however. Many certified companies never win diversity contracts because they don't market themselves hard enough. "You still have to get out there and tell people who you are, what you do, and what your product is, or they just won't know you're out there," says Gail Warrior, whose company is WBE and MBE certified.

Table 11: Top-of-the-Line Certification: ISO 9000

The International Organization for Standardization (ISO) is a network of the national standards institutes of 152 countries. Overall, more than 600,000 organizations adhere to the standards. Any company can obtain ISO 9000 certification, providing it fulfills specific quality-management requirements listed in the relevant standards of the ISO 9000. The certification standards deal with how companies meet customers' needs, deal with applicable regulations, and work to improve performance in these areas. Certification bodies in different countries issue the certificates of conformity. Lynne Marie Finn's Superior Staffing Services, Sharon Lobel's Seal-It, Inc., which manufactures shrink labels and other shrink products, and Cathy Newell's Mohawk, Ltd., which repairs telecommunications equipment, have this designation.

To obtain more information, contact:

Address: American National Standards Institute
1819 L Street N.W. Suite 600
Washington, DC 20036
Phone: 202-293-8020

New York Office: 25 West 43rd Street, 4th floor
New York, NY 10036

Phone: 212-642-4900

Fax: 212-398-0023
E-mail: info@ansi.org
Web: http://www.ansi.org

Source: http://www.ansi.org

Join your local chamber of commerce. A bastion of entrepreneurship, these organizations often sponsor one- or two-day small-business fairs featuring local companies. You pay for your exhibit space, but the chamber promotes the event for free, advertising on local radio and TV and in newspapers. Chambers also host other events to showcase member firms and to promote networking among entrepreneurs. At a Jupiter/Tequesta/Juno Beach Chamber of Commerce businesswomen's luncheon, just one of multiple "great" chamber events she's attended, Joanna Schmidt heard Deputy SBA Administrator Melanie Sabelhaus give an inspiring talk on women in business. Such settings are ideal for promoting your business if it's local in nature, such as a gym, salon, caterer, or jeweler.

Networking and referrals. It's easy to get overwhelmed by the amount of networking opportunities available. The challenge for today's woman business owner is to sort through the large number of organizations available to support women in business and select the one or two groups most likely to provide sales leads and peer support. Besides national and local organizations (see Resource Guide), there also are many groups aimed at a particular industry. Angela Drummond, for example, belongs to Women in Technology, a Washington, D.C., area–based organization that works to mentor, promote, and foster networking for tech-industry women. Denise Baker, coowner of D.R.B. Electric, Inc., in Albuquerque, New Mexico, joined the National Association of Women in Construction, a move that helped her meet other women in her field and to learn about what's going on in the industry. "The knowledge and information you learn from others—both good and bad—can be key to your success," she says.

Industry networking can be vital if you're new to your field. When Joan Coukos quit her banking career to start her chocolate-making company, Chocolat Moderne, she left behind years' worth of personal capital that she had invested in the financial world, where she belonged to several professional societies and had a wide network of acquaintances. To learn about how the chocolate industry worked, Joan joined the New York Women's Culinary Alliance. She made a point to attend conferences with culinary programs to hone her chocolate-making skills and to meet other chocolatiers and vendors. While, like many entrepreneurs, Joan had time for only a few meetings each year in her start-up phase, she found that networking proved invaluable as she grew her business.

Referrals are another free but powerful way to promote your business. Signature Events, Shelley Rote's New Orleans event-planning firm, landed its biggest assignment through a referral. A big company, looking to host a weeklong conference for 250 marketing managers, called the local Ritz-Carlton to ask for recommendations for the top three local event planners. Because Signature's staff networks regularly with hotel sales managers in the area, the Ritz included Signature on its short list. Shelley's presentation won the contract, and she put together a stellar program for the conference.

When I ran my own company, my sales directors also used referrals as a way to drum up business. We regularly asked clients whom we knew were satisfied with our work to write us a referral letter for particular new prospects, sending us a copy so that we could follow up with the potential new customer. Many clients are reluctant to share a good supplier, so you may have to reassure them that their business will continue to be a top priority for you. We sometimes had to answer questions on the spot when asking for a referral: "If I refer you, who will service the additional business if you get it? Do you have more people available who can handle more business without any disruption to my account?" Make sure you are prepared to deal with such questions. If your responses aren't well thought out and clear, understandably the client may turn down your request.

E-mail. One of the easiest and cheapest forms of promotion is e-mail. Sending out updates and reminders via e-mail will keep your company name constantly in front of your customers while providing them with useful information. Start by getting your customers' e-mail addresses whenever you get their mailing address, on order forms or through a signup sheet in your store. Then create digital marketing pieces featuring your name and logo. You can have a professional Web designer or online marketing agency do these for you, for a fee. To save money, when you commission your logo, be sure to get it from the graphic designer in digital format, so that you can include it in e-mail or online communications that you design yourself. In addition to promoting your products, you can also use e-mail to keep your customers and clients abreast of your company's growth, announce a new employee, or note that you've taken additional office space. These positive messages communicate your new company's progress.

Melissa Epstein uses e-mail as a marketing tool anytime she wants to introduce a new product or a new creative technique for her invitations. She sends out reminder e-mails to stimulate holiday card orders and to encourage clients to place orders a few weeks in advance for custom invitations. E-mail also allows Melissa to zero in on additional marketing opportunities such as Mother's Day and end-of-school-year teacher gifts. All her e-mails feature click-through links to her website, www.imadethis.net.

Be careful, however, to include on every e-mail provisions for unsubscribing from your e-mail list, should the customer be so inclined. Some people take e-mail privacy seriously and may consider your marketing messages spam, even if they have given you their e-mail addresses. Be sensitive to customers' online privacy concerns. You may also want to include a sentence in your e-mails stating that your company does not sell its customers' e-mail addresses to third parties, to assuage any fears.

Internet sites. The Web allows you to showcase your company's capabilities and products. All you have to do is put up your own site. If possible, try to buy or lease the domain name that corresponds to your company's name or the name of a well-known product. (For more information go to http://www.Webdeveloper.com or http://www.domainmart.com/leasing/lease_payment.html.) Ghislaine Bérubé, for instance, uses www.lbalm.com for her Lobsterman's Balm. Unless you have experience designing websites, to achieve a unified, put-together look, hire a professional website designer to set up your site for you. Make a list of the features you would like to see on the site and talk to your programmer about what content you need to create. Maintain the consistent color scheme, logo, and branding that you created for your company throughout the site. If you are marketing to consumers, like Ghislaine or Phyllis LeBlanc of Harbor Sweets do, your site should be easy to navigate, with frequent updates to make the content reflect your company's current specials or pricing. Ask your mother to test it out to make sure it's easy to use. Service companies such as Shelley Rote's event-planning firm or Himanshu Bhatia's IT consultancy need interactive sites aimed at corporate procurement officers. These sites can also feature case studies showing how you helped clients in the past. Once your site is online, add the Web address prominently to all of your marketing materials to encourage clients to visit the site.

Media advertising vehicles. If you need more marketing firepower, the next step up is advertising on television and radio and in national magazines and newspapers. This strategy is expensive and not always useful for the small businesswoman. None of the women I interviewed mentioned buying national TV or radio spots as part of their marketing plans. Print ads are also risky; Ghislaine Bérubé's ad campaign in *The New Yorker*, designed to reach her target audience of sophisticated skin-care-products consumers, fell flat.

Local ads can be your best bet, provided you are willing to pay for frequent repetitions of your ad. On the radio, for instance, ads work best when they are repeated several times a day for a week or longer. This strategy has worked well for Ilanna Ball, a twenty-five-year-old real estate agent who bought and runs her own RE/MAX realty franchise in Woonsocket, Rhode Island. She was so pleased with the results of her radio ads on local stations that she developed her own weekly half-hour show, which discusses mortgage rates and home sales in her area. Nancy Milby's Laguna Culinary Arts also gets a steady stream of students for hands-on cooking classes from local newspaper ads. Even ads in local media, however, can be pricey without leading to results. If you do decide to go this route, you will need top-quality, professionally produced ads, for which you should hire a well-respected ad agency. Consider also taking part in a group ad, in which a small group of area merchants take out an ad together to promote their shopping center or block.

Despite the expense, national ads do work for certain companies. St. John Knits places an ad in nearly every issue of top fashion magazines such as *Harper's Bazaar* and *Vogue*. Until recently, every ad featured the company's secret weapon, model Kelly Gray, daughter of founder Marie Gray, who left the company after a private-equity firm bought the family's majority stake. This large promotional outlay works because St. John already has a considerable following among the stylish, well-heeled readers of the fashion bibles. Most companies can grow for years before they reach the level where they need national advertising to support their sales.

Direct mail. Tweak your ads to turn them into direct mail pieces. To save money on envelopes, create a self-mailer by folding over the page on which your promotion is printed, labeling the back, and then running it through a postage meter before mailing it. Your message will begin to hit the customer as soon as the mailer lands on his desk.

In addition to the list you keep of your current customers, you will likely want to buy or rent other mailing lists targeted at your audience. When selecting these lists, make sure the mailing house has customized them for you, with all the addresses current and the customers matching the demographics you wish to reach. If you are promoting a prom-dress sale at your ladies' boutique, for instance, ask the mailing house to delete men's names and the names of women between the ages of twenty-one and thirty-five, who are too old to buy prom dresses themselves but too young to have prom-aged daughters. Have the mailing list company send the list directly to you for review, and check it carefully. You don't want your prom-dress promotion going to a list of expectant mothers.

When you hire a printer or mail fulfillment center to assemble and mail your promotional pieces, understand their procedures for reducing errors. This is especially important if you plan to launch several campaigns targeted at different customer groups simultaneously. A competitor of mine had this problem when her company scheduled two 20,000-piece mailings advertising medical educational seminars at the same time, one for cardiologists and the other for gynecologists. The printed mailing labels were sent to the printer, where the wrong labels were affixed to the brochures. The only way around this mistake was to reprint, relabel, and remail everything, while paying rush charges and angering the client sponsoring the seminar. Total cost: $20,000 extra, plus incalculable reputational damage. Remember, the cleverest direct mail piece is useless if fulfillment goes awry.

To get a positive response, send the first self-mailer and then follow up with a postcard. Send mailings to yourself and your staff as well, to verify that the pieces were sent correctly. Ask the printer for your postage receipts to check against your bill. Also, for the highest response rate, schedule your mailings so the pieces arrive on a Tuesday or Wednesday.

Although direct mail pieces take considerable forethought and incur costs for printing and mailing, they often pay off. Ilanna Ball has had so much success with her monthly promotional mailing to clients that she has hired a marketing expert to coach her agents on assembling the pieces.

Other advertising vehicles. If your business is local, scout out stores in your area for community bulletin boards or good places to put up ad posters. A popular variation on this idea is the racks of free ad postcards found in many restaurants and bars. A well-designed billboard ad can also bring business to your door. And don't forget the Yellow Pages. High-tech media aside, many consumers still turn to the phone book when looking for local services.

Publicity. Not to be confused with promotions and advertising that you develop and pay for, publicity is often free. But free press has a price: You have no control over what's said or where it appears. If you agree to do a

Table 12: Ten Direct-Mail Tips

A response rate of 1 percent to 3 percent is average with direct mail, unless there is an offer attached such as a free sample or a gift certificate.

1. Develop a self-mailer to eliminate the cost of envelopes and reduce postage.

2. Scrutinize the mailing list to make sure it is as targeted as possible.

3. Time your direct-mail pieces so they are delivered midweek, when the response rate tends to be higher.

4. Consider postcard mailers. They cost less to develop and print, the postage is less, and they're effective as reminders.

5. Avoid scheduling mailings when most customers might be away, such as close to school vacations, national holidays, and religious celebrations.

6. Use color whenever possible for a higher rate of response.

7. Spot-check your lists and select a few customers that you can contact directly to ensure that your direct-mail pieces are delivered on time.

8. After your mailings are completed, request the postage receipt to check the date and price against what you paid for the mailings.

9. Ask your printer or fulfillment center what checks they have in place to ensure that mailing list mix-ups don't occur.

10. Ask your list company when the list was last checked against the national change-of-address database. This should be done every two years to keep bounced-mail rates down.

magazine, radio, or TV interview, for example, you typically don't know what questions will come at you, nor do you know how your responses will be interpreted in print or on a broadcast. My advice is that before you attempt one-on-one interviews with reporters, first try looking for ways to get your company media exposure with minimal risk. State and local business events, such as trade shows, chamber of commerce fairs, or crafts shows, generally get generous coverage from area broadcasters and print media. Many local publications want to support commerce in the neighborhood, not crush it. It's more likely your company won't be mentioned at all rather than singled out for a poor review after one of these events. Read the coverage that follows these events to determine the general orientation of the various publications, and don't volunteer to be interviewed by a publication you think is antibusiness.

What should you do when publicity backfires? When the *Dallas Business Journal* listed Gail Warrior's 2003–04 revenues at three times less than what they actually were, Gail let the paper know about the mistake immediately. The paper subsequently printed a correction, but only after Gail provided the editor with a copy of the Warrior Group's audited financials. Don't let a problem like this one go unanswered. Address it as soon as possible.

When your company needs national publicity but you don't have the budget to launch an expensive campaign, think creatively. Susan Schadt wanted to move her beeswax candles beyond the gift stores and boutiques where they were sold when she first launched her business. To get attention, she came up with the idea of promoting her candles as "art in wax." She called and called until buyers at top New York shops agreed to meet with her. Then she sent free samples to the buyers and to several popular style and home decor magazines. If a buyer or editor asked for any more information, she got right back to her to fulfill the request. Her candle-as-art concept, along with her determined networking and follow-up over several months, won her mentions in *Architectural Digest, Elle Décor, InStyle,* and *House & Garden.*

You can also create your own publicity by letting others do the work for you. Each year, Nancy Milby gives away 200 gift baskets and certificates for her cooking classes to area nonprofits, all of whom acknowledge Laguna Culinary Arts in their program materials. Denise Baker's company, D.R.B. Electric, touts the national recognition it has received for its safety program from the Occupational Safety and Health Administration and from Associated Builders and Contractors. Similarly, both Angela Drummond and Doreen Marks are recipients of numerous business recognitions and awards that garner free publicity for them. Doreen has been written up in numerous newspapers and magazines for her achievements, including being recognized by the SBA as New York State's Small Business Person of the Year.

To announce a new product with a splash, consider hiring a professional public relations agency. You pay for the agency's services, based on either their standard fee or a fee you negotiate, and their staff puts together a publicity package for you. They will also work with you to assemble a press kit, usually a two-pocket folder containing a professionally written press release about your new product and your firm; the name of a contact in your company and at the agency for more information; your company's brochure; and biographical information on you and other key employees. In addition to sending this kit to journalists with whom they have relationships, the agents will also try to convince them to write a story about your business. Keep in mind, however, that your publicist can only advise you on what and what not to say, and how to appear and speak on camera. Once the media interviews are arranged, their job is over. They do not control the content of what is printed or aired, nor do you.

Return on investment (ROI). Track your promotional spending compared to your returns. If a $2,000 newspaper ad yields a few phone calls and one modest sale, consider that a poor ROI and channel your marketing dollars elsewhere.

Turning Marketing into Sales

Market your product yourself. Never underestimate the power of door-to-door and in-home selling. Most closely identified with Tupperware and Mary Kay Cosmetics, this sales style was also successful for Lane Nemeth's Discovery Toys, Inc., and Madolyn Johnson's The Homemaker's Idea Company, now Signature HomeStyles. If you don't have a large promotional budget, the next best thing is to get out there and sell the product yourself. Besides raking in sales, you'll also meet and build up your customer base. Joanna Schmidt, for example, began by traveling around south Florida providing samples of her homemade skin-care products to upscale spas and resorts. She also asked hotel sales managers to include some of her products in a complimentary gift bag at golf tournaments or as part of a hotel welcome package. When she felt she had exhausted those routes, Joanna visited Sassafras, a popular Jupiter, Florida, women's clothing boutique, to ask if it would display her line. Jewelry maker Elena Caldera doesn't have the marketing dollars for color ads in glossy fashion magazines, so she organizes trunk shows at resort hotels and at clubs in gated communities. She and her daughter go to every show to model and sell the jewelry.

Even when your company gets big enough that you no longer have to drive door-to-door yourself to make individual sales, you will still need to make your own contribution to the marketing strategy. Lynne Marie Finn, whose multimillion-dollar staffing company is five hundred times the size of Elena's or Joanna's, still spends one-third of her time on the road visiting her clients and satellite offices. Himanshu Bhatia also makes three trips a month to see clients of her thousand-employee IT services company. Identifying ways to build, enhance, and grow your relationships with your customers must be an integral part of your marketing plan. The methods you select depend on whether you are selling to consumers or to other businesses. Options for relationship-building include the simple monthly e-mail communiqué; a quarterly "news from us" direct mail piece; and directing clients to your website for their account information. In addition to these updates, try to encourage as much direct contact between your key staffers and your customers as possible.

Trade shows. Your presence at your industry's top trade shows will cement your company's place among its peers. At first, you won't have much money to spend on giveaways or snazzy booths, but don't let a small budget discourage you. Because she had no money for marketing, Doreen Marks distributed her handmade gun-cleaning kits for free to soldiers at trade shows when she first started her company. Once they used the kits in the field, she knew they would create word-of-mouth buzz about her product among its target audience. Hinda Miller did likewise, giving away Jogbras at trade shows. Joan Coukos pitches her chocolates at both the consumer-focused Chocolate Show and the Fancy Food Show, which targets connoisseurs. To promote her brand, she gives out samples to both ordinary chocolate lovers and the experts who can recommend her products to hotel gift shops and boutiques. Judy Galbraith, aiming to market her children's self-help books around the world, sets up a booth at major international book fairs in Bologna, Frankfurt, and London. Erica Zap attends eight to ten trade shows a year to promote her Newport, Rhode Island, gift and housewares boutique. While she spends much of her time traveling to the shows, this avenue represents nearly Erica's entire marketing budget.

Start with one or two trade shows a year and add a show annually until you are visiting all the major events in your industry. Spend as much time as you can on the show floor. Bring several staffers with you to man the booth so you can walk around, network, and familiarize yourself with the competition. And wear comfortable shoes!

Product Delivery

There are two ways to distribute your products: directly to the customer, as in a retail store or from a website, or indirectly, by selling to buyers for larger retail outlets. With direct sales, you own the relationship with your customer. Indirect sales force you to interact with buyers for chains such as Target or JCPenney. While this removes the responsibility for handling customer service, the downside to indirect selling is that the chains will negotiate you down on your price, arguing that they have multiple sites in which to sell your product. And while you need their business, they don't need yours.

Online sales. The key to selling on the Internet is to have a well-planned site that is easy to navigate, with dazzling graphics that don't take too much time to load on your customers' computers. The site should be professionally designed to make your products stand out. Make certain, as well, that all of your site's features work as advertised, and that your shopping cart function, if you have one, is simple to use.

Joanne Stoner, founder of eDressMe, designs, manufactures, and sells dresses from her retail store in New York City's garment district as well as on her own website. A women's apparel veteran, with experience at Lazarus, Saks, and Liz Claiborne, Joanne learned about the Internet at technology giant Lucent, where she became director of e-commerce, and later at a firm where she worked on sales-prediction algorithms. In her free time, Joanne, a passionate tango dancer, began designing dance dresses, and set up a website to sell them. "But I realized I really enjoyed this more than my regular full-time job," Joanne said, "so I decided to leave my full-time job, take my website out of the closet and launch it full-time." The site became a hit not only with tango dancers, but with other women who liked the feminine, ruffled styles. Thanks in part to a strong following for its e-mail newsletter, coupled with favorable publicity in *The New York Times* and the *Wall Street Journal*, which ranked the site No. 1 for same-day dress delivery in Manhattan, business at eDressMe has exploded. According to Google, Joanne's company ranks first among 1.3 million evening-dress sites and 770,000 cocktail-dress sites.*

Mail-order catalogs. In some instances, as in Lillian Vernon's mail-order catalogs, this method of promotion is the business. In other cases, such as

---

*Joanne went back to school when she was 38 and got her M.B.A. from Harvard.

Phyllis LeBlanc's Harbor Sweets, the business began with mail orders, with the original owner sending his first mailing to the seventy-five people on his Christmas card list, and mushroomed from there. Harbor Sweets has a retail store, Internet sales, and a direct-sales operation for fine gift and gourmet shops but, Phyllis says, still sends out more than half a million mail-order catalogs annually. And Phyllis adds more customer labels to her mailing lists each time she targets new markets (see chapter 5, Diversify).

Who does the selling? All of the businesswomen in this book sell their own products, and they have sales personnel on staff to push sales as well. You can hire outside representatives to do your sales calls for you, but I don't recommend taking this route while you're still in the throes of building your company. While you may increase sales in the short-term, independent agents will never know your product as well as you and your team do, and they will move on.

Pricing Strategies

Different businesses have different profit structures. Make sure you know your industry's pricing trends before you establish prices for your products or send proposals out the door. Every market is also subject to the laws of supply and demand. If a celebrity was photographed wearing one of Joanne Stoner's tango dresses, for instance, demand could skyrocket. The trick is to know whether a sudden demand surge or dip is a fluke or whether it represents a shift in market trends.

When setting your prices, first understand your expenses. Direct costs, sometimes called hard costs, are expenses for materials used to make your product. If you design greeting cards, your direct costs include paper, inks, envelopes, and photos. Indirect, or soft, costs are the overhead that supports your business, such as office rent, utilities, general supplies, and accounting and legal fees. Your margin is the difference between what it costs you to make the product or deliver the service and what a customer will pay for it. This margin is your profit, which your company keeps. Your break-even price is the price at which a sale will make back your costs without making a profit. Any price above breakeven allows you to make money on each sale.

Once you set your prices, customers will always want to pay less. Deciding when to hold the line on list prices and when to show some leeway is not always easy. In my company, we would not move more than 5 percent below our listed fees, believing our prices to be appropriate to our costs. You may feel that the only way to get a certain order is to lowball by cutting your margins below your normal profit levels. But bear in mind that a lowball cost quote only works the first time. In all subsequent negotiations with that client, you will have to explain why your fees are now higher. My firm had a policy of offering a lowball quote only when trying to win a new client, but never for an existing account. A solution to this dilemma is the introductory-price approach, often used to promote a new product or service. This tactic makes it clear to your customer that your initial price will rise for future business.

At the other end of the spectrum is premium pricing, in which you set a higher price and target customers who are likely to pay that price. St. John Knits, for instance, is aimed at high-income women who buy luxury designer clothing. While focusing on a small subset of the apparel-buying public leads to lower sales than a mass-market brand like The Gap might bring in, St. John can charge higher prices and generate a larger profit margin.

Bundling is another pricing concept worth considering. With this approach, you tie together a customer's purchase of several products from you with one price. You provide a discount from the individual prices of each product, and in return you get the guaranteed business up front. My company used this tactic successfully to encourage customers to look at their needs far in advance to take advantage of bundle prices. This allowed us to lock in the revenue and to plan our own staffing and delivery needs as well.

The bottom line on pricing strategies is to know your costs, know your industry's pricing trends, set a price plan, and sell. But don't forget to review your prices at the start of each year or to discount at the end of a season, depending on the type of business you're in.

Selling Past the Competition

Your competitors never quit. They are always out there, undercutting your prices, poaching your best people, or adding new products that make your own look stale. Staying in front of them takes finesse as well as perseverance. Shore up the core competencies that make you better than them.

Take stock. You can't improve your products and compete more effectively until you size up the competition objectively. In my company, we began the process of annual self-assessment by asking our regular clients to tell us what they thought we did that was outstanding and where they thought we could use some work. Typically, our clients would tell us, for example, about some additional services that a competitor might provide as part of their meetings-management fee and ask us to think about doing the same. They also suggested other services they would like to buy from us that would enhance our regular programs.

To keep tabs on the competition, we also circulated our industry's major trade news magazine among the sales directors and senior managers every month. My sales directors attended trade events to scout competitors' activities. Our meeting planners also aggressively sought out competitors' programs at medical conventions. They were diligent about gathering discarded direct-mail pieces and other printed materials at conferences. Upon their return to the office with a Santa-sack-size bag of brochures, the sales directors and I pored over the materials to evaluate program designs and content. If you don't know who the competition is and how good they are, you can't outpace them.

Spawning a competitor. When Lynne Marie Finn became president of Superior Staffing Services, then a small temp agency, her first stop was the Buffalo, New York, office, where four people were on staff. Lynne stepped out for a lunch appointment one day and when she returned, the entire staff was gone. Apparently, the group had been planning an abrupt departure for a few weeks, telling Superior clients that "a new company" would bill them for services shortly. Spooked by Lynne's arrival from headquarters, which they wrongly assumed meant the bosses were onto their plan, the workers simply walked out.

Once the baffled corporate office figured out what was going on, Lynne had some heated discussions with the ex-employee responsible for the mutiny. She realized that her arrival had inadvertently caught them up short, so she spent the rest of the day on the phone to Superior's clients doing damage control. As a result of her speedy thinking, the new company was unable to poach any of Superior's customers. Lynne had new hires in place within weeks in Buffalo, leaving the competition scrounging.

Deborah Millhouse, president of CEO, Inc., in Charlotte, North Carolina, also found that her competitors were within her own organization. One of her junior partners left her firm, violated his noncompete agreement by soliciting her clients, and even hired one of Deborah's key employees. Fortunately, Deborah's noncompete agreements were well written and specific, prohibiting employees who left from either calling on active clients of CEO or recruiting CEO's staffers. She sued her ex-partner and eventually settled with him.

Service businesses constantly have to deal with defections. It happens all the time, even when you have noncompete employment agreements in place. Lynne told me, for example, that it is standard practice in her industry, employment services, to have noncompetes, but as a practical matter it can be tough to enforce these agreements. Suing a noncompliant employee is a time-consuming, expensive process that requires a lawyer and diverts you from your primary goal of building your business.

Keeping Clients Loyal

Attracting customers is difficult. In the early-growth phase of your company, it's more efficient to focus on retaining the clients you have and convincing them to give you more business than constantly trying to recruit more customers. To do this, you need to have a close relationship with the right customers. Concentrate on those who pay on time and re-up frequently for more services. This is easier if your customers are large companies with institutionalized procurement procedures. The downside is that you'll have to compete with many other suppliers for these companies' business.

Keeping Your Customers Happy

1. **Start by reviewing Step 1.** Are your core competencies as good as they can possibly be? Probably not. Hitting peak performance is one thing; staying there is something else entirely. For the clients with whom you are building relationships, make sure the next job you do is a blockbuster. Show your clients you don't take their routine business for granted.
2. **Look for ways to increase value for your clients.** My company routinely competed against several other firms, all vying to provide meeting planning services to individual pharmaceutical products groups within the same drug company. But we noticed that a number of different product marketing groups at the company were all registering to attend the same major medical conventions. We quickly put to-

gether a group proposal showing the different marketing managers how we could manage all of their events at the same conference, since programs are scheduled over a few days, saving all the groups money by charging, for example, one set of airfare and hotel fees for our staff, among other duplicate expenses. Your client may not bite every time, but it does show you're thinking about ways to help them even more.

3. **Raise the bar.** A global consumer-products company hired Shelley Rote's event-planning firm for a multimillion-dollar contract to organize a weeklong forum for marketing managers from around the world. In contrast to the usual evening or two-day events they were used to planning, the Signature team had to develop up to seven events per day, including team-building exercises and New Orleans–focused tourist excursions. Every night featured a special theme dinner with entertainment. For several months Shelley's team worked so hard that "it felt like we were organizing events for the president of the United States," she says. They turned a theater into an authentic jazz club, created a Mardi Gras night complete with floats from the city's Carnival parade and celebrity chef demos, and planned a formal gala dinner dance with cocktails, jazz, and an orchestra playing through dinner. As their reward for a successful event, the Signature team won several enthusiastic referrals from their client. Your relationship with a happy client will only deepen over time.

4. **Customer service.** What would you like from us and when would you like it? Suzy Vasillov and her staff at Keesal & Mathews routinely log twelve-hour days at holiday time in her specialty shop on New York's Madison Avenue, fulfilling numerous last-minute gift purchases from customers. Much of Suzy's customer base is made up of walk-ins from the neighborhood whom Suzy knows by name and address. She delivers gift-wrapped boxes to their doors even after the store is closed, at no charge.

Both service and retail businesses can rise and fall on the quality of customer service alone. Almost nothing travels faster, or is more destructive, than negative word-of-mouth publicity. Whether your customers are down-the-block neighbors or Fortune 1000 managers, pay attention to their needs and come up with solutions to fill them.

5. **Flexibility.** Besides attentive service, flexibility also goes a long way toward winning loyalty. The quickest way to ensure your customers feel bound to you is to show your willingness to accommodate them. Multiple order changes from a client can be stressful, but demonstrating flexibility will earn your client's devotion.

6. **Coping with angry clients.** In retail, if a customer brings back an item, you can often solve the problem by issuing a credit. If the same customer complains routinely, this may be a customer impossible to keep. You may also learn what the problem really is. Perhaps your sales staff is rude or fails to follow up on your orders.

   In a service business, dealing with an unhappy client can be more complex. Is the client disappointed in your company's performance? Did your staff misunderstand what the client wanted? Sit down with your dissatisfied clients as soon as possible to listen to their concerns. Even if you disagree with what they say, hear them out, and provide solutions wherever you can. The old adage "the client is always right" is usually true. Assure them that you can meet their needs and close by saying you look forward to continuing a good working relationship with them.

7. **Take steps every month to nurture the relationship.** You travel, your client travels. Before you know it a couple of months have passed and you've done nothing more than trade e-mails. Make sure you talk to your clients on the phone and meet with them often, even if it's for just a brief update meeting. They need to know that the head of your company cares about their business.

8. **Maintain special client lists.** As your relationship with a customer grows, you'll share in their good news: the birth of a child, a graduation, or a business milestone. A thoughtful, handwritten card or note is appropriate, as is a small holiday gift. It's even better, of course, if you remember your client loves baseball, not football, and you can provide tickets to a good game occasionally. Beware, however, that while keeping a short list of key clients, their important dates, and their sports or hobby interests is acceptable, don't keep any type of document that records personal observations or details of client likes or dislikes. This list is not something you want in your files as it could easily be misconstrued.

9. **Maintain your customer relationships.** Joanne Piraino's promotional-products company lost Disney as a client when the entertainment giant changed its buyer, as it does every two years. By the time Joanne made it down to Orlando, the buyer she knew was gone, and a new buyer, with whom she had no relationship, was already in place. But the business was too good to give up. Joanne thought of a buyer she had known years before when he worked at the Orlando, Florida, theme park. Although he now worked for Disney in Hong Kong, she e-mailed him, and he passed her e-mail on to the right person in

Florida. When she visited Orlando shortly thereafter on her vacation, she was able, through this connection, to get an audience with the right buyer. She is now selling souvenir shirts to Disney's Animal Kingdom. Stay in touch with everyone you meet at your client companies. You never know where they'll land, or when, and how they may be able to help you.

10. **What losing a client or customer teaches you.** It hurts when a client leaves you. Use this injury to your advantage by thinking carefully about why the client gave up on you. It could simply be a change in focus within the client company, or a shift in market trends. If it's your company's fault, think about what you could have done, or what you can still do, to repair the relationship. Also consider what internal changes you need to make to avoid losing more business from others. This soul-searching can be useful, if painful, for your company.

Without customers, we are out of business. Good, durable relationships with key clients are as important as sturdy relationships with your partner and most valuable employees. Work on these connections throughout the life of your business and you can be sure your business will always have life. And now that you have some good customers, you can focus on growing the rest of your business.

SUCCESS

Himanshu "Sue" Bhatia grew up in New Delhi, India, and moved to St. Louis in 1987 after she earned her degree in architectural design. But when she arrived in the United States, it was too late in the year for her to start graduate school in architecture. Rather than sit out a semester, Himanshu instead went for a master's degree in management information systems, then joined McDonnell Douglas to work in technology for five years. She married, had two children, and then left her job to start Rose International, an IT services company that was born in her basement. Six months later she leased office space for the new firm. Her branding taglines are "We want to make it easier for you to do business" and "Our success depends on your success."

Himanshu says she was "keenly aware that many new businesses fail," but she was determined hers would not be among them. She also felt that there were few top IT service providers, and with hard work she believed she could create a company that could fill that market void. Himanshu tackled and exhausted every marketing avenue. She joined local business organizations and national professional societies; she worked with the SBA to obtain a business loan; she attended SCORE seminars, both for advice and networking; and she lined up a SCORE adviser to make recommendations as she went about building her firm. "At the beginning," Himanshu says, "I went nearly everywhere and attended everything." Himanshu wanted Rose International to provide quality service and performance at competitive prices. She got her WBENC certification, and made many cold calls, feeling good when she finally got Rose in, even if it was as a tier-three supplier. After a successful sales call, she followed up, waiting until the larger companies had worked through their first two tiers of suppliers and then convincing them to give Rose International a chance to perform. "It was much harder to work on the jobs that other suppliers had already let go or been passed over for," she says, but as those were the only opportunities, she took them.

Just twelve years after start-up, Rose International's revenues exceed $70 million, with eight hundred full-time employees and a host of Fortune 500 clients. In 2003, Himanshu received the SBA's National Entrepreneurial Success Award.

REGRETS

Jennifer McLarnon was shopping in the Boston College bookstore with her young son, looking for a children's book about eagles, her boy's latest interest, when she had a business idea. She realized that she could create such a book based on Boston College's mascot, the eagle. Contacting the Collegiate Licensing Company, which manages the logos of many schools, she obtained the licenses for ten schools, including Boston College. Her idea was to create coloring and activity books for children centered around the mascot of a particular college. Jennifer incorporated Odd Duck Ink in Seekonk, Massachusetts, hired illustrators, and then searched for a reason-

continued

ably priced printer. She started by producing books for her alma mater, Boston College, and then did a book for the University of Texas.

Marketing, however, proved more complicated than the book production process. "That is one of the tricky parts," she says, "because I don't have a distributor, so I just call on the college bookstores and local specialty shops around the universities." Jennifer has brought in Dunkin' Donuts as a sponsor at an athletic event at Boston College, convincing the company to buy and give away 1,000 books. She sold the same idea to AOL-TimeWarner, which also purchased 1,000 books and distributed them through a children's book club at the University of Texas. But Jennifer has had a frustrating experience marketing her goods. Despite her hard work, the limitations of the market and her lack of marketing muscle are a near-lethal combination for Odd Duck. She regrets that she didn't develop a solid advertising budget or learn more about how chain stores, on which she had counted for orders that have not materialized, buy books. Jennifer has decided to sell off her inventory and turn her attention to developing mass-market children's books, where she believes she'll have more success.

CHAPTER 6

Step 5: Diversify

Following the first four steps of the seven-step guide should take you between one and three or more years. At this point, you've established a core competency for your company, built a solid infrastructure, developed and maintained good financial procedures, and created a successful marketing plan. Next, focus on growth. To ensure your company remains viable and to insulate it from market trends and seasonal swings, you need to diversify. That's how you'll ensure that your company is still in business five years from now. Diversification is the pathway to both growing your revenue and protecting your profits.

What Is Diversification?

You execute diversification every day. For example, when you change from workout gear to a business suit and then to formal dress at night, you diversify your wardrobe. Similarly, you strive to diversify family meals, leisure activities, and the books and magazines you read. In business, diversification means adding different clients, products, or services to your core competency. It is a critical step in making your company more valuable.

Regardless of how much money your company makes, if you rely solely on your core competency, your firm is at risk if orders for one product fall off, or if a major client cancels a contract.

Diversification fulfills three objectives:

- Protects your company from overreliance on specific clients or a single product
- Smoothes out the seasonal peaks and valleys that occur in many types of businesses
- Provides a way to grow

A strategy to shield your company's revenues. Landing a marquee client is a feat to make any entrepreneur proud. Getting repeat orders is even better. But when you take on too much business from any one client, there's a risk that you might neglect the cultivation of new clients and the development of new products. In addition, if the client stumbles and has to cut back on its business with you, or if its relationship with your company sours, your company could share in the fall.

Joanne Piraino's company took a huge hit after the 2001 terrorist attacks because of her dependence on one family of products. She had been selling T-shirts and other promotional apparel to travel-industry clients such as Delta Air Lines and Avis Rent A Car. After the travel industry collapsed that year, Joanne realized her company needed to diversify. First, Joanne targeted a key trade group of meeting planners that could put her company in front of event managers for a wide range of big companies, among them Compaq and Cracker Barrel. She also developed other types of promotional items that her company customizes, such as coffee mugs, car sun-visor clips, and pillboxes for drug giant Astra-Zeneca. "We needed balance," she says. "We learned the hard way from 9/11 that your clients and products have to be diverse."

Unfortunately, once you have one large, lucrative client, it's easy to become complacent. This is especially true if you are working for yourself.

The single-client trap. After leaving Corpus Christi, Texas, Renee Skeels spent fifteen years doing catering for Martha Stewart and Paul Newman's The Good Food Store. Then a colleague asked her to help plan a weeklong medical meeting in Puerto Vallarta, Mexico. Renee became adept at it and soon became a freelance planner with a steady stream of business. Unfortunately, most of her assignments came from a single client. The work allowed her to make meaningful money as her family moved around the country, and she and her husband, Dennick, used the extra income for vacations, gifts, and savings. Eight years ago, however, Renee's income became more important to the family. Since starting her business, she had had two children, and now her two daughters had entered private school and she and her husband were beginning to plan for their college education. Because business from her biggest client evaporated when that company was sold and downsized, and a smaller account also slowed down, Renee was forced to think creatively about where to find new clients. She has been networking hard to drum up more medical-meeting planning jobs as well as pitching big companies such as banks and hotels in Atlanta, where she lives, to diversify into both catering and planning other types of meetings.

Being a sole proprietor doesn't have to translate into dependency on a few major clients. Tammy Baldwin moved to New York's picturesque Hudson Valley from New York City, where she had worked as a corporate events planner. Looking for a way to market her skills in her new, rural location, Tammy noticed ads for a business called Charmed Places, which specialized in organizing customized, nontraditional weddings in unusual settings. Tammy used all the money in her IRA to buy out the owner. She has expanded the company's exclusive relationships with numerous estates, farms, and local historic sites in a bid to attract sophisticated couples who don't want just another hotel-ballroom affair. She advertises in the major bridal magazines and also relies on word of mouth to bring in business, pitching the idea of a one-of-a-kind wedding limited only by her imagination and a client's budget. By advertising nationally, and representing a diverse range of venues, Tammy has reduced the risk of her business dropping off dramatically.

Larger companies also feel more than a pinch when a big client walks away or an industry sector takes a plunge. Ellen Bates says she learned "not to put all the eggs in one basket" years ago, when the banking industry stopped spending money on office furniture while the health care sector was booming. "I learned to diversify early on," Ellen said, "because I realized that when one portion of the economy dwindles, another sector picks up." Office Interiors now has a diverse client base that includes corporate, medical, and public sector work in New Hampshire.

Diversifying away from seasonal peaks and valleys. In Wendy Goldstein's first year in business, her revenues spiked in October, then fell back to a flat line for the rest of the year. She realized that, with half her sales coming around Halloween, her costume business was dangerously seasonal. After considering what other types of costumes she could offer, Wendy zeroed in on the "slump months" and decided to add tuxedo rentals and dance wear. These new lines filled in the gaps in her cash flow; tuxedoes rented mainly at prom time and for summer weddings, while sales of dance clothing peaked during the spring recital season, in the back-to-school months, and during the holidays. Wendy learned the importance of diversification in her third year in business, before a seasonal slump could put her out of business. Since then, Wendy has diversified further. Her company manages the tour schedules of the character costumes she creates as well as providing maintenance, storage, and delivery. In addition, she now manufactures both foam and inflatable costumes to complement her costume rentals and costume management business.

Joanne Stoner started off selling tango dresses, a business that mirrored her personal passion for the dance. She designed her own line as well as offering dresses by other brands. But she knew this strategy was risky, leaving her open to the whims of tango dancers. She took advantage of a shift in fashion trends toward feminine, flirty styles, and began selling dresses that were not specifically made for dancing. Moving slowly, she selected different styles from a variety of manufacturers and developed her own private-label product. This diversification plan is working, bringing new customers onto the eDressMe website site. During prom season, for instance, the average age of her customers drops from the usual twenty-five to forty down to eighteen as teenage girls log on. Her website also sells cocktail and evening dresses, which sell best in late spring, fall, and at holiday time, and sundresses for the summer. Next, Joanne plans to diversify into bridesmaids' dresses.

Diversification can help retail shops avoid getting tied to the seasons as well. Suzy Vasillov's housewares boutique does most of its sales during the fourth quarter as customers buy holiday gifts. To even out her revenue during the spring and summer, Suzy now features decor items aimed at beach-house owners and their houseguests, including hand-painted picnic baskets, decorated flower vases, silk flowers, colorful floor mats, and playfully patterned table lamps. Elaine Moffitt uses a similar strategy at Periwinkle's, her gift store in Westfield, New Jersey. Like Suzy, Elaine finds that her third and fourth quarters are the strongest. To keep revenues up throughout the year, Elaine created sections in her store for party goods, baby gifts, and golf presents. She also sells inexpensive but attractive gifts for teachers, such as pretty stationery. Periwinkle's also offers afghans and painted pottery with images of local landmarks, which real estate agents buy as welcome gifts for their clients.

Whether you sell gifts, clothing, or chocolates, it's critical for you to be aware of seasonal swings in your industry, and formulate a plan to offset them. Also, make sure the percentage of business from one client doesn't go above 30 percent.

Your Diversification Plan

To begin to diversify, write a formal diversification plan (see table 14). Ideally, diversification has already been addressed in your start-up business plan. If not, start thinking about how you can grow your business through diversification. Ask your senior managers, accountant, and advisers to make recommendations. You can think on a grand scale or in smaller steps, but be sure to address the following first:

- Is your core business sufficiently established to undertake developing new clients, services, or products?
- Do you have adequate management in place to support the company while you turn your attention to a new product?
- Do you have the capital you will need to execute your plan successfully? Even if your goal is to add one new client a year, you may need to add another staffer to help run the new business, and another full-time employee means more work space, more equipment, and more supplies.
- Is your management enthusiastic about growing the company through diversification? Personnel in small companies often don't like change, so work with your employees to ensure that your diversification plan is implemented smoothly.
- Have you set down how long you will pursue your diversification strategy before you determine whether or not the plan is working?
- If your diversification plan doesn't take off, do you have a backup plan?

Table 13: Before You Diversify: A Checklist

A successful diversification plan means more than dreaming up a new product or service. Develop a vision, make sure you have the staff in place to execute it, and review your financials to ensure that you can support it.

Vision

- Conduct market research and evaluate the competition, barriers to entry, and regulations.
- Assess the target market. Are you addressing an existing need or creating a need? Define what market testing you will need to do.
- When will you launch? Define your timetable.
- What trends support your diversification plan?
- If your plan fails, is there a backup plan?
- Focus on generating new customers for an existing product line, and look for new customers as you add new products

- Identify new locations for stores or service territories
- Acquire a different but complementary type of company
- Start another company
- Consider a joint venture

Logistics

- Do you have the skills? Or senior staff who can work with you?
- Do you have the time and energy?
- Do you have the personnel who can manage a new product once it sells?
- Can you train your employees in your new line?
- What is the marketing strategy?
- How will you price your new product?
- Do you have the office space, equipment, and supplies that you need?
- Is your infrastructure ready to support a new product?

Financing

- How much money will your diversification plan, including the research stage, require?
- How will you finance it? Can your cash flow support it, or will you need to take a loan?
- What are the estimated costs, revenues, and projections?

Metrics

- What is the break-even point?
- Are the projected returns satisfactory?
- What are the synergies with your existing products or operations?

There are numerous ways to diversify your company, whether you're in a service or products business (see table 14). To begin, consider these options:

- Add one to three new clients a year. Project the revenue from each new client for the next three years, and determine your staff needs as a result of the new business. If you are in a product business, look for one to three additional customer bases, or begin plans to develop a new product.

■ Develop a plan to create and add one or more new products each year to your core product line (see box 5).

Table 14: How to Diversify

Diversification means adding clients, customers, products, and services.

■ Add a new product or service to your core competency
■ Add new clients or customers
■ Add new locations
■ Acquire a company in the same industry
■ Acquire a company in a different industry
■ Start a new company
■ Enter into a joint venture

BOX 5: CASE STUDY: MD/TV

When my partners and I started TransMedica in 1981, we formed the business around quality medical editorial products such as clinical abstracts of papers and clinical slides for use at medical education symposia. The company was also set up to manage the logistics for medical conferences. Our clients, the pharmaceutical companies who sponsored the conferences as a way to introduce physicians to their new drugs or new indications for existing drugs, demanded top-notch editorial products and perfectly orchestrated meeting planning services. That was our core competency.

After our first year in business, we talked about a second vision for the company. We wanted a product idea that would accomplish several objectives, goals we could not achieve just by getting better at meeting planning or ratcheting up the quality of our editorial services. We needed something that would do the following:

■ Be unique in the marketplace
■ Attract pharmaceutical clients to us
■ Enhance our reputation in our industry as well as in associated fields
■ Lead to spin-off products

continued

- Attract the very best employees
- Attract the attention of larger companies

It wasn't long before my partner said "television," a eureka idea, and MD/TV was born. It had never been tried before: Put advertising for prescription drugs on television. (This was before cable took off, so we were talking about drug ads on network TV.) The plan was to produce a weekly half-hour program on a specific disease or condition, to be broadcast on network TV once a week in the early morning, before doctors left the house. We would sell drug companies three advertising slots on each show, each for a drug targeted at that disease. We would also produce a program guide that would be mailed to physicians in the show's markets, as well as distributed by sales reps from our pharma advertisers.

The idea came with several serious drawbacks. First, we didn't think the Food and Drug Administration, which regulates drugs and their advertising, would permit drug ads on TV, where consumers could see them. If the FDA did give us the go-ahead, we might then have to contend with the FCC and other broadcasting regulators, governmental bodies we knew nothing about. We also lacked experience with advertising. Drug companies keep ad agencies on retainer and use them as gatekeepers for all ads and promotions. We would have to get these agencies on board with our idea, or they would surely tank our prospects with the pharmaceutical companies. Then there were the logistical issues. We were not in the television production business, but to develop and broadcast a TV show, we would need studio recording space, a professional TV host, an audience, and graphics. We might even need guest appearances by patients. Clearly we would need to hire or partner with a production company. In addition, we would have to sell the program to TV broadcasters in the top fifty markets, requiring tough and time-intensive negotiating. We would also need ways of promoting the programs to physician viewers, as well as a compelling pitch to sell our pharma clients on the idea. Despite these obstacles, we were determined.

While I continued to manage our editorial and meeting-planning business, my partner worked on the new project. At this point, when we were about to venture out into an unknown business, our third partner, who held a minority stake in TransMedica but had the strongest relationships of the three of us with the pharmaceutical companies, decided to leave. The partnership upheaval was over within a week and our firm was able to continue much as before with our core business. We had lost a third of our executive manpower, however. While I ran the editorial side and my remaining partner handled operations, the defecting partner had been in charge of sales and client relations. Now we were faced with launching a new product in the midst of pervasive rumors that our company would collapse without our former partner's sales experience.

The only way to get around the whispers, we agreed, was to sell as hard as we could, absorbing the dropped responsibilities ourselves. I became the head of business development. Although I was very apprehensive at first, I found that I enjoyed presenting ideas to clients. To my surprise, I also discovered that I liked handing off the editorial work to the new editorial director we hired to take my place. Once we determined that our core business wouldn't suffer, we were able to refocus on launching MD/TV.

As the two of us and our top staffers became more and more excited about the idea, we worked overtime on the development plans. We drafted a list of program ideas. My partner negotiated for airtime while I tackled lining up an advisory board of top-rated physicians in a variety of specialties, from cardiology to pediatrics, immunology, and oncology. The doctors, who all liked the idea, agreed to serve on our board for free, taking only a $500 honorarium for reviewing individual ads within their specialty. We also designed the program guide, a glossy magazine-format booklet featuring a month's worth of programming schedules for MD/TV as well as articles complementing the broadcasts.

The next step was to hire sales reps to work with us as we sold the concept to the ad agencies and drug companies. We invited several top sales agents in our field into our offices to hear about MD/TV. We hoped to convince at least some of them to join the project. But we struck out. After hearing our presentation, not a single one signed up. They found the idea creative and innovative, but felt it would never work coming from a small start-up like TransMedica. This could have been a sign for us that the concept was flawed, or that our execution was lacking, or that MD/TV was sure to fail. But we knew it would work.

We went back to work. My partner continued working with the local TV markets and concluded a deal with a TV production company. We presented our idea to several ad agencies, which saw the marketing possibilities immediately. In what was a coup for us, the agencies agreed to develop the ads for MD/TV while giving our physician advisory board final

continued

say on the content, graphics, and wording. This hands-off arrangement, we thought, would help us with the FDA approvals and, more generally, with promoting our fledgling network. We also sold the FDA on the idea after showing it sample storyboards for several programs and giving it the list of doctors who had agreed to advise us.

These drawing board stages took a full year. By the time we were ready to sign up pharma companies, we heard that a new cable network called LifeTime was debuting with several clinical and medical-education programs for doctors. It seemed we weren't the only ones with this idea.

We scheduled our first client presentation with one of our major customers, a pharma company with which we had worked closely for years. If we were off course on MD/TV, we knew they would tell us. When we arrived for the early-morning meeting, the conference room was packed with the company's most senior marketing executives. My partner took the floor to describe our project. He was barely finished before the ranking client executive signaled us to step outside the room with him.

"It's great," he said. "How much do you need to get under way?" I gave him a number, and he replied that his budget was $200,000 short. "Not a problem," I said. "Just let me see the spending and I'll be happy to make suggestions for appropriate cuts." He declined my offer, but on the spot he agreed to become our first advertiser for MD/TV.

My partner and I left the building euphoric over our big score. As we went out through the lobby, we saw the sales team from LifeTime waiting to make their presentation to our client. It was exhilarating to know we had competed against a well-funded giant and won. That first meeting inaugurated a string of successful sales pitches. We soon had a variety of pharma advertisers, and both the network and the program guide took off. Our next step was to think of ways to repackage the programming we had already developed to generate more revenue. Line extension ideas that became popular with our clients included videos and audio tapes of individual programs and of sets of programs, patient education brochures based on our shows, and reprints of articles from the program guide.

Our elation at how well MD/TV did was matched a year later when CBS decided to acquire our company. Without diversifying into TV, we would never have been able to attract a serious offer from a major broadcasting company. (Our company became part of the publishing division of CBS, and that division was sold to the publisher Harcourt Brace Jovanovich two years later.)

Add new clients. You can't rely on one or two big clients to grow your business. Nurturing your existing clients is the way you *stay* in business, but to grow your company you have to add more customers.

Cuban native Adela Gonzalez started Future Force Personnel Services in Miami Lakes, Florida, after more than a decade in the staffing business. For her first client, a large health care services company, Adela provided home health aides, nurses, and clerical workers. Business was good but Adela worried about dependency on one customer as well as a growing number of rules and regulations for home health care companies. Looking outside the health care industry, Future Force landed a large warehouse account. Word spread quickly that Future Force could provide large warehouses with a range of personnel, including truck drivers, forklift operators, quality control supervisors, and manpower to load and unload goods. But even this market niche seemed too small for Adela. She is now focusing on developing a competency in clerical support staff, lining up workers and identifying new clients who need this sort of help.

Add new products. Bonnie Swayze has been working in her family's business, Alliance Rubber, since the age of twelve, dropping out of college at age nineteen to work full-time for the Hot Springs, Arkansas, rubber band manufacturer. When she started at the company, manufacturing traditional pale gold rubber bands was the core business. But Bonnie and her brother and sister, who took over Alliance from their father, knew that diversification and innovation were key to survival and growth (see box 6). They pushed the company to focus on technological innovation and new product development. For example, in 1986, long before the Lance Armstrong bracelet arrived, Alliance introduced Ad-bands, rubber band bracelets imprinted with ID information, motivational phrases for children, or branded promotions. More than 14 million bracelets sold in 2004, thanks in part to Bonnie's efforts spearheading sales and marketing. Alliance also created ProTape, the world's first waterproof UPC-imprinted tape to bundle flowers and produce for supermarkets and florists, together with a line of tape dispensers. In 1998 Alliance moved into office supplies, introducing a line of paper, binder clips, and pushpins. Shipping and mailing products such as mailing tubes and packaging tape followed. In 2000 Alliance targeted the corporate and at-home office market with rubber band products called Cable Wrapz™, designed to organize the tangle of computer and cable wire under desks and behind TVs. A similar line for consumers, Gear Wrapz™, aimed at binding garden hoses, jumper cables, and marine lines, followed, as did a pack of bands, STRAC ComboPack™, designed to silence and secure military gear. Most recently Alliance began selling new types of imprintable bands called Flexbands, including glow-in-the-dark (Glowbands™) and perfumed versions (Fragrancebands™). Bonnie and her family-member colleagues meet often to discuss when and how to introduce new products based on their return-on-investment analysis. "We know our Thai and Chinese competitors have incredibly cheap labor and no fringe benefits, so to stay ahead in the marketplace we have to have better technology, create innovative products, and market them effectively," Bonnie says. Today, Alliance's five major product groups bring in more than $30 million in annual sales.

Phyllis LeBlanc, president of Harbor Sweets, a chocolate maker in Salem, Massachusetts, developed a line of chocolates with equestrian designs, Dark Horse Chocolates, because of her own love of horses. She thought this novel chocolate gift would be perfect for the blacksmiths, trainers, and others who took care of her horse. Her diversification idea was a hit. Sales of Dark Horse Chocolates paid for all of the development costs in the first month on the market; revenue tripled in the first year, and

---

BOX 6: DIVERSIFICATION: THE ALLIANCE RUBBER STORY

The Alliance Rubber Company went from one core product, pale gold rubber bands, to five major diversified product groups. Here's how the products evolved.

1923: Alliance Rubber Co. is started in Alliance, Ohio

1973: Bonnie Swayze and her sister and brother take over the firm. The company's sole product is opaque gold rubber bands.

1986: Introduces "Ad-bands," used to promote brands

1995: Introduces ProTape and ProTape dispensers

1998: Adds new products for the office supplies market, such as Brites! Paper and Brites! binder clips

2000: Introduces Cable Wrapz™ and Gear Wrapz™

2002: Introduces Gear Strapz™ and price-marking guns

2004: Introduces Flexbands™, Glowbands™, and Fragrancebands™

now makes up 10 percent of Harbor Sweets' total sales. This success led Phyllis to introduce another specialty line, Perennial Sweets, chocolates that have a gardening theme. In creating these lines Phyllis is moving the company away from its core competency, nautical-styled chocolates, into other motifs.

While working for a well-known dermatologist in California, Nina Montee developed a special skin lotion. The doctor allowed her to turn the lotion into a skin care line, which he stocks for his patients. He also referred her to other dermatologists who carry her products. From there Nina sold her products to salons in Southern California. Word of mouth helped build her sales, and, eight years after launching her skin care line, Nina was ready to grow her business by fulfilling a dream of opening her own spa. She bought and renovated a turn-of-the-century bungalow in Santa Ana to create a Japanese-style day spa, Nina Montee Spa, complete with Zen gardens and a large koi pond behind the gates. The spa offers massages, facials, and yoga classes, attracting an upscale clientele. Most important, the new business brings in clients for Nina's specialty skin products.

Donna Sosnowski approached starting a business from a lifestyle standpoint. She left a twenty-year banking career in human resources when she decided she wanted the flexibility to spend more time with her teenage daughter. Donna joined the South Shore Women's Business Network in southern Massachusetts, and talked through her business ideas with other members. Her husband grows irises, inspiring Donna to create a mail-order catalog with iris-themed items. Through her catalog business, Everything Iris, Donna sells decorative home and garden wares, gifts, collectibles, and fashion accessories from her home in Foxboro, Massachusetts.

Add locations. Once your company is doing well, you can look at developing business in another location and managing it from your head office or opening another office in a different location to generate more new customers. This option requires considerable planning and a large financial and emotional investment on your part.

Ellen Bates, at the instigation of Haworth, the office-furniture giant, which wanted her to represent it exclusively in Maine, cultivated more clients in her neighboring state. Ellen found her home-base office in Dover, New Hampshire, could manage the core business, so she focused on new business development in Maine, and brought in a slew of Maine companies that she could not have reached previously, including L.L.

Bean, Merrill Merchants Bank, Portland Federal Credit Union, T.D. Bank-North, and the new Auburn municipal center.

Taking on clients in a new location or opening an office in a new city raises financial questions as well as quality-of-life issues. Begin by talking with your accountant to determine what you can manage financially. Adela Gonzalez relied on her CFO, who is also her sister, to guide her when she brought up opening another office in Dade County, in addition to her headquarters in Miami Lakes. Adela and her sister determined that they could afford to take on the new office because it would be easier to service nearby clients. Although Adela put a manager in place to run the new office, she visits often to check in. Next, she hopes to open a third office in nearby Broward County to supply more clerical staff to new clients there.

Despite setbacks that would have sunk all but the most determined entrepreneur, Donna Cabrera now has a successful string of gyms operating in the Miami area. But so far Donna is limiting her business development and diversification plan to Miami. With two small children, she knows that between business and family demands she doesn't have time to launch gyms all over Florida, let alone the Southeast. But to minimize her dependency on revenue from the gyms, Donna keeps an eye out for a building where she might locate one of her gyms. Becoming your own landlord allows you to diversify away from your core business and into property management.

Purchasing the real estate where you house your company is often overlooked as an effective diversification strategy. Judy Wicks took this approach and now owns a row of five brownstones in Philadelphia: three for her restaurants and two for her gift shops. Wendy Goldstein also bought the building where she maintains her corporate offices, and Madolyn Johnson's Signature HomeStyles owns a two-story building in Chicago.

Starting up in a second location does not always work out, even if the new branch does well on its own. When Suzy Vasillov decided to tackle a second location after several years of successfully running her store on Madison Avenue in New York, she zeroed in on the Hamptons, the fashionable summer colony popular with New Yorkers, where she and several family members had homes. When her accountant gave her a green light, she promptly found space and staff to open a new store catering to the tony summer clientele. But by year two Suzy found herself sitting on a Hamptons beach with her young nephew, worrying about how the less-experienced staff in her new shop were doing. Before she knew it, she was at the new store, checking on inventory, meeting new customers, and en-suring that her employees were up to the task. This wasn't how she wanted to spend her summers. Not long after Suzy decided that her original bou-tique in Manhattan was enough for her, and that after years of working seven days a week, she didn't need the angst of worrying about a new en-deavor. Suzy closed up her second location within six years of opening it.

When your additional locations are nearby and you're comfortable with the added responsibilities of a new staff, landlord, and clients, then it is still relatively easy to oversee multiple office sites. But when your diversifi-cation plan includes adding offices or new services in faraway locales, the stakes rise.

Brenda Loube and Sheila Drohan, Corporate Fitness Works partners in Montgomery Village, Maryland, started out with a nearby corporate client, Sprint, in Reston, Virginia. From there they secured Sprint's world headquarters in Kansas City. But both partners knew that to grow the busi-ness they would have to court and win corporate clients around the coun-try, and then service them effectively. To do this, they targeted major companies and worked with large current clients to get referrals and rec-ommendations. They also developed a brochure, and marketed aggres-sively to the top 100 U.S. companies. They simultaneously focused on their infrastructure, ensuring that solid managers were in place to help them manage three new, distant corporate accounts: Gillette, Humana Health Care, and two retirement communities for The Episcopal Min-istries of the Aging, among others. They now have thirty-five centers in eleven cities and manage more than 150 full-time employees. For them the key to operating locations across the country is a strong, centralized headquarters staff that administers client contracts, electronic payments of gym membership fees, and payroll and benefits for all the locations, as well as uniform training for gym employees. An East Coast and Midwest operations director working from the corporate office oversees regional di-rectors, and a national safety coordinator ensures that staff members at all locations follow standardized safety procedures and OSHA regulations, as well as the specific requirements a particular client may have. This well-defined structure has allowed CFW to add new facilities while keeping control firmly at headquarters.

Acquire another company. Large corporations often diversify at a rapid-fire pace by simply gobbling up companies. A major drug company, for ex-ample, will buy a much smaller but promising biotech firm, or a bank will buy a brokerage house. In other cases, companies opt for more radical diversification, so that over time they have substantial business in several different industries. This approach also protects shareholders if one sector of the economy tumbles. General Electric, for one, now owns everything from the NBC television network to manufacturers of lightbulbs and high-tech medical imaging equipment.

For small business owners, acquisition may be the most challenging approach to diversification and growth. Buying a company forces you to deal with employees you didn't hire, clients you didn't recruit, and an infrastructure you didn't create. You must learn how all these components work together before you can integrate them into your own homegrown company. Most crucially, you must do this without disrupting the success of the company you acquired or alienating its workers and customers.

Wendy Goldstein tackled this challenge when, after more than fifteen years in the costume business, she decided to purchase The Costume Factory, a small company in California that makes inflatable costumes. Wendy moved the company's offices to her headquarters in Ohio, and managed the transition so well that she didn't lose a single client. Because the inflatable costumes are sold at a different price point and appeal to a different corporate market than her original costumes, the acquisition allowed Wendy to diversify her customer base as well as her products.

Another means of diversification is the acquisition of a company in a different line of business. Beware, however, that a company that is not in some way linked to your core business requires even more work. First, it means you have to do extensive research in a whole new field, exactly as if you were starting a company in that industry from scratch. You need to do the following:

- Understand the new marketplace
- Learn the language of the new business
- Familiarize yourself with the industry's trade shows and publications
- Identify competitors
- Understand how the new business functions: how sales are made, jobs are billed, and employees recruited

Second, with the possible exception of accountants and operations executives, you may also have to hire or get to know an entirely new staff, with expertise different from your own. Finally, you have to address how your current employees and customers will view your new undertaking.

Will you have to create a new, integrated infrastructure of some kind, marrying the new company to your existing firm? What about marketing your business and the new business? What effect will the acquisition have on your company's cash flow? All of these questions must be examined in detail with your lawyer and accountant before you acquire another company.

Buying a company, even a small one, isn't for everyone. It typically involves months of negotiations and requires a significant amount of cash. Then there's the daunting task of managing an existing enterprise, often somewhat set in its ways and resentful of any new ownership. Finally, there's the tremendous responsibility you will have of keeping your flagship company afloat and growing, and keeping your key employees in place, while growing the new business as well.

These caveats aside, a diversified acquisition can be done well. Cathy Newell, who owns and operates Mohawk, Ltd., a company started by her father in upstate New York that provides repair, refurbishment, and calibration services to telecommunications, cable, and public utilities customers, has diversified successfully out of her core business. Cathy bought out her father in 1991, moving from the bookkeeping department to the owner's office. "Mohawk wasn't given to me; I had to pay my father before I paid anyone else," she says. Under her leadership, Mohawk got orders from several local phone companies, as well as Bell South, Verizon, and Qwest. Cathy began planning for diversification soon after taking over the company. Her first move was into snow-grooming, which Mohawk now does in ten states. Next, she branched out into contracting and construction, all the while maintaining the utility-service business. To keep control of operations, Cathy centralized all the oversight functions at her seven-acre headquarters complex. Her business units are all loosely related, with the exception of a nearby specialty toy store she bought in 1999 from the retiring owner. While she has hired a professional manager to handle the store, she supervises the buying herself, focusing on educational toys that her two small children would enjoy. While Mohawk grows, Cathy hopes the toy store can one day blossom into a national chain.

Start another company. You won't find this advice in many business manuals, but it is another effective way to diversify. My company, AM Medica, was eight years old when a British competitor approached me to discuss having us sell one of their products, strategic publication plans. A strategic publication plan is developed years in advance of a new drug getting FDA approval; a team works with the pharmaceutical company to look at the results of clinical trials, discuss possible journals in which to publish and a timetable for publication, and then plan how to communicate the new information to practicing physicians around the world. I knew this firm had succeeded with this product, and to diversify into this new area was tempting. I worried, however, that my sales directors might spend more time on the new product rather than continuing to grow our core business and develop new clients for my company. I also feared that a partner fight would have disrupted my core business, AM Medica. The solution seemed obvious: start another company. Joining forces with the British company, I found office space and handled all employment matters, payroll, and invoices. My new partners provided a senior staff member to New York to work in our new office, develop sales, and train new staff in publication planning. A few years later both my company and my British partners received unrelated exit offers for our original companies around the same time. We came to an amicable agreement to split up our company before we sold our firms.

Brenda Loube and Sheila Drohan also started another company, Equip, Inc., some years after they launched Corporate Fitness Works. Equip, which sold training equipment and set it up for clients in their homes, complemented their original corporate fitness-services company. They eventually decided to merge the two companies. Since they were the sole owners of both firms, there wasn't any meaningful business reason why they should keep Equip separate from CFW.

If you have multiple areas of expertise or interest, you can even start a company that doesn't mesh with your original business, provided you are willing to split your energy between them. Nancy Allin ran her own hypnotherapy center in Bellevue, Washington, for years, preparing women to give birth using hypnosis. Shortly after her marriage, she and her husband opened Newport Furnishings, a retail home-furniture franchise. Nancy has been sewing since she was twelve, and has always enjoyed working with colors and fabrics, so she found the new company fulfilling. The franchise hit nearly $1 million in sales in 2005. Meanwhile, Nancy continues to own her hypnotherapy center, subleasing space to two hypnotherapists and working there two nights a week to stay involved. Similarly, Melissa Epstein, a mother of two who started her custom-party invitation company a few years ago in Chicago, also decided to diversify by starting another, unrelated company with a partner, yoga instructor Sharyl Fishbein. Together the pair created www.yoga-mom.com, a site that shows moms, and their young children, how to incorporate yoga poses into daily tasks. The site will also offer apparel and gifts with yoga themes. If you have passion and vision, you can venture into an entirely different market, providing your core business has a solid performance record, a stable management team, and a sound financial footing.

Geralyn Kasmer followed a similar course, maintaining two careers, one as a nurse, the other as a specialty-coffee shop owner. Geralyn had spent most of her adult life in Seattle and Oregon, where she loved to visit the coffeehouses. In 1991 she returned home to southern Florida, but she felt frustrated that she "couldn't get a decent cup of cappuccino anywhere," she says. Geralyn thought about opening her own coffee shop, similar to the ones she'd seen in the Northwest, but she wasn't prepared to quit nursing. By 1995 Geralyn had identified a business partner, a woman who could run a shop all day while Geralyn was at the hospital. They created Belle and Maxwell's, a coffee shop that they named after their dogs. Located on Antiques Row in West Palm Beach, the shop sold premium coffees and cheeses. Geralyn worked full-time as a nurse for another year, but by the third year she had cut back her nursing hours to a per diem basis so she could work more hours in the shop. Geralyn was able to do both successfully: nursing is a profession well suited to per diem work and she had a partner in the coffee shop with her.

Starting another company for diversification is challenging, but it also has advantages. It protects your flagship company in the event that things do not work out with the new company. As long as you don't pull personnel from your existing company to build the new one, your flagship company's stability won't be jeopardized by trying to incorporate a new acquisition into your existing firm. The downside of starting another company to meet diversification objectives is that you will most likely need a partner. Keep in mind that the majority of partnerships experience difficulties that could distract you from your primary company. Details of any partnership agreement are important. They're even more important when you and a partner start another firm. Such agreements must spell out as clearly as possible exit strategies for both parties.

Joint ventures. A joint venture is a partnership or a strategic alliance with another individual or firm. In such an arrangement, each partner shares profits, losses, and control. Company owners enter joint ventures for various reasons, including:

- Shared economic risks
- Increased presence in a market
- Access to more capital

- New products or customers
- Access to a foreign market where regulations require a joint venture with a local firm

A joint venture can provide an opportunity for diversification, but it can also lull you into a false sense of security. Alliance Rubber initiated a joint venture with a British firm with the hope of expanding into the U.K. market. Relying on the partner's assurances, Alliance didn't take care to manage the venture's inventory carefully from their headquarters in Arkansas. When Alliance staffers visited the venture's U.K. offices to check on its progress, they discovered its inventory had vanished. Alliance was forced to close the venture within two years of its launch.

Whether your business plan to diversify is large scale or small, successful diversification always translates into growth. What happens when companies grow, and how you manage that growth, will determine whether or not you enjoy long-term success.

SUCCESS

When Kalika Yap launched her graphic design firm, Santa Monica, California–based Citrus Studios, seven years ago, the Getty Trust became her first client. The company started by designing websites, and for a time it had only the one product and the one client. But Kalika said she knew that even though Getty was a "fantastic" client to have, she had to make a "concerted effort" to diversify both her client roster and her products. She networked aggressively with Getty staffers who had moved on to other local nonprofits, including USC, the Fowler Museum at UCLA, and the mammoth Cathedral of Our Lady of Angels. She also focused on developing new products. Today, Citrus Studios also designs corporate logos, product brochures, press kits, and trade show posters, with more than thirty-five different projects going at any one time.

REGRETS

For a company that provides temporary workers, Adela Gonzalez's Future Force Personnel Services has offices in the perfect location. Miami is filled with enormous warehouses to hold the goods that arrive in the busy port daily. All of these facilities need workers. Relieved at first when she picked up her first warehouse client, Adela believed that she could leave behind the tightly regulated world of home health care, the bedrock of her core business. Staffing warehouses, she thought, would allow her to move into an industry without such strict work rules and away from serving one major client. But after a few years of providing truck drivers and forklift operators to warehouses, Adela discovered that this industry had ever-changing regulations too. Workmen's compensation issues cropped up, forcing Adela to spend time dealing with insurance issues and leaving the company perilously close to losing its coverage. "It was really scary," Adela says, and, when Future Force got insurance, "the very high premiums we had to pay ate into most of our profits." It took over a year for Adela's company to bounce back from the steep expenses associated with the insurance premiums.

Adela neglected to research the warehouse business before taking on these new clients and, as a result, she failed to realize that liability and workmen's comp insurance rates could climb so quickly. Had she known, she says, she would have focused her diversification plan on clerical workers, who do not require this level of insurance. And that is what Adela is working on today.

CHAPTER 7

Step 6: Plan for and Manage Growth

Once your company is settled on a path to increased revenue and profit, your next hurdle is to handle the growth so it doesn't overwhelm your start-up or your staff. Some companies arrive at this point sooner than others, but ultimately all entrepreneurs grapple with growth issues and challenges. Women business owners have to face these trials as they address some questions that their male counterparts don't face. The biggest difference, any female CEO will tell you, has to do with the tension between business and babies.

Can You Really Balance Your Business and Your Family?

Wendy Goldstein's two children grew up spending weekends in her costume shop. Although her business didn't require her to travel often when they were young, she spent seventy hours a week working, a challenging situation. "I'd work a full day, go home and feed them and put them to bed and then start working on the stuff I'd dragged home," she says. Because she was always working, Wendy, who divorced when her children were preteens, felt that they were in some sense shortchanged. Growing up with a CEO mom did affect their outlook, however: "My children became much more empowered and independent individuals because of their experiences," she says. Today, Wendy's daughter is in medical school and her son is in college.

Entrepreneur mothers frequently look back in amazement at the feats they accomplished. "I don't know how I did it," says Lynn Marie Finn, who took over Superior Staffing Services in her early thirties, just before her son and then her daughter were born. Lynn didn't travel then as much as she does now, but she says she was just "really lucky" that her company solidified by the time her children were three and five. Coupled with "wonderful child care and a very supportive husband," the company's move out of the early growth phase made it possible to take care of her children and her business, she says. Cathy Newell feels the same way. "I have two small children, two and seven; it's a mission to get through it," she says. "I've got a phenomenal husband, but it's still not an easy road by any means."

Madolyn Johnson had a more harrowing experience. After working as a teacher, she quit to stay home with her first child but quickly grew to hate not having her own money. She started her business from an apartment and moved it soon after into professional office space. As the company, a retail store and party-planning business called the Homemaker's Idea Company, grew, Madolyn had a second daughter. But the baby, Cathi, was diagnosed with a life-threatening lung disease before the age of two. The family crisis put the company's growth stage on hold as Madolyn struggled to maintain the business at a stable level while shuttling her daughter to and from the hospital. Thanks to loyal and helpful employees, the company survived the ordeal and was still profitable when Cathi finally stabilized at the age of sixteen.

Once she adjusted to the demands of her daughter's condition, Madolyn went to her office files and pulled out all of the letters from prospective customers asking when her products would be available in their area. "We packed our two girls into the car, drove across the Midwest, took hotel rooms, and made sales, contacting the people who had written us," she says. Soon, sales in the new areas had surpassed sales in the Chicago region, her home.

Although the couple later divorced, Madolyn bought out her ex-husband and built the company, now called Signature HomeStyles, into a multimillion-dollar enterprise. Today, her older daughter, Cari, heads marketing for the company. Cari says that her mother was a role model, showing her that "women can be successful and do whatever they want to do." She learned at an early age to be responsible and manage time well by watching her mother's example. Growing up with a CEO mom also taught her about balancing choices and maintaining priorities.

Dolly Peters learned similar lessons herself as she built a career in real estate sales. Trained as a nurse, she was a stay-at-home Florida mother of three with a packed schedule of charity commitments when a friend suggested they both get real estate licenses. Dolly's husband, an orthodontist, was ill at the time, and the couple feared he had lung cancer. Even though she did not want to go into business, a hedge against the expense of raising three children seemed prudent, and she enrolled in the realty courses.

Soon after getting her license, Dolly took a full-time sales job with Investment Equity Realtors and sold her first home within two weeks. A few years later, she and three other employees bought out the company's owners. Devoting all of her attention to her company only made her home life more complicated. Working in partnership with other women helped her to handle the compromises of her life. For logistical matters, she was able to rely on her mother-in-law, who lived nearby and helped out with the children. Her husband was also supportive, never bothering her about missing family dinners and never acting threatened by her success. Despite this solid support system, however, Dolly recalls feeling guilty when she was with a customer but had promised a child she would be at a ball game or school function. "I never said anything to a client," she says, "but inside I always felt extremely stressed."

The family survived the turmoil of Dolly running a company, and she is proud of the fact that her children, now adults, have made their own way in life. One is a physician, one a V.P. in a financial services company, and the third, following in Dolly's footsteps, is a Realtor.

Even if you're a sole proprietor working from home, the balancing act can be difficult. Artist Lisa Goddard recalled that when her three children were small, she thought an at-home printing studio would resolve conflicts between working and being with the family. Instead, she found that the distractions—laundry, a ringing phone, the doorbell, and children running in and out—hampered her ability to stay focused on her work. Sometimes days would go by before she got back to her studio. "I thought being able to set my own work schedule would be a tremendous advantage," she says, "but it didn't really work out that way, even with a very supportive spouse." When Lisa's children were a bit older, she partnered with an artist friend, Regina Partridge. They leased professional space, opened Studio-GoddardPartridge in Pawtucket, Rhode Island, and bought a printmaking press. Now Lisa enjoys driving to work. The partners keep a strict schedule for themselves and, when they aren't working in their studio, they let it out for minimum fees to other artists.

But now that Lisa's youngest child is in college, she's encountered another hazard: People who don't understand that she is not always available. "When you work by yourself and your children are gone, people think you're really free," she says. "It's hard to say I'm not available for lunch or some other function, because a lot of people don't understand that for me, painting is working, and to earn recognition as an artist and to make some money, I have to be in the studio."

No one has come up with a solution to the inevitable conflicts of running a company and a family at the same time. "The truth is, it is sometimes hard to do, but you just do it; you have to manage both, and you get through it," says Doreen Marks, a CEO and single mother to two young teens. Regardless, here are suggestions to ease the way:

- **Enlist your husband's help and support.** If he won't pitch in as much as you would like, either work on it together or accept it and build a support network elsewhere. If your husband doesn't support your success, the situation is only likely to worsen as your company prospers. Consider peer-to-peer or professional counseling for help.
- **Build a support network.** If you don't have relatives nearby who can help you on a regular basis, you need a network. Many local women's business organizations can guide you to groups of working women with small children, single working mothers, or others who support each other. Local church groups are also helpful. If your church or synagogue doesn't have such a group, start one.
- **Secure backup child care.** Even if you have full-time child care, things can and do go wrong. Know the quality of your local day care centers, and work with a couple of babysitters—preferably ones who might be able to step in for a couple of weeks if necessary. If your children are older, investigate available after-school programs.
- **Learn to say "no."** Women aim to please. Women running their own companies often work far too hard trying to please their customers, build their businesses, and keep their families happy. While saying "no" to customers isn't advisable, it is acceptable to let your husband and children know that as a business owner, you have increased responsibilities and you have to meet them. Reiterate this message, then review your calendar with your husband and children and see what you can do that works for them—and you.
- **Get a solid infrastructure in place at your company as soon as possible.** When you have strong managers in place to back you up, you have less to worry about if you need to leave the office unexpectedly for a family emergency.
- **Build in breaks.** Sometimes, it's easier to get fifteen minutes to yourself in your office than it is at home. One of my colleagues, who owns a demanding business in New York City and has two young children, goes for a walk in a nearby park at lunchtime almost every day. When

the weather's bad, she closes her door, doesn't take calls, has a salad, and flips through nontrade magazines. "Anything to take it down a couple of notches," she says, "before I gear up again for afternoon work, a commute, and a whirlwind evening making dinner, cleaning up, and putting the kids to bed."

Managing the Growth Curve, and Life's Curves

No matter how well-planned your company's trajectory, life will always get in the way. The ability to deal with the unexpected is part of an entrepreneur's job description. How you handle desperate situations will affect whether your company survives them.

When Lane Nemeth discovered an $800,000 loss on the books of her Discovery Toys company in November 1982 due to corporate mismanagement, she realized that she needed professional managerial help to sort it out. She hired Jim, an ex-CFO, who fast became her friend, colleague, and ally. Jim came out of retirement to work with Lane, planning to spend a year at most getting the company's financials back on track. But as year-end 1983 rolled around, Lane pleaded with Jim not to leave. He agreed to stay through April 1984. Jim became her key adviser, helping her run her operations and bringing in Doug, a former colleague who had successfully sold two businesses for $40 million, to reorganize Discovery's computer systems after they crashed. Doug organized the twelve techies who worked from March through December 1984 resolving Discovery's computer catastrophe. Meanwhile, by May 1984, Jim and Lane also knew that the $2 million Security Pacific Bank had infused into Discovery Toys a few months earlier wouldn't hold them. The company desperately needed cash. Jim strong-armed Doug into writing Discovery a $1 million check in exchange for options. But at the end of 1984, Jim died suddenly of a heart attack, leaving Lane without a trusted sounding board.

Several months later Lane met and hired Mike Clark as her new chief operating officer. An operations whiz, Mike helped Lane grow the company over the next ten years. Revenue peaked in 1994 at $100 million. Then, at forty-five, Mike died of melanoma. "After Jim, Mike was the second greatest loss in my life," Lane says, and "I think that after he died I was in a clinical depression that went undiagnosed and untreated." A couple of years later Lane sold her company to Avon.

The death of a close business associate, or a family member, can force an entrepreneur to choose between the health of the company and her own grief. Susan Marie Thibedeau discovered this unhappy dilemma when she became a widow. After working as a legal secretary after high school, she returned with her husband to her home town of Fargo, North Dakota, where he bought a printing business, Richtman's Press Club. For several years she stayed home with their three children. Then she decided to join the business, working in administrative roles while her husband handled sales and marketing as well as the press operations.

In 1996 Susan's husband passed away from a sudden heart attack. "It was very difficult for me because I still had two children at home and just one at college, a freshman," she says. "I stayed home for a week and then I felt like I couldn't stay there by myself." She returned to the office and called her managers in to discuss the company's future. With the help of her brother, who lived nearby, she intended to keep the company running, but she was afraid her best people might defect, thinking the business leaderless or doomed. She was right: Within a short period of time, most of the key managers quit. She realized that they expected her to pay them more to stay. Instead, Susan promoted some of her junior staffers to more responsible positions, earning their loyalty. "They've been behind me ever since," she says. Richtman's has since opened additional offices in Bismarck, North Dakota, and Des Moines, Iowa.

Nan Sharp also found that personal and business difficulties can intertwine in a family-run company. She had a series of food-service jobs—running a $3 million restaurant; working for hotels like Hyatt, Holiday Inn, and Marriott; and doing catering in Boston and Chicago—before deciding, in 1983, that she would rather spend the hundred hours a week she was working running her own company. Nan, her husband, and her sister started Food for Thought, a Chicago catering company, drawing on her family's expertise, her strong sales and operations experience, her sister's culinary background, and her husband's financial skills. It took them five years to get the company rolling, but word eventually spread, leading to orders for weddings, parties, and other special events. In addition to owning several buildings, the company grew to fifty-five employees, forcing the owners to think about being a sophisticated employer rather than running the company "mom-and-pop" style.

It was at this point that the partners began to reach the limits of their managerial abilities. Nan realized that her salespeople were better at selling than she was. The three of them, along with other family members who had joined the firm, were all running into each other trying to manage the company. To solve the problem, they hired a professional business consultant to advise them. Finally, the partners agreed on an eighteen-month plan in which they would work on becoming better leaders with defined roles, develop their senior managers, and write a strategic plan. "It was a painful but wonderful time for the company, because the greatest growth came in those eighteen months," Nan says. The company expanded and picked up a $3 million dining and concessions contract for a museum.

Once the company was moving in the right direction Nan, her husband, and her sister concluded that they were no longer the right people to continue to run the business. "Entrepreneurs get in their own way; they forget that the business comes before they do," Nan said. After much discussion, they reluctantly agreed to hire a young CEO who could take the company through the next twenty years. Nan began looking for this new executive, interviewing more than a hundred candidates.

Then she learned her husband had lung cancer. For two and a half years Nan shuttled between the businesses and taking care of her husband and two children, remaining at home for several months because her husband could not be left alone. Nan's sister was transitioning out of the company, leaving the senior managers to run things. But Nan saw that they were making some shortsighted decisions, and leaving the company paralyzed while the staff worried about how her husband was doing. "It was a very sad situation, so I had to go back in. I sat everyone down and said, 'Things are going to change. I love you all and I can't thank you enough for standing by our side, but we're hurting the company, and without the company none of us have paychecks, so I am going to step back into a leadership role,' " she says.

Nan found help to take care of her husband so she could work. She fought to rebuild the business, hiring a new president, vice president of catering, and operations head. But while the company thrived, Nan's husband passed away, leaving her with their two teenage children. She is grateful that the company, however, is once again healthy. The firm has added another twelve contracts and now has 170 full-time employees and 450 part-time workers. Nan's goal is to make the company a regional player before moving Food for Thought onto the national field.

The struggle to combine difficult career and personal circumstances also caused troubles for Jeanette Schwarz-Young. She wanted to be in television, but her husband convinced her to quit a job at NBC to take up teaching, which she hated. (Her husband thought it was a more appropriate career.) Instead, she ended up as a full-time mom, tied up in diapers, pets, and housekeeping, and unhappy in her marriage. But when she left her husband, a bankruptcy attorney, he managed to maneuver his finances out of her reach. Jeanette realized that she had to move quickly or start taking food stamps to survive. She obtained a real estate license and began showing houses. In 1981, a friend suggested she become a stockbroker, a job that would dovetail with her lifelong interest in investing. She managed to push past the antiwoman attitudes in the field to get hired at a New Jersey branch office of the company that hired her, eventually becoming a top broker and technical analyst.

In 1986 she married another attorney and had another child. But within four years she found herself in a disastrous marriage, one that left her both emotionally and financially drained. Jeanette ultimately took her four children and moved out, relying on a friend's house for shelter because her mother, who lived nearby, was dying.

As she was dealing with these setbacks—finding a new place to live, caring for her mother, raising her children—Jeanette found her calling as a commodities trader, working at the New York Board of Trade in the options pits. She executes orders for clients and also trades on her own account as JA Schwarz LLC, wearing her signature animal-print blazers to stand out from the sea of male brokers. In addition, she also appears on TV as a market commentator and distributes her own free newsletter about the stock market.

Lane, Susan, and Nan all navigated their companies through the growth-stage years despite staggering personal losses and business challenges that would bring down all but the best CEOs. Both Lane and Nan agonized over the steps necessary to move their companies from the "mom-and-pop" stage to the next level. A maturing company naturally grows its management team and works on increasing its market share, but with that comes often daunting personal and financial issues. No one is ever adequately prepared for the death of a spouse, nor do most business owners expect to lose a key manager. Serious personal issues can occur at any time, threatening your ability to run your company. You can't have a contingency plan for every possible scenario. To help safeguard your company as it grows, remember the following:

- **Infrastructure and network.** If you don't have solid management in your company and a good network of family and friends to support you through life's trials, you're more vulnerable if your company is challenged—especially in the growth phase.
- **Insurance.** Start-up companies often postpone insuring on their facilities and employees. But both small and midsize companies can be crippled by the sudden loss or disability of a key manager, and they can be put out of business without adequate replacement insurance.

Discuss policies with your accountant and select an appropriate plan. Some insurance companies offer group rates to small businesses. Check with your local chamber of commerce or your trade organization. You can't afford not to be insured.

- **Monitor revenue and earnings.** As your company expands it's critical for you to review your financial statements monthly or at least quarterly, depending on your business. If your sales are growing faster than your earnings, it could be a red flag that the growth is being managed improperly. Discuss the statements with your accountant and make changes as soon as possible, if necessary.

- **Review your management team and systems.** Throughout the growth years, take a hard look at your infrastructure. On paper it might look great, but do you have the managers who can keep growing the company with you? Similarly, are your IT and accounting systems up to the task?

- **Hire management expertise.** Rapid growth or sluggish profits? Look for a professional consultant with expertise in your industry who can advise you.

Hairpin Turns and Other Business Problems

While a death in your personal or professional circle can be one of the most trying events an entrepreneur can face, more common issues include business slowdowns, a sudden influx of orders, and the personnel swings that typically accompany these cycles.

Layoffs. In the summer of 2001, Judy Galbraith took on substantial debt to buy a building and renovate space to house her publishing company. In August, she sent out tens of thousands of dollars in catalogs to generate mail-order sales. Then, in September, the economy fell apart. She had to lay off workers, a task she found extremely difficult. But the company emerged stronger after these trials. "I focused on economizing, being as resourceful as possible—like I was when I started the company—and I found that employees who were given new responsibilities really rose to the occasion and enjoyed their new challenges," she says.

Denise Baker, president of D.R.B. Electric in Albuquerque, New Mexico, found herself in the same position as Judy that year. Earlier in 2001, D.R.B. Electric had added a new division, D.R.B. IT Technologies, spending more than $100,000 for new equipment, employee training, and remodeled space to accommodate new staff. But several government and city contracts were canceled immediately after 9/11, and not long after Denise had to start a round of layoffs and expense-cutting. Still, Denise and her husband hung on, aggressively courting new contracts. They recovered, and their IT department has expanded rapidly, with several new contracts throughout New Mexico. In addition, they have grown their core electrical business.

Staffing up. Many companies experience periods of robust growth and manage it well. In some cases, though, rapid growth can spiral out of control.

AM Medica had a scary encounter with too-fast expansion a few years after I started the company. One late fall, a senior sales director received a call from a top pharmaceutical executive at a Midwest pharmaceutical giant, asking us to bid on a multistate medical-education program. After we made our pitch, their marketing managers decided they wanted to give us some of the assignment, splitting the multimillion-dollar contract between us and their favorite vendor. We fought hard to win the entire program and prevailed.

The good news was the size of the contract. The bad news was the entire program had to begin in January and run through April, a drastically shorter schedule than the normal cycle of nine months to a year. We knew the job would put a strain on our company, with the need to organize seminars for 250 physicians every other weekend in the Southwest and West, far from our New York City headquarters. But we were thrilled to have secured the business.

On the first day of work after the holidays, the sales director on the account told me that she was pregnant and would not be able to travel. Suddenly we were without a hands-on, on-site leader, just three weeks before the first seminar. The remaining planning staff was already booked for the first half of the year on prior jobs. We quickly hired a freelance meeting planner to be our full-time, on-the-ground supervisor, and we added the slew of supporting temps she needed, including database programmers and assistant meeting planners. Once these people, and their computers and desks, moved into our offices, no one had a spare inch of work space.

The first event took place in Arizona in late January. I flew out to cover for my sales director. Things began to go wrong quickly. From the moment the physicians arrived, they complained that the meeting had been scheduled on too short notice, a client decision beyond our control. Our top three people on the job—a newly hired senior staff meeting planner, and the freelancer we had brought in, and I—barely knew each other, a factor that mattered far more than I realized.

The backlash was immediate. The client's marketing managers in Phoenix called their management at headquarters in Chicago to say we were too stretched, and continued to lobby to award half of the remaining program to their preferred vendor. Senior managers from the drug company's headquarters called my senior sales director at home in New York during the event about "problems in Arizona." She in turn called me Saturday morning in Phoenix, demanding that I come to the phone immediately and threatening to quit if we didn't get "the issues" resolved that day. At the same time, the client's marketing managers were unduly hassling my editorial staff. They wanted us to cave in, to ask them to bring in another vendor to ease the workload.

To compound our misery, Phoenix had its first snowstorm in years. The temperature plummeted to 35 degrees. Our staff and attendees had to navigate the resort in golf carts under hotel-provided rain slickers. Most of the physicians scrambled for early flights, only to discover that even their scheduled departure flights had been canceled. The meeting felt like anarchy, and this meeting was only the first of eight more to come.

By April's end we had completed all of the meetings for our client. A total of 1,600 physicians attended. Despite the early setbacks, nearly all of the physician speakers and attendees thought we did a terrific job, helping to soothe our client's frayed nerves. Our first-quarter revenues that year topped some competitors' annual revenues, putting us on the path to even more success. But the whole program could have been disastrous. The tenacity of my meeting planners, coupled with the extraordinary professionalism of my editorial director, kept our reputation for strong meeting planning and editorial services intact. But we also learned that an avalanche of business is a double-edged sword, and you can sink your company as easily as grow it with rapid-fire expansion. Table 15 outlines steps to reduce the risk of this happening in your company.

Table 15: How to Reduce the Risks Associated with Rapid-fire Growth

1. **Look at your infrastructure.** If anyone falls off your organizational chart, can you still make a steady go of it? If you don't have significant strength and depth, rein in your growth.

2. **Review your physical space.** Rapid growth requires more staff, full-time or temporary, and adequate space to house them. Make sure you don't bump your loyal employees by giving the newer employees updated computers and office furnishings. As my company grew, I learned to ask the old employees if they wanted to move into newer space. Surprisingly, many opted to stay put but appreciated my consideration for them.

3. **Review your IT system.** Even if you have up-to-date programs, new clients may have demanding reporting or accounting systems. Make sure you discuss a large new client's needs well in advance so you don't get caught short on delivery.

4. **Befriend your competitors.** This advice may sound odd, but in a pinch, it's better to share a large piece of business with a trusted colleague than to let the entire contract get away, or, alternatively, to end up sharing it with an unknown competitor.

5. **Look for local solutions.** A large order can tax your staff and subcontractors. We would have fared better lining up local meeting-planning companies to assist us when we ran our multi-state program. Similarly, know your local suppliers even if you rarely, if ever, order from them. A vendor across town might be the one to help you meet a sudden surge in orders.

Pay attention to morale during either escalating growth or layoffs. While you may think the growth is stimulating, some employees may be overwhelmed by it. If they want to talk, hear them out. And once you move the company into a high-growth phase, survey your staff and make sure they've bought into the plan and feel up to the task. Our multimillion-dollar contract could have broken us apart. Our company survived because all of us wanted to succeed and use the experience to grow (see box 7 for tips on smart hiring and firing).

BOX 7: HIRING AND FIRING: A GROWING COMPANY'S
DREAM AND NIGHTMARE

Staffing up feels great; it means there's a new influx of business. But there are steady, professional ways to hire, even if you are just bringing a temp

continued

or two in for the week. The same is true for firing. Here are some tips to help you make both procedures run smoothly in your company.

Tips for Hiring Right

1. **Use your professional network.** Trade meetings, women's business groups, and other professional organizations are an invaluable source for contacts and referrals. Let your colleagues know what position you are trying to fill and follow up on any leads. If one works out, be sure you acknowledge it with a thank-you.

2. **Ask your employees.** Some of my best employees came to the company via another employee's recommendation. Reward employees who help grow your company this way by giving them a dinner voucher to a good restaurant, or a small bonus payable when the new hire has completed six months with your company.

3. **Advertise.** Newspapers, trade-association-run Internet job boards, and trade magazines are the most useful. Be specific and honest in your job description.

4. **Interview.** Nothing beats the one-on-one interview for evaluating the candidate. Provide him with a written job description, review the key points, and gauge his level of interest and ability. Look for good eye contact, social ease, and professional presentation. And don't violate any laws by asking inappropriate questions (see page 73).

5. **Check references.** Many entrepreneurs overlook references, and it's a big mistake. In addition to calling the references the applicant provides directly, try to locate someone you know, discreetly, who has actually worked with the candidate, and get his or her opinion of the applicant.

6. **The hire.** Make sure your new employee has a job description on the first day. Give the employee a brief letter of employment, which states the employee's salary, benefits, reporting structure, performance-review schedule, and policies on sick leave and vacation. Make sure the letter says the employee is hired "at will," which means he or she can be terminated without cause. Both you and the employee should have signed copies of the employment letter, and the employee should also sign that he has received the company's employee manual.

7. **The introduction and follow-up.** Have a formal "introductory plan" that can be used for every employee, even a temp. We assigned someone from the appropriate department to "look after" the new employee

for the first full week, including taking him to lunch. This approach is just as important to do for temp workers and will earn your company a reputation that makes temps want to work for you.

Tips for Firing Right

1. **Evaluate and re-evaluate.** Is firing your only option? Can the employee be trained for another position within the company? Before you proceed, make sure you've looked at this option, and that the employee's supervisor agrees with your decision.

2. **Check with your attorney.** Most small business owners know the laws in their state, and some unwritten rules in their industry. It never hurts to let your attorney know what you are planning before you let someone go.

3. **Reverse your hiring procedures.** When you interview someone you want to employ, you move quickly and professionally to get him. Do the same thing in terminating an employee. If you've decided an employee must be let go, do it as soon as possible. Prepare termination information for the employee in writing, such as information on continuation of health and other benefits, severance pay, and whether or not you will provide a letter of reference. If the employee has office equipment at home, make arrangements in advance to pick it up, and ask for the keys to the office. Offer to provide transportation home to help him ferry personal effects.

4. **Keep it professional and brief.** You hear everything. Some employees know a pink slip is coming, while some don't have a clue. Either way the conversation is always emotional, and sometimes unpleasant. Be courteous, direct, and use the word termination—more than once, if possible—so that the employee is clear on what is occurring. A box of tissues sitting squarely on your desk and easily accessible doesn't hurt, either.

5. **Do damage control.** Even when an employee has repeatedly demonstrated incompetence, or is genuinely disliked, don't be surprised if other staffers show empathy or are afraid for their own jobs. After terminating an employee, it's a good idea to take a couple of "walk-arounds" during the day, to see how the rest of the staff is doing.

Navigating Financial Issues

Most small business owners are diligent about bill collection in their start-up years, checking the receivables list regularly and cheering every time a check comes in. But as the business grows, each new payment appears less crucial to the company's future. As the business owner functions more and more as a leader and strategic thinker, the mundane task of tracking receivables is appropriately delegated to a bookkeeper or accountant. The owner stays abreast by reviewing financial statements.

Bad debts. At Hire Expectations, Inc., in Michigan, Mary Anne Pompea's staffing company was prospering until a new client approached her company. Mary Anne felt uncertain about the client's financial status, so she set the following terms: Hire Expectations would only provide weekly staffing provided it got paid weekly. Payments progressed smoothly for several months, with the client increasing its order for additional staffing. Then Mary Anne's contact at the company left, and a new person stepped in. Mary Anne let a couple of weeks go by without receiving payments because the new employee assured her he was simply trying to "get on top of things." The delay seemed reasonable to Mary Anne, who was busy servicing other clients. But the client soon owed her $83,000, two months overdue. When Mary Anne moved to collect it, she discovered its doors had closed.

When Himanshu Bhatia started Rose International she wanted business, large or small. "In the very beginning I did not have the business experience to distinguish the pros and cons," she says. "I was so eager to get started that I took on business from a very small company." Rose completed the work and sent the invoice, but the client did not have the cash to pay the $23,000 it owed.

Malfeasance. Although you work hard to choose the right employees and business partners, sometimes you pick the wrong people. Lane Nemeth will never forget the financial statement that showed an $800,000 loss. Her new CFO told her that she was likely the victim of internal theft, but she didn't have time to divert energy from running the company to pursuing the thief. "Rather," she says, "I simply had to work with Jim, get our bank loan in place, and get my company back on track."

Gail Warrior wasn't so fortunate. She and her husband and business partner, Wayne, are currently in arbitration involving a subcontractor and $800,000 to $900,000. Fortunately, Warrior had established a strong line of credit that they were able to tap to see them through the crisis. "When we realized what was going on," Gail says, "I was a basket case because I thought we would have to lay off a lot of people." As an accountant herself, Gail knew that many businesses could not withstand such a loss and still survive. The Warrior Group has made it through financially, but the outcome of the arbitration is still pending.

The risk of dealing with the wrong people is magnified if people are your product. Mary Anne Pompea's staffing firm was hit with a $12,000 bill when an accounts payable clerk they placed with a client wrote checks to herself from her new employer's account. The damage to Mary Anne's reputation was considerable, and she lost the embezzled money as well.

Bad debt, embezzlement, and petty theft can occur in any company, regardless of size. Businesses that work with Fortune 1000 companies rarely encounter clients who renege entirely on bills. Rather, there may be a dispute regarding final payment on an invoice due to a disagreement over services rendered or products delivered. If this scenario occurs at your company, as the business owner you should speak to the client directly to be sure you know why they are withholding a payment. Other ways to avoid collection issues are:

- Review your receivables list weekly, and be aggressive about collecting payments.
- Have your accountant call on overdue payments. If he doesn't get a satisfactory response in the course of a week, you should make the next round of calls yourself.
- If you're unsure about a customer's ability to pay you, initiate a strict payment schedule and enforce it.
- Don't let a client fall behind in payments. It's your responsibility to invoice—and collect—in a timely manner.
- Take steps to know your clients. Himanshu suffered in the start-up phase because she wasn't really sure with whom her company was working. If it is too time consuming for you to run reference and credit checks on subcontractors or customers, ask your accountant to develop a form for new clients and subs to complete that will allow them to qualify financially to work with or for your firm. This procedure is relatively common today.
- Ask your accountant to outline the best safeguards for your company to protect against embezzlement.
- Open your bank statements when they arrive and review the canceled checks yourself. You don't have to reconcile the statements but you do need to see that the signature on the check is yours or a designated employee's.
- Don't use a signature stamp on checks. These are too easy to locate and abuse.

- Require employees to hand in expense reports accounting for cash advances before they receive another cash advance.
- Have a strict policy that all items of more than $5.00 submitted for reimbursement must have a receipt.
- Don't permit employees to take a cash advance from a hotel where they are traveling, or to borrow cash from each other to be reimbursed by the company.
- If you run a service business, set your policies on cash gratuities, including which staffers are allowed to distribute tips. Don't let staff make these decisions for you on an ad hoc basis.
- Don't be afraid to question an employee's expense report. It shows them you review it carefully. If you find a mistake in their favor, be sure to give them the extra money they are owed.
- Review your petty cash expenses monthly. If they vary wildly from month to month for no apparent reason, investigate.

Going Global

Entrepreneurial companies know they must move from the local or regional playing field onto the global stage. International expansion provides significant advantages:

- Increased sales
- Increased profits
- A buffer against domestic market swings
- An enhanced professional network and public profile for your company

How you "go global" depends on the type of company you have and how much time and money you want to invest in the effort. It doesn't have to be a mind-boggling exercise in international logistics and finance, but you must have your core competency down and a stable infrastructure in place before you tackle global expansion. You can start out slowly, with a small office in another country, or begin with a small joint venture, as I did. My companies were service providers to the world's largest pharmaceutical companies, all of whom have offices throughout Canada, Europe, Latin America, and Asia. In my first company, we organized a small, profitable joint venture with a partner in Montreal. That experience prepared me for creating a larger joint venture in my second company. I entered a partnership with a British company to service one of our shared international clients more effectively. We provided the staffing for the medical education programs in the U.K. and Continental Europe, and my partner in London contributed the office space, materials, and general supervision. Housing and other expenses were shared by the joint venture. This successful partnership lasted for several years, and when the programs concluded, AM Medica was able to reference our experience for future international marketing. Our European work experience led to future sales and profits.

Similarly, both Wendy Goldstein and Judy Galbraith expanded their respective businesses internationally. After several years in business, Wendy's Costume Specialists started to ship costumes around the world. About six years ago Judy Galbraith moved into international book sales. Identifying distributors in Australia, New Zealand, and South Africa, Judy worked hard to license foreign language rights to publishers around the world. Today her books appear in more than twenty languages. Judy also cultivated international business by participating in the major European book fairs annually for the last several years. In 2005 she went to Beijing, China, to showcase her children's self-help books at the Beijing Book Fair, a gateway to the Chinese market. Lynne Marie Finn is also in the start-up and planning stages of taking her enterprise, Superior Staffing Services, around the world, beginning with a small satellite office in London. She is also selling personnel services to a large client with offices throughout Canada, and she plans to move into India and China within five years.

When Myriam Chen started her second company, San Francisco–based music production firm MidniteSun, in 2002, international expansion sat at the top of her priority list. Myriam bet that with the 2008 Olympics on the horizon in Beijing, demand for music fusing East and West will surge, sparking business for the company's blend of modern rhythms and ancient Far Eastern sounds. In addition, Myriam says, "We saw an opportunity to expand the business into China's emerging corporate world. Many major corporations there are organizing concert tours as a means of promoting their products. We are planning and organizing the events for them." MidniteSun has opened branch offices in Beijing and Wuhan. Myriam and her partner, Wuhan native Benjamin Sun, realized that they could not only work to promote China's corporate world through arts and music, but also they could use their business know-how to help catapult Wuhan to center stage. This strategy is paying off. MidniteSun was recently nominated by the government of Wuhan to be its sole representative to facilitate international trade commissions on behalf of the city.

The company is also working with major broadcasters to produce music sound tracks during the Olympic events.

While you don't have to invest a fortune in manpower or funds, you should, before you step onto the global business stage, do the following:

- Consult with your advisers and determine where you should expand first. Both Lynne Marie and I tried Canada and the U.K. first, bypassing language-barrier concerns.
- Know your target market. Do your research first and make sure you know what customers in the new market expect.
- To start off small, and slowly, and to minimize risk, consider a joint venture.
- Plan for a minimum of eighteen months to two years to penetrate your new market.
- Develop a timetable and budget for the expansion plan.
- Visit your new office or joint venture facility several times a year in the start-up years, or send your senior managers.
- Make sure you spend time at the outset understanding a foreign market's customs, professional interactions, and sensitivities. Avoid culturally or contextually insensitive mistakes, such as printing Spanish-language marketing brochures for distribution in Portuguese-speaking Brazil, or serving cigars at a dinner for health care executives who don't smoke.

Once you're on a progressive growth curve, it's time to think about Step 7: Understand Valuation and Organize an Exit Plan.

SUCCESS

Once Wendy Goldstein got Costume Specialists' finances back on track, she charted a course of planned, deliberate growth. After adding tuxedo and dance costume rentals to her retail store, Wendy beefed up her custom theatrical work. In addition to renting out costumes for operettas and musical theater, her firm added wigs, makeup, and accessories. Wendy also created life-size book characters and started a costume-management division to develop and market each character's appearance schedule. Finally, she acquired an inflatable costume company. Today, her company handles "walkabout" costumes for a dozen publishers, as well as amusement parks, department stores, and restaurants. Wendy's successful growth is attributable to her careful planning, her consistent attention to her clients' needs, and her close attention to the financial management of her company.

REGRETS

Anne Cunningham* has enjoyed gardening since she was a child. By the time she married and had two children, Anne felt landscape gardening was an ideal business for her, enabling her to work from her home, control her hours, and do what she likes to do. As the years went by, Anne's business flourished, with a steady roster of upscale clients. She took on a couple of major landscaping jobs every summer in the booming New England area where she lived. Over time, Anne was also able to log more hours working because her children were older. More than once her husband suggested that she hire a few capable, full-time people, but she insisted she liked working directly with the clients, and she still loved the landscape design and gardening work. The income was terrific.

Just as last year's spring plantings were to begin, Anne injured her back. Unable to perform her job, she also had considerable difficulty directing her unseasoned temporary workers. As a result, she lost three major clients and is struggling to get the work done for her remaining clients. Even as a sole proprietor with a small business, it is important to manage business growth. By hiring even one full-time professional gardener to work alongside her, Anne probably could have held on to all of her clients. Instead, her income dropped by more than one-third.

*Name and location have been changed.

CHAPTER 8

Step 7: Understand Valuation and Organize an Exit Plan

A major goal of child-rearing is to raise children to be independent enough to thrive on their own. Mothers spend years preparing their children to leave the nest one day. Yet many mothers who own companies neglect to plan for the day they will have to let their business go, and watch it fly without them, too. Remember, of women entrepreneurs, nearly 73 percent lack an exit plan for their companies (see figure on page 169). (1) Why do so many entrepreneurs fall short in planning their exits with the same passion, vision and round-the-clock vigor they put into starting and running their companies? After careful planning and years of execution, why do so many neglect a phase in the business plan that is as crucial as the initial phases? (See figure 7.) The costs to women business owners of this oversight are considerable; without proper planning you may deprive yourself of thousands or even millions of dollars. A MassMutual Financial Group Study reported in *The New York Times* in 2004 found that "most business owners who plan to retire within five years have not laid out what will happen to the company after they leave." Unfortunately, experts say that neglecting to plan the sale of a company usually means the owner will not receive full value for it.(2)

Two Great Start-Ups: No Exit in Sight

Tricia Clode and Donna Cabrera both have stories typical of women entrepreneurs who forge ahead and build companies with no exit strategy.

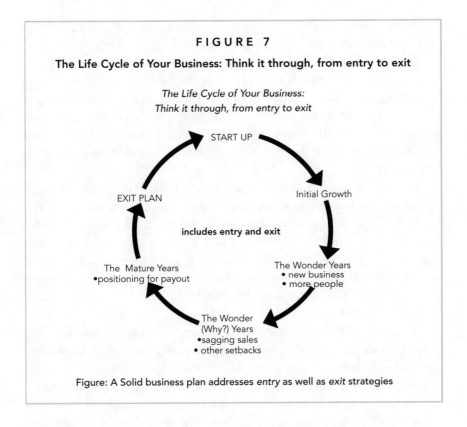

FIGURE 7

The Life Cycle of Your Business: Think it through, from entry to exit

The Life Cycle of Your Business:
Think it through, from entry to exit

START UP

Initial Growth

EXIT PLAN

includes entry and exit

The Mature Years
•positioning for payout

The Wonder Years
• new business
• more people

The Wonder
(Why?) Years
•sagging sales
• other setbacks

Figure: A Solid business plan addresses *entry* as well as *exit* strategies

Tricia, a successful hair colorist in Rhode Island, competes in the multi-billion-dollar beauty-salon market. After working for ten years in a busy up-scale salon in Providence, she decided to head out on her own. She opened a salon called Mars Attracts, in Wakefield, Rhode Island, in 2003. Her reasons for venturing out on her own, at forty years of age, mirror the reasons so many other women today are now starting companies. She wanted control of her own schedule to spend more time with her husband and two daughters, and she wanted to make more money. She wasn't particularly fearful about failure, as she knew her reputation as a superb colorist, and she knew that many of her regular clients would follow her. In addition, she timed her seaside salon opening to coincide with the start of summer, when many of her regular clients took up seasonal residence in the same area.

Tricia spent months talking to her husband and working on developing her business plan, which properly addressed funding and staffing issues, supplies, and accounting and legal questions. She negotiated the lease for her salon space herself, designed her own opening day announcement, and sent out promotional mailings heralding the new salon.

From the first day, everything went smoothly. Tricia's only complaint was the realization that she was back in the trenches, oftentimes doing everything from answering the phone and sweeping the floor to bringing coffee to a client. There was no assistant to mix formulas, fetch lunch, or clean the sinks. Still, Tricia was sure her salon would succeed, so she took on another stylist from the start. A year after opening day, Mars Attracts was prospering.

Amid the chatter of clients in her salon, Tricia felt happy just to get through every busy week, never mind about long-term plans for the business. She hadn't considered that she had found solid business success, and that with a little more thought and planning she might be able to grow Mars Attracts into a statewide or even regional chain, one that could ultimately draw an even larger chain or spa owner to buy her out. The thought of a lucrative exit, or an exit of any kind, had never occurred to her.

For Donna Cabrera, too, an exit is a fleeting thought. Now opening a fourth gym in Miami, Donna already owns and manages three always-open fitness centers. It wasn't easy for Donna to get to this stage. After obtaining her college degree in physical education, Donna went to work at a string of gyms in Miami. She worked days, nights, and weekends and soon the older man who owned the gym noticed her skills and commitment to her job and her clients. Meanwhile, rumors were flying that the owner was going to sell or close the gym. On top of that, the landlord arrived and posted a three-day notice on the door for nonpayment of rent. Donna knew she could run the gym successfully so she went to the owner and offered to buy him out. He agreed, but only if she could complete the transaction in a week. Donna then learned just how much rent was owed. The owner balked, and Donna realized that in order to keep the gym, she had to bring the rent current. The landlord also demanded her personal guarantee on the lease. She no sooner took ownership when Hurricane Andrew swept through turning her gym into a pile of rubble. Within minutes, exercise treadmills were thrown across the gym; they looked more like scrap metal than training equipment. Potted plants were overturned, and light fixtures dangled from the walls like earrings.

Donna felt she had no choice but to start over, beginning with cleanup. She didn't have to worry about filing insurance claims; she hadn't had the time to get any insurance in place. She and her husband patched up the gym, and Donna took a loan to buy new equipment and see the gym through its first months, until she could focus on bringing in more clients. Donna's work paid off. Her gym became so popular that she was able to open a third location in 2005 and a fourth in 2006. She and her husband, Tod, are also busy raising two small children.

But despite her expansion plans, Donna has given no thought to putting her string of gyms in a position to attract a buyer someday. Although she's the owner of a growing company, Donna hasn't given any serious thought to identifying exit opportunities, nor does she feel she has the skills in place today to execute one successfully. Donna still thinks of herself as a superb exercise trainer, wife, and mother, not as the very skilled business-woman she has become.

The typical woman business owner simply gets too wrapped up in day-to-day operations and growing her business to think about much else. Intense focus on growth leaves precious little time for something as seemingly remote as an exit plan. In addition, although many women have started and are building strong businesses, pulling out a solid paycheck month after month, they often find themselves adrift in a sea of complacency, comfortable with the salary, relieved that the start-up jitters are over, and at a total loss to plan and execute a financially rewarding exit from the business they struggled to start. But it doesn't make sense to take

BOX 8: STOP: WHERE IS YOUR EXIT STRATEGY?

"Where is the exit?" How often have you said that shortly after entering a new movie theater, an unfamiliar restaurant, or a concert hall? The reason you ask is simple: You need to know how to get out. Providing exit information is so commonplace today we barely notice it. It is mandatory for flight attendants to point out all aircraft exits during takeoff, and lifeboat passenger drills are required as a ship launches from dock. When you think about it, there are few things in life that you truly enter into blindly without having any idea whatsoever as to how you will exit, be it a sports stadium, an amusement park ride, college, or a job. In fact, when you overhear someone shriek, "How did I get into this?" generally what they are really saying is *How can I get out?*

So it is with your business. You need to plan your exit with as much care as you did your entry.

the risk of starting a business, work through the initial years of sleepless nights, cope with everything from meeting a monthly payroll to hiring and firing employees, and then wind up neglecting to design an exit plan. Unless you've unearthed the elixir of youth, at some point you will have to exit from your business (box 8).

Valuation: What Is Your Company Worth?

Like Tricia and Donna, a lot of women who own small- to-medium-size firms think their businesses are solid if the firm provides them and their employees with a steady paycheck and the possibility of a nice year-end bonus. And that's it. But what many of these women don't realize and appreciate is that a company that adds customers, employees, and products, and grows significantly in earnings every year, is a company that may be of considerable interest to a serious buyer. If you own or are building such a company, you need an exit plan. How do you know if you have such a company? How would you assign a value to it? Do you need to be concerned about valuation if you have no intention of selling your company anyway? Even if you don't have concrete plans to sell, you should know what your business is worth. You'll likely need this information at some point in your company's future:

- If you decide to buy out your partners
- In the event that your company is considered a marital asset in a divorce, as happened to Wendy Goldstein
- For estate and tax-planning purposes, especially if you plan to pass your company on to your children or you plan for them to buy you out
- If a minority shareholder sues you
- If you wish to raise capital for your firm
- If you plan to introduce an employee stock ownership plan (ESOP) in the company and need to file a valuation with the IRS
- If you are a C corporation and you are converting to an S corporation

Valuation is the process of determining what your company is worth in today's market. For legal proceedings or a sale, hire a professional business appraiser to value the company for you, but you should understand yourself how the valuation is assembled. There are a variety of methods used to value companies. Criteria considered include your company's line of business, tangible assets, income statements, likelihood of future earnings, caliber of customers, management strength, industry sector, the book value of your stock (assets minus liabilities), and intangible assets such as goodwill. An accounting term, "goodwill" is the difference between the fair market value of a company and the purchase price. Goodwill is based on nebulous concepts like a company's reputation, strong brand, or a track record of customer loyalty. Privately held businesses are challenging to value, and final valuation often depends on what the buyer wants and how well you negotiate. Unlike companies listed on public stock exchanges, where stock prices are listed daily, determining a company's value, no such information is available for privately owned companies.

Determining a Valuation for Your Business

Before you begin, to save time, meet with your accountant and make sure that your corporate and financial records are in order (see table 16). Next, be clear about why you are getting a valuation for your company. This will determine what sort of valuation calculation you should perform. Do you want to know what the company is worth before you solicit offers to buy it? Do you need an investment value to help you court investors? Do you want a liquidation value so you can close up shop entirely? The most common type of valuation is fair market value, the amount of money you would get in a sale. For tax purposes, fair market value is the price that the buyer and seller agree on, given that both have accurate information about the company's performance and neither is under pressure to act.

A professional appraiser looks at not only all of your corporate and financial records over the last several years, as well as your forecasts, but also at your industry sector in general and companies similar in size to yours, in order to evaluate trends and see where your firm fits in. Is your company sluggish, or a leader for its size? Decide whether a simple meeting with the appraiser to discuss the completed valuation is sufficient, or whether you will require a detailed report. Partners who are separating and suing each other and divorcing couples usually need thorough, written valuation reports for the settlement process.

It's a good idea to get a valuation every two years as part of your own estate-planning process. Think about it. If you were suddenly disabled or died, what would happen to the company you own today? Don't leave this important decision in limbo. If you have partners, your buy-sell agreement should address buyout provisions, establishing how valuation is determined. Many partners opt to have their companies pay for life insurance policies so that the remaining partners will have the cash they need to buy the estate out. As such, the valuation needs to be updated regularly.

Table 16: Checklist: Records to Review and Put in Order Prior to Valuation

_____ Three to five years' worth of financial statements
_____ Three to five years' worth of corporate tax returns
_____ Up-to-date list of your receivables, payables, and inventory
_____ Details of your collection methods
_____ Annual budget
_____ A three-to-five-year forecast
_____ All customer contracts
_____ Major leases (office space, cars, equipment)
_____ Minutes of board of directors meetings
_____ Curricula vitae of board members, including length of time on board
_____ Curricula vitae of senior managers, including ages and salaries
_____ Organizational chart
_____ Employee manual
_____ Company brochure and other marketing materials
_____ Sample budgets for job orders
_____ List of job orders

Methods of Valuation

Valuation of a business takes several factors into consideration. In addition, the accounting methods used vary. One of the most common valuation methods uses a multiple of earnings before interest, taxes, depreciation and amortization (called EBITDA, and pronounced "EE-bit-dah"). The multiple used depends on several factors, including your industry's growth prospects, your negotiating skills, and how eager the buyer is to own your company. The multiple may be applied to last year's EBITDA, or a valuator may average the last several years of your company's EBITDA (see box 9).

Valuation is also affected by market factors. During the late-1990s Internet boom, investors valued dotcom companies with no profits or even revenue based on their projected future earnings, or even on factors unrelated to their financial performance, such as the number of visitors to their websites. Those days are over, but hot industries such as biotechnology or Internet security still benefit from high multiples due to their perceived

BOX 9: VALUATION METHODS: AN OVERVIEW

Like a piece of art a business is worth whatever the buyer is willing to pay for it. But, generally, both buyers and sellers look to established valuation methods to determine a fair market value price. Profit and sales multiples are the most commonly used methods, but other methods may be used as well. Here are some of the more common methods used.

EBITDA Method

EBITDA stands for earnings (the amount of money your company makes) before income taxes, depreciation, and amortization. A buyer may average the previous three to five years of EBITDA and then apply a multiple to the average EBITDA number to arrive at a valuation. Multiples range from one to five or even more. If your company's EBITDA is $400,000 and a multiple of three is used, your company is valued at $1.2 million. Multiples are negotiated and vary, depending on the industry you are in. A good adviser will research past deals in the same industry to determine a fair multiple. Even when the relatively simple EBITDA method is used, both buyers and sellers weigh other factors before they finalize a price.

EBIT Method

EBIT stands for earnings before interest and taxes. This method is commonly used for businesses that have substantial fixed assets, such as manufacturers.

Sales Multiple or Market Valuation Method

Some companies are bought based on their sales rather than their earnings. Legal and accounting firms and other service businesses such as public relations and advertising agencies may be sold based on a multiplier or market valuation. Both buyers and sellers use an "industry multiplier" determined based on recent comparable sales in the same industry. If the industry multiplier for a public relations firm is 0.80, and the annual gross sales of a public relations company is $9 million, then the value of the company is $7,200,000 (or 0.80 × $9,000,000).

The "Leapfrog" Start-up or Cost-to-Create Method

This approach is implemented when a buyer wants to establish a presence in a new market quickly or simply wants to save the time and trouble of

continued

starting another business. A sporting goods store that wants to diversify into retail athletic clothing and buys a retail athletic clothing store is an example of a company pursuing the "leapfrog" approach. The buyer establishes a valuation for the business but may pay above fair market value because buying the existing business saves the buyer the start-up costs and the considerable time required to enter a new market.

Valuation Based on Synergies

This is the 1 + 1 = 3 approach. A toy company with a superb distribution network may look for additional products to pump through its channels, such as sports equipment for children or educational toys. The new products will give the buyer access to additional customers and create economies of scale. In this case, the buyer may pay above market value for the company because of the immediate benefits of acquiring it.

Value of Specific Intangible Assets

This approach may be used when a buyer is after a specific asset that a company has, such as databases, customer lists, licenses, or patented technology. Buyers determine how much it would cost for them to create the intangible asset themselves and then establish a value for the business.

The Tangible Asset Method

Buyers often use this method to set a price for a company that is losing money, such as a retail store or a manufacturing company. Buyers look at inventory, the lease for the space, and equipment, and set a price based on those factors. If you own a retail store or manufacturing company that is break-even or losing money and you want to sell it, seek out buyers in the same business first. A store that is set up for retail or a manufacturing firm with equipment and supplies in place has more value to a buyer in the same industry than someone who may simply want your retail space lease or selected pieces of equipment.

Discounted Cash Flow Method

A buyer looks at the free cash flow that a business generates (net earnings plus depreciation and amortization less fixed asset additions) to determine the size of a loan (at current interest rates) that can be serviced by the cash flow of the business. For example, Cathy's Catering Service generates $100,000 in annual cash flow and the going market interest rate is 10 percent. A buyer wants to pay the loan back in five years. The total cash flow over five years is 5 × $100,000 = $500,000. The total cash flow is then discounted, to figure out how much the cash flows are worth in today's money. A shortcut for figuring out the discounted value of these cash flows is to divide the number of years of cash flows (in this case, five) by two, to arrive at an average cash flow that is 2.5 years away from the present. Then simply multiply 2.5 by the going market interest rate of 10 percent, to arrive at a discount factor of 25 percent. Subtract the product of the total cash flows ($500,000) by the discount factor (25 percent) to arrive at the total discount ($125,000). The total cash flows ($500,000) minus the discount ($125,000) equal the value of the cash flows in today's dollars, which in this case equals $375,000. This is the amount of money that a buyer could afford to pay for the business.

Asset Valuation (Tangible Book Value)

Valuation for manufacturing and retail businesses is often established using this method. The buyer examines assets such as accounts receivable and inventory (including work in progress), improvements in the facilities, and the fair market value of the fixed assets.

Book Value

The book value of a business is the net value (assets less liabilities) as stated in the company's accounting records. This method is often used for a company that has little or no earnings and does not have significant tangible assets.

Liquidation Value

This is a "rock bottom" approach to selling a business. The assets of the business are assigned liquidation values (below fair market value) because the owner needs or wants to cash out quickly. This amount less liabilities is the liquidation value of the business.

Other methods such as adjusted book value (similar to asset valuation), excess earning method, income capitalization valuation, cash flow, and debt assumption methods may be used. Lastly, the "rule of thumb" is often worth knowing, even though it's unlikely to be used as the sole method of valuation. This multiple is based on industry averages for similar deals, and can be obtained from trade groups and professional societies.

prospects, while the grocery or textile industries, for instance, are valued at lower multiples. A copy of *Small Business Valuation Formula Multiple, 2005 Edition*, is available at Amazon.com for $17.50. The report provides valuation multiples for nearly two hundred industries, and the focus is on smaller firms valued at less than $1 million. If you obtain a copy of this report, keep in mind that you should simply refer to it as a starting point for information. Remember, buyers consider numerous variables in evaluating a company, and a specific buyer may not adhere to industry multiples.

Organize an Exit Plan

An exit plan should be an integral part of your overall business plan (see figure on p. 169). Developing and executing a successful exit strategy depends on your goals and the steps you've taken thus far to meet those goals. Exit strategies consist of the following options. Don't get wedded to one; it's important to remain open-minded.

- Sell your company to another company
- Sell your company to a family member or friend, or to your employees through an employee stock option plan (ESOP)
- Sell shares to the public via an initial public offering (IPO)
- Identify additional positioning-for-exit strategies (such as looking outside your industry for a buyer who might be interested in your company)
- Close your company, selling off tangible assets and/or patents

Begin organizing your exit plan by determining which exit fits into your long-term goals. Whichever option you select, each exit strategy requires preparation if your exit is to go smoothly.

Preparing your company for sale. In order to sell your company, whether to another company, family members, or employees, you'll need to ready your company—and yourself—for the process. (See table 17.)

Table 17: Checklist: Before You Prepare to Sell

Infrastructure

- Do you have a portfolio of business successes assembled that highlights your core competencies?
- Do you have a sound corporate infrastructure?
- Do you have an organizational chart and an employee manual?
- Are your personnel records in order, including employee stock options and vesting schedules, if you have them?
- Is your company in compliance with all federal, state, and local regulations?
- Do you have sales contracts and leasing agreements available?
- Do you have records of any intellectual property you own or royalties you pay?

Marketing and Growth

- Are your marketing materials current?
- Can you present an overview of your market, market trends, a competitive analysis, and your company's marketplace advantages?
- Do you have a five-year business plan in place?
- Where do you see your company in the marketplace five years from now?
- How will you stack up against the competition?
- What specific ideas do you have to stimulate aggressive growth?
- Do you think a complementary business should be acquired?

Financial and Legal

- Do you have your seal of incorporation?
- Do you have copies of partnership agreements; client and subcontractor contracts; leases; employment contracts; personnel records; insurance policies and records?
- Are your company's financial records in impeccable order?
- If earnings declined one year, do you have a detailed explanation why?
- Can you talk through your financials comfortably?
- Can you demonstrate company growth through diversification of customers or products?

To ready your firm, begin by reviewing the six previous steps in this book's seven-step guide. In addition, start reviewing how well your company really operates. For example, a buyer will recognize immediately if, despite an infrastructure that ensures employees report to your managers, you still have day-to-day control of your firm. Starting and running a business requires different skills than exiting the company (see box 10). In particular, a buyer needs to be convinced that your management team can run the show without you. Many entrepreneurs struggle with this step, severely limiting their ability to sell their companies. "I can't tell you how many people come to me and ask me to buy their restaurant or catering business," says Nan Sharp, "but they're not worth anything." "Usually, it's a woman-owned company and she approaches me to sell her firm; she's burned out, late forties or older, and her name is on the door and wrapped around everything the firm does. In other words, the company is only worth the equipment and the walls it sits in," Nan says. Many entrepreneurs don't appreciate that without learning to delegate and creating a structure that doesn't depend on their steady presence, they have positioned themselves for ultimate failure.

BOX 10: AS YOU ASCEND THE SEVEN STEPS, PLAN TO DON A DIFFERENT HAT

Starting and running a business requires different skills than exiting the company. Here's a preview of the different roles of the entrepreneur.

You Own and Run the Company	You Are Molding the Company for a Sale
■ You have day-to-day control of operations.	■ You delegate to your managers.
■ You work hard to ensure employees are loyal to you, from a company picnic to annual in-house lunches with each employee.	■ You have lunch with key personnel, and you encourage them to have lunch with others in the company.
■ You have input on every company hire and fire.	■ You are only involved in a hire or fire of senior personnel.

■ You see every proposal before it goes out to a client.	■ You've established a company style, format, and generic budgets; your senior sales personnel are responsible for their proposals.
■ You review every invoice before it is sent.	■ You only review a final invoice, or delegate it to the accountant and a senior salesperson.
■ You oversee the company retirement plan and are involved in company employee health insurance claims.	■ Your accountant updates you on the status of your company's retirement plan; you never see employee insurance claims.
■ At the end of the year, you meet with each employee to discuss a raise.	■ You review senior personnel only, and provide a copy of the review in writing. Your executives review other employees.
■ You and your accountant managethe company finances; he gives you financial statements when you ask for them, but you don't have a set accounting schedule.	■ Your accountant provides quarterly financial statements to you.
■ You review every bank statement and check on a monthly basis.	■ You review every other bank statement, and perform occasional spot-checks.
■ Employees know your company has rules, but there is no formal record of them.	■ You have a written employee manual that every employee receives upon starting.
■ You personally oversee all of the finances and have the company financial statements certified every year.	■ Your finance staff prepares the financials. You review their work and oversee the certifying of the financial statements.

Next, think about why a buyer would want your company: Is it the strong relationships you have with major clients? The long-term business contracts you have in place? Consistently impressive earnings growth? Do you have a unique or particularly strong position in the marketplace? Do you have intellectual property (a production process, a recipe) that is unique? Keep managing your company to make these relationships and positions even stronger.

Next, have a heart-to-heart with yourself and ask the following:

- Do you believe you are ready to prepare your business for sale now, or is it something you want to plan for in a couple of years or more?
- Are you ready to let go in the next few years and watch someone else run your show?
- Have you, and your family, thought about what you would do when your business is no longer a part of your life?
- If you want to sell your company, are you amenable to a range of possibilities?
- Do you think your employees will adapt comfortably in time to new ownership?
- Is your business in the strongest position to sell now, so you can maximize value? If it isn't, can you correct the deficits, such as lack of infrastructure or diversification, in a timely manner?
- Are you amenable to working for someone else, someone who may tell you how to run the company you founded and built?
- Will your customers deal with the change of ownership well?
- Is your company on track to keep growing? If not, can you take action?
- Do you understand that once you sell your company, generally there is no turning back?

All of the above need to be addressed if you are seriously thinking about putting your company up for sale. Selling your firm will have a significant effect on you, your family, your employees, and your customers. If you think your employees might revolt en masse if you sold your business to a publicly traded company, then start dealing with that now by talking with them from time to time to see what the issues are. Incentive plans are customary for senior managers to encourage them to stay on when a company is sold; let your top execs know that. Assure them that you plan to remain with the company for a specified period, typically one to three years, after the sale. Finally, you can hire an additional manager or two whose goals will be more aligned with your own.

Letting go. After working for years to build your organization, letting go can be difficult, even when there is a sizable offer on the table. "If you are in love with your business, you need to fall out of love ASAP," says Rosalind Resnick, who took her company, NetCreations, public in 1999. She advocates addressing exit strategies early on: "If you don't, you may find your emotional attachment to your business will result in your biggest business mistake, selling your company six months too late or missing the boat altogether."

Selling to a family member. Selling your company to a relative can be immensely rewarding or problematic. In family buyouts, the key is to agree upon the business appraiser who will provide the valuation. Both Cathy Newell and Lynne Marie Finn bought their fathers out at an agreed-upon price and went on to build much larger companies. Madolyn Johnson and her daughter Cari, as well as Melissa Caldera and her daughter Elena, are still working together and discussing the transition process. Once valuation is determined, the owner and the purchasing family members need to consult with an estate and tax attorney, to ensure that company ownership is transferred with minimum tax liabilities for both parties.

If one or more of your family members wants to buy your business from you, start with a financial valuation, set a price, and establish the buyout schedule. Meet with your lawyer and accountant to address legal and accounting issues. Next, put together a transition team and allow sufficient time for the transition process (see box 11). How long will you remain as CEO? Will you depart when the payments are concluded? Will you serve in an advisory capacity after that? Or do you plan to cede day-to-day management responsibilities quickly, but maintain financial control as long as you can? Don't assume that you'll be able to come and go as you once did. If clear boundaries were ever important between parents and children working together, it is in cases like this.

BOX 11: PASSING THE TORCH: SUCCESSFULLY TRANSITIONING YOUR BUSINESS TO THE NEXT GENERATION

Today, many well-known privately held companies, such as Cargill, the Bechtel Group, and Schnuck Markets, are family-controlled, along with approximately 40 percent of Fortune 500 companies, including Wal-Mart, the Ford Motor Co., Loews, and Koch Industries. But fewer than half of family-

continued

owned businesses survive when the torch is passed to the second generation. Here are some tips to help you improve those odds.

- Meet with your lawyer and accountant to structure the business
  transition and minimize taxes. The Independent Women's Forum,
  the Center for the Study of Taxation, and the National Association
  of Women Business Owners released an important study in March
  2000 which showed that four out of ten women business owners
  surveyed expected that all or part of their business would have to
  be sold in order to meet the federal estate tax. More than one-third
  of women business owners say family members will have to borrow
  money to pay the estate tax. Advance planning can reduce the tax
  burden.
- Get a financial valuation. Sit down with your successor and discuss the
  buyout price and a timetable.
- Assemble a transition team that includes the family successor, board
  members, and key senior managers. Lay out the steps of the transition and timetable carefully. If conflicts arise in the planning stages,
  bring in a management consultant or hire a professional manager
  who can help you integrate the transition plan into operations
  successfully.
- Don't be too quick to hand over the reins. Let your successor know
  you're implementing a transition plan and monitoring its success. If it
  doesn't work out, let the successor know you can reclaim the reins and
  look for management outside of the family.
- Who will be in charge? If you have more than one family successor lining up, define their respective roles and responsibilities now.
- Evaluate family successors as objectively as you would other employees. If a family member doesn't make the cut, say so. Remind them
  that ownership doesn't spell management. The family can own the
  company while a professional CEO and management team run the
  firm.
- If your successors haven't grown up in the company, now is the time to
  put them through a program that exposes them to every aspect of the
  business and lets them work with key employees in all of your operations.
- Hold board meetings and transition team meetings on a quarterly
  basis.

Next, recognize that when you do pass the torch, a new chapter begins for your company. Your child may not be as goal-driven as you were, or he may steamroll past your wildest dreams within a few years. Whatever the scenario, your role—if you still have one in the company—should be defined, and you must remain within those limits to ensure the smoothest transition.

Finally, if your company is large enough, consider introducing professional managers as part of the transition process. Make sure your board of directors is involved and supportive, and schedule quarterly meetings with them, as well as your key managers and family members, to keep the channels of communication open.

Employee Stock Ownership Plans (ESOPs). This exit strategy is sometimes overlooked by small business owners. Often, employees think they have to come up with a substantial amount of money quickly to buy the owner out, something that most employees don't have the financial muscle to do. But an ESOP doesn't work that way. Some small business owners find this route the most attractive exit vehicle because it offers distinct tax—and emotional—advantages.

How an ESOP works. Consult your attorney and accountant and explore an ESOP as an exit option. If you want to pursue it, then talk to your senior management team. If you and your employees decide to proceed, here's what to do:

An ESOP is a tax-exempt trust that must conform to a number of legal and financial regulations, so plan on numerous meetings over a few months with your lawyer, accountant, banker, and employees to set up the ESOP properly. If your business is a Sub-S corporation, you may want to convert it to a C corporation; this change is not a time-consuming or expensive endeavor but it will provide you with tax advantages down the road.

First, choose trustees for the ESOP. An annual independent business valuation is also required once an ESOP is in place, so set up a budget of $15,000 to $25,000 per year to cover the expenses associated with administering the trust. Your company will then take a bank loan and put the money into the ESOP. The funds are used to buy the owner's shares and distribute the stock to the employees, likely based on management seniority or some other mechanism you set up. The company pays back the loan with tax-deductible contributions from the firm's revenues; the company can deduct up to 25 percent of the annual payroll for contributions made to an ESOP.

Advantages of an ESOP. Owners who sell to an ESOP get fair market value for their companies. This strategy also allows your company to remain independent, and you can remain as CEO for an agreed-upon period, sometimes a few years, depending on the terms of the plan. Your company uses tax-deductible dollars to buy out your shares. You also get tax benefits on a personal level. As the owner of a C corporation, when you sell more than 30 percent of the company to an ESOP, you can defer the capital gains taxes, providing you reinvest the money from the sale of your shares in qualified U.S. securities. Stock in the company is distributed into employee accounts, which usually vest over time. Employees who retire from the company or quit can sell their shares back to the company. Finally, you get to reward the people who built the company alongside you. This feature is especially valuable if you are running a local company, where the favorable publicity around an ESOP enhances employees' job performance and could bring in more customers.

An ESOP in practice. Irma Mann and a Sonesta International Hotels colleague founded Boston-based Irma S. Mann Strategic Marketing, Inc., years ago. The firm created and managed direct-mail campaigns, websites, business-to-business advertising, and strategic planning assignments for corporate clients such as Four Seasons Hotels and Resorts and Best Western. By the time Irma began thinking about an exit, her company had one hundred employees, $85 million in revenues and clients in fifty-six countries. Rather than sell her company to a larger one and risk seeing it swallowed up, Irma, her partner, and a few top managers worked together on an employee buyout plan. During the yearlong negotiations, lawyers for Irma, the employees, and the bank, along with ESOP consultants, met to settle on terms. The employee group has met its payments to Irma every year over the five-year buyout period, even though she left her firm not long after the ESOP was in place. She recently gave her former employees permission to change the company name to ISM Strategic Marketing.

An ESOP works well when you want to preserve your company, protect the people working for it, and keep your company name alive. "If it doesn't work out," Irma says, "you get your company back: lock, stock, and barrel—and debt." When you know your managers are honorable, Irma says, there's a lot less to worry about.

Disadvantages of an ESOP. Going to the bank for a loan means taking on debt, which can complicate your company's expansion plans. Next, the ESOP is legally obligated to repurchase stock from employees who retire, quit, die, or become disabled, requiring the trust to pay out money from its reserves. Your accountant and attorney can discuss with you ways to minimize these drawbacks. An ESOP is also a vote of confidence in your managers and workers, but if you don't feel they are up to the task of growing the company and paying your money back, don't sign onto this option.

Initial Public Offering (IPO). In an IPO, the company "going public" raises money by issuing equity in the form of stock. An IPO makes the most sense for companies growing at an accelerated rate, as high as 30 percent annually for services or manufacturing firms and even higher for tech companies. Such businesses need access to large amounts of capital to continue growing.

Less than 1 percent of the companies in the United States are publicly traded. But the glamour of a public offering, with its promise of riches and a chance to ring the opening bell at the stock exchange, attracts many entrepreneurs. An IPO is a lofty goal, one that many companies will be unable to achieve. Only companies that meet certain requirements can go public. The New York Stock Exchange has the strictest requirements, with a minimum number of shareholders and revenue or earnings floors as well. Listing on NASDAQ is less restrictive, but companies must have net tangible assets of $6 million, net income in the latest fiscal year, or two of the three past fiscal years, of $1 million, and a minimum of 400 shareholders (see box 12).

BOX 12: IPO-BOUND: U.S. EQUITY MARKET LISTING/QUOTATION REQUIREMENTS

(From most stringent requirements to least)

Markets	Requirements
NYSE	
www.nyse.com	(A) *Minimum Quantitative Standards—Distribution and Size Criteria:*
	(1) Shareholders: Any of the following may be satisfied:
	(a) 2,000 Round lot holders; *or*
	(b) 2,200 Total shareholders with an average monthly trading volume of 100,000 shares for the most recent six months; *or*

continued

(c) 500 Total shareholders with an average
monthly trading volume of 1 million shares
for the most recent 12 months
2) Public Shares
  (a) 1.1 million Outstanding
3) Market Value of Public Shares
  (a) $60 million for spin-offs, carve outs, IPOs,
  affiliated companies
  (b) $100 million for public companies
(B) *Minimum Quantitative Standards—Financial
Criteria:*
Any of (1), (2), or (3) below may be satisfied:
(1) Earnings Criteria
  Aggregate pretax earnings over the last three
  fiscal years of $10 million, with $2 million
  minimum earnings in each of the two most
  recent years (must be positive in the third year);
(2) Valuation with Cash Flow Criteria
  For companies with more than $500 million in
  global market capitalization and $100 million
  in revenues in the last 12 months: $25 million
  aggregate operating cash flow over the last
  three years (each year must report a positive
  amount);
(3) Pure Valuation Criteria
  $75 million Revenue for the most recent
  fiscal year
  $750 million Global market capitalization

*Note: Affiliated companies, REITs and funds have different financial stan-
dards. View: http://www.nyse.com/Frameset.html?displayPage=/
listed/1022540125610.htm*

Nasdaq

www.nasdaq.com   In order to be listed on the Nasdaq National Stock
Market, one of three standards must be met.
Standard 1 will be explained in full because it is the
easiest standard to meet. For the particulars on

standards 2 and 3, please visit http://www.nasdaq.com/about/nasdaq_listing_req_fees.pdf

Standard 1:
— $15 million in stockholder equity
— Pretax income of $1 million in latest fiscal year or in two of the last three fiscal years.
— 1.1 million publicly held shares.
— $8 million market value of publicly held shares
— $5 minimum bid price
— 400 shareholders
— 3 market makers
— Compliance with corporate governance rules
— Entry fee of $100,000 for up to the first 30 million shares
— Annual fees based on shares floated. The annual fee is $24,500 to remain listed for up to 10 million shares

A Nasdaq Capital Market also exists for smaller companies. The standards are as follows:
— Stockholders equity of $5 million or market value of listed securities of $50 million or net income from the last fiscal year, or two of last three years, of $750,000
— 1 million publicly held shares
— $5 million market value
— $4 minimum bid price
— 300 shareholders
— 3 market makers
— Operating history of one year or $50 million in listed securities
— Compliance with corporate governance rules

AMEX
www.amex.org   Companies seeking to be listed must meet all

continued

requirements of one out of four *quantitative* standards:

Standard 1:

— 4 million in shareholder equity

— Pretax income of $750,000 or more in the last fiscal year or in two of the last three years

— 800 public shareholders and 500,000 shares publicly held

  or

  400 public shareholders and 1 million shares publicly held

  or

  400 public shareholders, 500,000 shares publicly held, and average daily volume of 2,000 shares for previous six months

— A price per share of at least $3

— A public market value of at least $3 million

Standards 2–4:

— Standard 1 is the easiest standard to meet. Standards 2–4 change certain variables, which may be advantageous for some companies (i.e., standard 2 replaces the pretax income requirement with a business history requirement of two or more years, but requires a public float of at least $15 million). Standards 2–4 are best fit for larger companies that are worth at the very minimum $15 million. For specific information please see: http://www.amex.com/equities/howToLst/Eq_HTL_ListStandards.htm1

— *Qualitative* standards are also considered. Although the quantitative standards serve as a general requirement, the exchange exercises some discretion. It also evaluates potential companies via a set of qualitative standards. These standards may include (1) the nature of the business, (2) the market for company products, (3) management reputation, (4) the historical record and pattern of growth, (5) financial integrity, and (6) the future outlook.

OTCBB
www.otcbb.com (1) Company must be current in filings with SEC or applicable regulatory authority.
(2) There is no fee for being quoted. For specific information, please see: http://www.otcbb.com/issuerinformation/issuerinfo.stm

General Description of Exchanges/Quotation Providers:
The NYSE is the most reputable exchange in the United States and arguably the world. This is mainly due to its having extremely stringent criteria—the most stringent of the four exchanges discussed above. The Nasdaq exchange lists many technology companies. Meanwhile the American Stock Exchange is the least stringent of the three exchanges. The OTCBB is not an exchange, market, or even a listing service. Instead, it is referred to as a quotation provider for the shares of a company that has issued over-the-counter shares.

Benefits of the Exchanges:
The benefit of being listed on the NYSE and Nasdaq is that your company is exposed to many more market participants and, in turn, investment dollars. This exposure comes from analysts who may cover your company, large brokerage houses who may take positions in your company, and from the national media. Being listed on such an exchange helps ensure a greater level of financial security and flexibility, as a company may choose to issue more shares and, perhaps, float bonds in order to obtain financing. In essence, a listing on such an exchange gives your company a high level of credibility because of the requirements each has. The AMEX features many of the advantages that the NYSE and Nasdaq provide their listed companies and is an alternative for smaller companies. Companies which may one day seek listing on the NYSE or Nasdaq but are too small to meet

continued

its listing requirements, may list on the AMEX and be bound by the above-mentioned regulations. Finally, the OTCBB provides a fast and easy way for companies to raise money through the equity markets. However, these over-the-counter shares are often avoided by investors and analysts alike because the size of the company and the integrity of the corporation are a constant question. The requirements are extremely lax; in fact, compliance with SEC filing requirements is all that is required to be listed on the OTCBB.

If your company meets these criteria, or you are growing your company to qualify for an IPO exit, keep in mind that the financial and legal preparation for an IPO is expensive and time consuming, typically taking more than a year. In addition to registration and filing fees, you will need to hire an investment banking firm. Your bankers will help you write your prospectus, a required document that provides historical financial data on your company and explains your products, competitive advantage, and growth strategies, as well as introducing your management team and detailing how the funds that are raised will be used. Before your stock goes public, you will be expected to accompany your bankers on a road show, a nationwide and sometimes global tour to meet prospective investors and sell them on buying your company's shares.

Advantages to an IPO. An IPO can raise substantial investment capital quickly without interest or debt repayment. This infusion of money can fuel growth and provide the foundation for national or global expansion and for acquisitions. In addition, the majority shareholder in a company that goes public often becomes rich overnight, since a share in a publicly traded company is usually more valuable than a share in a privately held company. When the exchange's closing bell rang on October 19, 1999, Martha Stewart's 30 million shares in the company she founded and had just taken public were valued at more than $1 billion.

A publicly traded company also has a level of legitimacy that a privately held company may not. As such, public companies may find it easier to secure good loan rates. It is often easier for them to recruit the best staffers as well, because of perks such as stock options that are available only when the company's stock trades publicly.

Disadvantages to an IPO. Even if you own a company that qualifies for an IPO, there are disadvantages to consider. First, you lose control of the company. Your board of directors can fire you if they aren't satisfied with your performance, and Wall Street becomes a major player in your life. Your company's earnings, which may have been irregular, will be scrutinized heavily. Next, the Securities and Exchange Commission (SEC) has demanding reporting schedules; once a company goes public, in fact, usually at least two accounting staffers must be hired to create and provide the financial documents required by the underwriters, analysts, lawyers, and regulatory bodies on a quarterly basis. Finally, you're accountable for everything that goes on in your publicly traded company. Failure to report critical information properly, from compensation packages for executives to revenues and debt, can lead to civil and criminal investigations. Regulations were tightened further with the passage of the Sarbanes-Oxley Act of 2002. Among the new regulations is a section on "corporate responsibility for financial reports," which states that the CEO and CFO must prepare a statement to accompany the audit report to certify the "appropriateness of the financial statements and disclosures contained therein." Many publicly traded companies reported significant increases in accounting fees in order to comply with the Sarbanes-Oxley Act. If you remain as CEO of your company, these regulations will apply to you. (Privately owned companies are also affected by the Sarbanes-Oxley Act; for example, if you plan to take your company public, your accounting documents must comply with SOX upon filing. Similarly, several government agencies rely on SOX regulations as the standards for corporate governance and internal controls. If your company is regulated by a federal regulatory agency you may be asked to conform to these regulations. Lastly, SOX forbids improper document "destruction, alteration, or falsification of records with the intent to impede or influence a federal investigation of records." This applies to privately held as well as publicly traded companies.)

To consider an IPO as an exit plan, set up a meeting with your attorney and accountant. Be prepared to discuss your rationale, and review the listing criteria with them to see whether or not your firm qualifies, or what steps you can take to ensure your company meets the guidelines. Once this meeting is complete, you should write up your company's IPO plan and then review and refine it with them. Your IPO plan should address the following:

- Getting your management and board of directors to buy in to your proposal
- Deciding who will handle your tasks within the company while you spend a year working with your advisers on the IPO

- Planning a budget for the necessary audits and investment banking and legal fees
- Identifying underwriters, ideally a top-tier Wall Street firm that has done successful IPOs in your industry recently
- Evaluating the IPO's timing to maximize the value you get
- Registering with the SEC and a stock exchange, a process that takes upwards of three months

Once you have cleared all these hurdles, discuss the offering price and market timing with your investment bankers. Be prepared to join them on road shows. As the CEO, you will be the main exhibit at these presentations, and your enthusiasm is crucial.

Identify additional positioning-for-exit strategies. If you don't have family members or employees interested in acquiring your business, and you've ruled out closing your business or an IPO, there are other options to consider. In fact, if your company goes up for sale and you don't get the price or buyer you want, then it's time to either look elsewhere for a buyer or find ways to make your company more attractive to potential buyers.

Begin by researching trends carefully in your industry. Who has recently bought a company like yours? Once you have a list of the buyers of similar companies both in and outside of your industry, look around to see what other types of buyers might make sense, and add them to your list. Work with your investment banker and ask him to search out companies that may want to break into your industry by buying a company rather than starting one.

Look at your products or services. Can you add products relatively easily, or add a service if you have a products business, or tweak an existing product or service to have more market appeal? Emma Durand, a Rhode Island engineer and cofounder of American Biophysics, worked with her team to fulfill a contract for the U.S. Army, which wanted a machine that would capture and kill mosquitoes so it could subsequently track mosquito-borne diseases such as malaria. American Biophysics delivered a working machine, but it was difficult to work with; still, Emma and her colleague recognized that the device had potential for backyard home use, provided it could be made more manageable to use. The development team went to work and, approximately two years later, with $1 million more invested in product development, Emma and her team had a machine for at-home use. The device, The Mosquito Magnet, is featured regularly in mail-order catalogs, and American Biophysics was recognized as the number-one company in 2003 on *Inc.* magazine's list of the fastest-growing privately held companies. By making its device easy for consumers to use, Emma and her team are in a stronger position to sell their company.

Closing your business. The reasons women close their businesses are as varied as the reasons women open them. For some, the process is often as easy as notifying a landlord, telling a couple of employees, paying some bills, hanging up the *"Closed"* sign, and organizing a farewell dinner. For others, "breaking down" a business is both procedurally and emotionally more complex. Even if you aren't planning to close your business as your exit choice, you can find yourself having to do so for numerous reasons: Your husband's job may be transferred to another city; your family can no longer tolerate your prolonged absences; your husband has an opportunity to take early retirement, and he wants you to retire too; after several years of running your own shop you realize it's much more than you bargained for; health issues; "acts of God"; or an economic slowdown might be your incentive to wrap it up.

If there's no buyer in sight and you want out, then closing may be your only option. Begin by meeting with your lawyer and accountant. Draft a closing plan, a timetable of events noting who will handle what and when. Discuss tax implications and severance pay for employees with your accountant. If you have inventory, will you sell it? How will you dispose of office furnishings? Can you move and store the financial files elsewhere? Review your leases, contracts, receivables, and payables. Then plan to close when you have the minimum amount of financial exposure. Finally, the type of business you have may influence how much advance notice you give to your employees, customers, and suppliers. Plan to be in the office and available full-time during the last few months you are in business. If possible, organize a dinner or similar event for the key employees who remained with you through the closing. And if you have several employees, take every step you can to help them find new positions elsewhere.

SUCCESS

Prior to her mother's death, Lois Silverman spent some of her childhood in a home for children, and then lived with her father and grandmother until her father remarried. With a stipend from a local Jewish charity, Lois was able to attend the Beth Israel School of Nursing in Boston, graduating first in her class. For several years she worked in an acute-care hospital before leaving to raise her two young children. Once both were in school, Lois decided to return to work. She opted for a different career, taking a position with Philadelphia-based International Rehabilitation Associates, a provider of case management services of workers' compensation claims, where she could use her nursing skills in a new way.

After five years with the company, Lois decided to go out on her own. She incorporated Comprehensive Rehabilitation Associates (CRA), anticipating that Don Larson, a former colleague, would subsequently join her. The company provided case management services to insurance firms that covered workers' compensation claims. Teams of vocational specialists, registered nurses, and managers worked to evaluate employees' needs—from physical therapy to emotional support—and get them back to work.

Lois chose Don because they had complementary skills and had always worked well together. He handled operations, staffing, and finances, while Lois focused on business development and opening new offices. Fourteen years after opening their first office in Boston, CRA had more than 1,000 employees in eighty-five offices throughout the U.S. and Canada, and revenues of $80 million. The largest privately held company in its industry, it was one of the most profitable as well, with a five-year annual growth rate north of 30 percent. But with more than a decade under her belt running a fast-growing company, Lois was ready to start thinking about an exit strategy. Don, who was ten years younger, would be unlikely to be as enthusiastic about exit options, Lois knew. But both partners communicated openly and finally agreed to look into exit alternatives. Two years passed, during which time the pair met with different venture capitalists, learned about IPOs, and considered a direct sale of the company in 1992, when they turned down a $90 million offer because it was an all-stock transaction. (All-stock transactions carry risk because the stock can decline dramatically.)

Finally, in April 1994, Lois and her partner sold a 49 percent share of the company to venture capitalists for $51 million. This transaction meant they did not have to surrender control of their company, they gained liquidity, and they weren't immediately subjected to the demands of an IPO. But Lois and her new partners agreed that an IPO was the next likely step. The venture capitalists had the knowledge, network, and skills to help Lois and Don take CRA public. Several months later, Lois and Don were working round-the-clock with their venture capital partners to prepare CRA for a public offering. The venture capitalists brought in a sophisticated CFO to help CRA formalize and streamline its accounting systems. Next, they interviewed several investment banking firms and chose Alex Brown as the lead banker, with Dean Witter and JPMorgan also involved. After countless all-night rounds the team completed its prospectus and filed it with the SEC in March 1995. The following month, Lois and her team headed out on an investor road show, making presentations to forty-two companies in two weeks. CRA raised $35 million with its public stock sale, and Lois remained as chairwoman until the fall of 1997. Today Lois is active in philanthropic activities (see chapter 10).

REGRETS

Liz Manning* has a robust service business in Boston. She came to see me recently to talk over how to prepare her company for a sale. Her firm has an excellent reputation in its field, $15 million in revenues, and a stable roster of corporate clients and staff. But the more we talked, the more I realized she still had quite a bit of work to do to prepare herself and her company for a successful sale. Nearly all of the company's business is tied to Liz personally, a major flaw in the eyes of any potential buyer. In addition, although Liz has experienced people on staff, she hasn't actually delegated meaningful responsibilities to any of them. Finally, her business is strong but her cash flow is poor; receivables often sit for months with little attempt made by anyone to collect them. Liz is coming up on her fiftieth birthday, and is beginning to think about sailing around the world with her husband. But before she can do that, she told me, she needs to cash out. Liz's firm is not in a position to net her maximum dollars. But with steady work on building up her infrastructure, focusing her accountant on timely collections, and hiring additional salespeople who can bring in new clients, Liz will have a company that should attract several possible buyers.

*Name and location have been changed.

PART II

Putting the Seven Steps

into Practice

W hat does it mean to ready your company for sale? First, you have to build a strong and growing business using the seven steps, and while you're accomplishing this, design the company around what a potential buyer might someday want. If you do, one day you may be able to sell your company for a lot of money.

An unlikely expert on this process is Susan Matthews, a nurse and mother of four grown sons, who started and sold her own company. As Susan and other women entrepreneurs who have sold their businesses successfully will tell you, nothing happens overnight. She launched her firm, Corporate Health Dimensions (CHD), with a physician partner in Memphis, in 1988, to provide outsourced on-site employer-sponsored health care services to Fortune 1000 companies.

"It certainly wasn't your M.B.A. textbook model," starting out, Susan says. "But we were sure to put an infrastructure in place early on, and we made sure that we dotted our i's and crossed our t's every step of the way." Susan said she and her partner "loved what we were doing . . . we believed passionately in what we were doing, and we were focused on building a solid, sustainable business, one that we could be proud of." By 1991, tire maker Goodyear was a client, buying primary care, occupational health care, and pharmacy services from CHD. Once Goodyear was on board, Susan and her partner continued to sign up more corporate clients. They realized that if they grew the company's revenue and profit quickly, they would be in a favorable position to earn a large return selling the company later.

By 1993, CHD had a fast growth rate, compelling earnings, a roster of blue-chip contracts, and a strong infrastructure. With all these components in place, the company could start to think about taking on investors or selling. "An impressive performance history and good client references are a must," Susan says, "and you can't get that in just a couple of years. The truth is, when you first start your business, and in those early years, it's just all air. Typically you have to travel down the road for five or six years or more to demonstrate that you are a very real and growing business, one that survives and has a real future."

In her case, the strategy paid off. Susan and her partner sold just more than 50 percent of their firm to a venture capital group in 1997. In 2000, with revenues of $85 million and 800 employees, CHD merged with a major competitor, Meridian Occupational Healthcare Associates. Both companies had been pursuing the same clients, but Meridian was stronger in occupational health while CHD dominated primary care delivery. The merged company became the nation's largest provider of outsourced on-site, employer-sponsored health care services to Fortune 1000 companies and the federal government. Susan left two years later but remained a shareholder. In March 2004, Philadelphia-based I-Trax, a health management solutions company, merged with Meridian Healthcare in a transaction valued at $80 million.

Susan's story illustrates the idea of positioning for payout: building and growing your business by executing the seven steps as flawlessly as possible. It's a process that is repeated in the offices of women CEOs everywhere, a quiet but fiercely determined quest to create the best, most well-run company and cap it off with a spectacular exit.

CHAPTER 9

Put Your Company in Play

S elling your company or lining it up for an IPO will most likely be the biggest business move of your entire career. You have to get it all right, or you could lose the deal. To start, you need a team on your side. Start by thinking about the type of deal you want, and then consider advisers who can ensure that you execute the deal of your dreams, and that you and your employees can live with it after it is completed.

Assembling the Team and Putting Them to Work for You

Smaller companies typically have a lawyer they use for day-to-day consultations, an in-house bookkeeper and accountant, and often an outside accountant as well, for annual audits. This team may have been with you from the day you started your company. But if you are seriously considering selling your company or preparing for an IPO, the first thing you have to do is review your lawyer's and accountant's professional transaction experience.

Identify legal and accounting deal-makers. If your lawyer has provided you with excellent service reviewing employment contracts, client agreements, and leases, he is clearly familiar with your business and how it operates. But does he have solid experience sitting at a negotiating table representing clients who want to sell their companies? Does he know how many deals in your industry have been completed over the last two years, and does he understand their transaction structures? Ask the same questions of your accountant. If, like many other women entrepreneurs, you rely on a core team for your company's daily operational support, when it comes to making what is possibly the deal of your life, you may have to retain additional representation. (See table 18.)

My company was my accountant's largest client. He had quick, absolute command of my company's numbers, knew our business inside out, and even spoke directly with some of our clients on lengthy, detailed invoices. He certainly had to be present for any meeting regarding the sale of my company. My lawyer cautioned me, however, to be careful of relying on him too much, as the first thing a buyer would do after taking over my company would be to integrate our accounting function into theirs, leaving my accountant minus a major client. Although I saw the risks in this scenario, I was reluctant to lose the services of someone who understood my company so well. When negotiating is under way, that's no time to try to bring your new professional staff up to speed on your industry's jargon or your company's financials. I decided to use my accountant and be as upfront as possible with him, advising him that I would make every attempt to ensure that a reasonable transition time was part of my deal.

Table 18: Questions for Your Advisory Team

Choosing the right team is much like finding a good hairdresser: Just because a stylist is talented doesn't necessarily mean that he is good for you.

- Have you done deals in this industry?
- Can you identify players in my industry?
- Are you familiar with my industry's accounting procedures, contracts, and jargon?
- Can you work with the other members of the team?
- What is your availability on evenings and weekends? Where can I reach you at these times?
- What is your fee structure?
- Can you provide references from similar deals?
- Do you have support staff in place to process and assemble documents quickly?

Similarly, I rarely used our company lawyer, who had a small practice. When it came time to retain representation to sell my company, I went to a friend and colleague at a major New York City law firm who knew me, my business, and our industry well. He also had years of experience making deals and had represented major pharmaceutical companies. After him, all I needed was an investment adviser.

The Investment Adviser

The next step is to hire an investment banker to broker the deal, or to underwrite the IPO, if you choose that route. Research your industry to determine which firms have experience and which have made the most successful deals for their clients. Set up meetings with different bankers and take your lawyer and accountant with you. Feel free to grill the individual bankers on how they would pitch your company and on how well they know your industry. Regardless of the firm you choose, you will be working closely with one senior banker and his team, so make sure you are comfortable with his style, his contacts, and his method of running the sale process. After you have met with a few bankers, review their credentials and qualifications, discuss them with your lawyer and accountant, and select a firm to represent you. Whether you are preparing your company for sale or an IPO, the bankers will work with you to prepare materials for prospective buyers. These will include:

- An overview of your industry
- Your company's place in the industry
- Historical information on your company, such as the founding date, office and factory locations, corporate officers, number of employees, major customers, and product lines
- A survey of the competition
- Financial statements and forecasts
- Growth potential and expansion plans

Investment banking fees for selling your company range from a negotiated flat fee to a negotiated percentage. When taking a company public, investment banks typically charge 7 percent of the IPO's gross proceeds as their fee; if your IPO brings your company $100 million, you will owe the bank $7 million. If the IPO does not go through, the bank does not collect a fee, although you will most likely be billed for expenses, which can run to hundreds of thousands of dollars, including legal and auditing fees, printing costs, and road show charges.

One major difference between taking a company public and going through a private sale is the confidentiality issue. There is nothing secret about an IPO. Once you file your IPO prospectus, known as a Form S-1, with the SEC, it becomes public, and you can assume all your competitors will pore over it for clues to your strategy. If you don't want your industry blanketed with information about your company—including the fact that your firm is up for sale—then you need to pursue a private sale. In this case, talk with your bankers about handling the sale process discreetly, making direct phone calls to buyers whom they think might have a genuine interest in the company, and requiring all potential acquirers to sign a confidentiality agreement before they are allowed to see your financials and projections. Many small business owners opt to keep the sale process confidential so as not to disrupt routine business. If a competitor hears that you are selling your company, for instance, they may begin aggressively soliciting your clients or staff.

Another route is to get your accountant and lawyer in place and then put feelers out in your industry to see who might be interested. You can do this by simply attending industry events to learn more about which companies have been sold, or to meet people from larger companies who may be looking for smaller firms to acquire.

In my case, an investment banker whom I had met socially years before my transaction took place called me to ask how my company was doing. Based on the information I gave him, he suggested we meet to talk more about a possible deal. He knew that a larger company was looking for a medical communications firm. After a couple of meetings with him and one meeting with the potential buyer, I realized this process could get serious quickly. I lined up my transaction lawyer, negotiated a fee with the banker who had made the introduction, and retained another investment adviser who had worked previously with my accountant. This path was not traditional; my investment adviser did not have to prepare materials, do mailings, or present my company to possible buyers. But I wanted an investment professional with me at the negotiating table to watch for things my lawyer, accountant, and I might miss. Because my adviser's role was limited, we settled on a flat fee for services instead of a cut of the deal.

Rose Saia and her partners knew they would need stellar advice as they explored selling their computer software company. They hired a top CFO from a top-tier accounting firm as a consultant and put him on retainer. He had a seasoned network in place, and Rose found that their international business and their licensing and royalty deals moved along quickly with his help. By the time they reached the negotiating table, Rose felt her CFO had helped them maximize the price, often calling in a specialist at the last minute when the buyers had questions on tricky licensing agreements. The way to go about it, she says, is to get the best team of deal professionals you can afford: "I've seen other businesses make mistakes simply by using accountants and advisers that don't have any aptitude for the business they're representing, and that's a big mistake."

Planning a Timetable and a Budget to Sell Your Company

Your full-time job is to be the CEO of your firm, but when putting your company in play, you add another job to your workload: presenting your business to potential buyers by sitting at a table for hours and days at a time discussing your company's growth, its five-year forecasts, and its management team. And you have to do all of this while looking and talking your best. Then you have to return to your office and make sure your company's revenues and earnings are on track. Any downward deviation from the data you've presented to a buyer could unravel the deal or cause the sale price to fall.

Selling your company or preparing it for an IPO is a time-consuming, intense, and stressful process; it's both exhilarating and frustrating. A sale is never done until the purchase and sale agreement is signed, and an IPO is not complete until the stock price is established and shares in your company are sold. (Steps to an IPO are provided in box 12; since selling a company is far more common than an IPO, the remainder of this chapter focuses on executing a sale.) The entire process of selling a company can take anywhere from six months to more than a year, depending in part on how long it takes you to put together your team and get your company up for sale. If your investment adviser is managing the process for you, screening and identifying possible buyers, set a timetable with him. Bankers usually manage several clients simultaneously, so be sure you know where you fit into the schedule. Ask how long it will take to execute a mailing presenting your company, what is a typical response time, and when will they schedule you for an initial meeting and a presentation with a potential buyer. Check how many buyers they think you should see. These meetings normally take a few weeks to organize. You and your team—lawyer, accountant, and banker—meet with the CEO and CFO of the potential buyer company as well as their advisory team. If both you and a particular buyer want to continue exploring the acquisition of your company, your investment banker will schedule another round of meetings and the selling process will begin.

BOX 12: STEPS TO AN INITIAL PUBLIC OFFERING (IPO)

Lois Silverman had a successful IPO in 1994. Her IPO took a few months, but sometimes it takes a year or longer to take a company public. Here are the steps.

1. **Does your company qualify?** Consult with your advisers, but to go public you need diversified products, a strong management team, annual earnings growth of 25 percent to 30 percent, and a need to raise capital to keep growing.

2. **Get your core advisory team lined up.** If they don't have experience doing an IPO, ask them to recommend a lawyer and accountant who do. As you move forward, seek estate tax–planning advice as well.

3. **Identify a lead investment banking firm.** This firm will work with you and underwrite the offering. Talk to your lawyer and accountant and interview more than one firm. Select a firm that has experience in your field and one with whom you feel comfortable. The lead investment banker assesses market demand and oversees distribution of shares.

4. **Organize your team.** Set up a timetable and responsibilities. Pull together your corporate documents, including all financials and information on your internal systems.

5. **Start work on your prospectus.** The prospectus is the investment banker's tool for promoting your company to potential investors. It includes detailed information on the offering, including your company's financials for the past five years, a description of management, an overview of your company's products, and the target market. The prospectus goes through several drafts before it is finalized.

6. **Submitting the prospectus to the SEC.** The investment banker will submit the prospectus to the SEC, which reviews the document. Queries are addressed to your investment banker, and you.

7. **Registration.** Prior to floating shares on the open market, a corporation must register with the SEC. The registration requires both a registration statement and a prospectus. The registration statement describes what the business is, who manages the business, where the business is located, and other relevant information.

8. **The presentation.** Prepare your presentation for your investment bankers to give to prospective investors.

9. **Filings.** The investment banker files the registration statement and prospectus with the SEC.

10. **The "road show."** You and the investment bankers travel the country to garner institutional investor interest. Prepare for long, intense days of presentations and queries.

11. **Set the price.** The lead investment banker evaluates the demand he anticipates for your company's shares and sets a price per share.

12. **Effective date.** Following the price being set, and within two days of the prospectus being filed and distributed, the SEC will declare the offering effective.

13. **Trading begins.** After the stock begins trading, the offering proceeds are delivered.

Throughout the course of the sales process, you should plan to spend substantial amounts of time away from your office. If you want to keep your meetings confidential, as I did, this becomes challenging. Start putting a schedule in place that allows for your periodic, unexpected absences. You can prepare your most senior staffers by setting up meetings with your accountant and lawyer, out of your office, to review the financials and other key data and inform your senior staff that you're exploring ways with them to grow the company. You can also simply say you are meeting with business professionals to explore ways to grow your company, and leave it at that. Be sure you know who will keep running your company and be making decisions in your absence.

Before you can reap the money from an exit, you have to pay for all the advice you receive. Rose Saia and her partners entertained one offer and participated in negotiations for a few months before they called it quits. Then they realized they still had to pay the advisers their fees. When Rose's team went out for a second round of buyers, they consummated a deal. The advisory team had to be paid again. "I don't think most entrepreneurs realize how much money flies out the door while you are in the negotiating stage," Rose says. Add funds to your operating budget a year before you engage your advisers, so you can cover your exit costs. If you're uncertain about how much you will need, look at the market data and determine a minimum-maximum range.

What type of buyer do you want? There are strategic buyers as well as financial buyers. Strategic buyers can be your competitors, larger companies in your industry, or firms in an adjacent industry. By the time they approach you, they have done their homework and already believe that your firm will fit into their long-term business objectives. A financial buyer is a professional deal-maker who uses debt financing for at least 50 percent of the purchase price. These firms, typically private equity funds or leveraged-buyout funds, don't operate businesses of their own; they buy and then oversee a portfolio of operating companies before selling them off through an IPO or private sale. Financial buyers target companies with strong cash flow; they want to know that the company they buy will generate sufficient cash flow to service the debt.

When thinking about selling your company, discuss with your lawyer what you want the outcome to be. For example, if you want to stay with your company and help it grow within a larger organization, then you're looking for a strategic buyer. Similarly, if you are looking to protect the jobs of your employees, you don't want to sell to a financial consolidator that is rolling up a large number of similar companies in your industry; such a transaction is likely to lead to layoffs within your company. Guide your investment banker accordingly.

A Seat at the Negotiating Table: Meet the Buyer

A sale begins to feel real the moment your adviser informs you that he has a buyer who wants to meet with you and talk about your company. This buyer will have many questions for you. But don't forget that you also have an obligation to ask questions too. Many small business owners get so excited about their company that they forget to ask the most basic questions (see table 19 for a full checklist).

Table 19: What to Learn About Your Potential Buyer

- Who is the buyer?
- Is it privately held or publicly traded?
- Do you have its annual report, or other background documents?
- Does your investment banker, or anyone in his firm, know the management in this company?

- Who will attend the meeting from the buyer company? What do you know about those individuals?
- Why is the buyer interested in your company?
- The history of the company
- Its product lines or services, and its pipeline
- Its reputation. Does it deliver quality products or services?
- Strategic trajectory and growth prospects
- A general sense of its corporate culture
- A general overview of its plans for your company
- Ability to pay you
- Stock structure and performance

Management

- Do your short- and long-term objectives coincide?
- Can you work with its people for the duration of your employment contract?
- What will your new position in the company be? Do you have room to grow?

Personnel Issues

- What incentives can it provide to help your key employees stay?
- How do your benefits and compensation programs compare?
- Will it retain your entire staff?

Strategy and Operations

- Does your culture and strategy fit with the company's?
- Do your growth plans agree with its growth plans?
- Where will you and your staff be located?
- Do they have plans to change your products and services?
- Will your clients view the deal positively?
- Are the synergies being talked about real?
- Who are its competitors?

Financials

- Does the company have enough cash to complete the acquisition?
- If it is a publicly traded company, how has its stock performed in the past year? And what is the forecast?
- Are there any restrictions on the stock?

- What is the consistency and quality of the company's earnings?
- How healthy is its balance sheet?

Legal

- Does the company have litigation pending against it?
- Can it legally deliver what it offered you?
- What is the company's litigation history?

Mechanics of the Deal

- How does the company plan to manage the integration?
- What is the new reporting structure for you and your team?
- Will the company need additional resources—or will you—to complete the integration?
- Has the company completed other acquisitions? If so, what have been the results?
- Is there buy-in within the company about acquiring your company?
- What is the timetable?

Navigating the Introduction: The Nondisclosure Agreement (NDA)

On the first meeting, it's usually just you (and your partners, if you have them) and your investment adviser shaking the hands of the buyer's management team and their investment adviser. Before this meeting begins both parties generally sign a nondisclosure agreement (NDA). A preliminary but crucial agreement in the deal-making process, the NDA protects the confidential information of the parties to a transaction, identifying the type of confidential information that will be disclosed, to whom, and under what conditions. The key provisions of the NDA are:

- Proper identification of the parties to the agreement
- Purposes of the NDA, for instance, for evaluation purposes or for a particular transaction
- Definition of confidential information, including both oral and written disclosures
- How confidential information will be protected
- Who can use the confidential information

- How long the NDA is operative
- Exceptions to confidential treatment
- Governing law
- Remedies for breach of the NDA

In the context of a potential company sale, the NDA is a tool that allows the parties to share information freely for the purpose of deciding whether to enter into a particular transaction. If both parties go forward with the sale, the NDA may be superseded by the confidentiality provision of the final purchase agreement. A sample NDA appears in the appendix, on page 277.

At this stage, you are simply presenting your company in person. The buyers already have your company brochure and an overview of your financials. Now they want to see what you have to say about your firm, where you see it going, and why you are exploring a sale. This meeting is as much about chemistry as it is about the hard data you'll present. Typically, you will be asked to present an overview of your industry in general, where your company fits in, your organization, and your financials. Make sure your financials illustrate growth, and point out in the meeting where your company is strong, for example, in EBITDA growth or in customer wins.

As the seller, you want to convey enthusiasm, commitment to your business—whether or not a deal takes place—and confidence in your firm and your industry. But you don't want to say more than you have to on the first outing. Although both parties generally sign nondisclosure agreements, which often include an agreement that one party will not recruit employees from the other, it is still wise to avoid listing the names of your key employees and clients, as well as the exact revenue you get from each client. Talk in advance with your lawyer, accountant, and investment adviser about exactly how much you should reveal, and when.

At my initial meeting with the buyer who ultimately bought my second company, AM Medica, I grouped together several clients and their revenues. Within each group, I listed the drug products we worked on alphabetically, without disclosing which products gave us the most revenue. The buyer could see we had blue-chip pharmaceutical clients without knowing which client was the largest. It was enough information to keep the buyer interested, but not enough for them to walk away and use the information inappropriately.

After you present your own company, inquire about the buyer firm. Ask where your company would fit into their overall growth strategy, how their management structure works, and whether or not they see synergies between your firm and theirs. When the first meeting concludes, both buyer and seller determine whether or not a second meeting is desired. Not to trivialize the significance of selling your company, but a first meeting is very much like a first date; if you feel good about how it went, you may want to pursue another meeting. If you're not so sure, it still may be worth one more go-round. But if the buyer turned you off, even if it was just the chemistry, then pass and look for another buyer. As in dating and marriage, so in company sales: better a breakup than a divorce.

More Meetings

If you do like what you've seen at the first meeting, then move on to the next one, ideally as soon as possible. Momentum matters during your sell period, and you have to do as much as possible to drive the process (see box 13).

BOX 13: IN THEIR OWN WORDS

The best people to tell you what it feels like to go through a sale transaction are the women who've done it. Here's what some of them have to say.

Harriette Waldron and Judy Kelly
Cofounders, Kelly/Waldron & Company
   "Selling your company is a very emotional time, a whole process, and unless you've done it before you're never really prepared for it. It's your baby, and the buyer is never going to do it as well as you did it. I think that's normal. So you have to figure out what else you are going to do, knowing that you're going to have to leave your company behind. It still may be worth the payout—it was worth it to me—but there was so much emotion involved in moving forward, and leaving the company behind. It's a process that takes time."—Harriette Waldron
   "Think about your future before you sign your company away. Understand how it will affect you. Do you want to continue to work, and work in a situation in which you don't have control anymore because the new owners are in control? It's emotional. You've created a baby, and now the baby

is adopted by somebody else and they don't have the same rules as you do. They stop listening to you as a valuable source of information to guide them. If it's possible, get a deal whereby you can leave as soon as possible. Sign the papers, walk out the door, and don't look back."—Judy Kelly

Rose Saia
Cofounder, Trilogy, Inc.

"I know business owners who say they want an exit, but then they just dabble around the edges. This approach doesn't make an exit happen. Even if the perfect buyer does show up, the business owner's lack of clarity about their intentions related to a realistic outcome can sabotage an exit. Women business owners have to be really honest with themselves. And for women in particular, you have to have a sense of your life and what it will be after the sale. If you're really wrapped up in your company, the future can look terrifying to you."

During subsequent meetings, you learn more about your buyer, and they learn more about you and your firm. It is customary at the second or third meeting to bring in your lawyer and accountant, and the buyer's lawyer and accountant will attend as well. (Anytime their lawyer is present, yours should be too, and vice versa.) These meetings are longer than the introductory one; one session can last for several hours. More financial details are disclosed, such as exactly who your largest clients are, what your profit margins are on various lines of business, who your subcontractors are, and how your accounts payable and receivables are managed. At this point buyers will generally look for documentation, such as signed contracts with clients or purchase orders confirming that orders have been placed.

Buyer/Seller Language: More Financial Language You Need to Know

More than one woman entrepreneur who sold her company successfully and talked with me about it confided that some of the terms used in dealmaking as well as the posturing at the negotiating table were often foreign to them. As Rose Saia points out, you don't want to be in the position of trying to climb the language curve while you are simultaneously running your business and negotiating the deal of your life. If you're at the bargaining table, it's likely you've been in business for several years. But to get through a sale process as successfully as possible, you need to know more than just how to interpret your own financial statements and explain your company. You need to understand the contracts you are signing and their potential impact on your payout and your company's future. (See the glossary for definitions of terms commonly used in the negotiating process.)

In 1998, when Harriette Waldron and Judy Kelly sold their firm, Kelly/Waldron & Company, a pharmaceutical information and marketing company that included a sales force automation software division for $100 million in stock, the shares of the acquirer, McKesson, were peaking in the mid-90s. But just two months after signing the sales agreement, McKesson announced accounting problems in its software unit, due to issues at another company it had acquired previously. The disclosure resulted in multiple class-action lawsuits and the stock plummeted to the low 30s overnight. Harriette, Judy, and their other two partners had considered the possibility that the stock they received in exchange for their company could decline by 20 percent, but they never anticipated a drop of more than 50 percent. "We weren't educated in making deals," Harriette says. "If we hadn't been so afraid that the deal might get nixed, we could have put in some controls." Instead of asking questions that might jeopardize the deal, she and Judy looked to their two male partners. In addition, they negotiated only with McKesson, rather than multiple interested parties. Because they were dealing with a huge industrial company, "Judy and I felt totally out of our element in the negotiations with McKesson," Harriette said.

Regardless of the buyer, it's your company on the block and you want to make sure you secure the best possible deal for yourself and your employees. If you're uncertain about whether or not you should ask certain questions, jot them down, wait for a break in the meeting, and review your queries with your attorney and accountant. And don't let any adviser talk you into anything that doesn't feel comfortable to you. For example, if you are talking with a solid potential buyer who offers you a combination of substantial stock and a little cash, you may want to reduce your overall sales price, increase the amount of cash on the table and reduce the amount of stock you receive. You are the only one who has to live with the deal when the deal is over.

After my third meeting with the buyer of my company, I insisted on rehearsals with my accountant, lawyer, and investment adviser, to help prepare me for subsequent meetings. They reviewed terminology with me, and my investment adviser took me through a few different scenarios, letting me know when I should respond directly to a query and when it was perfectly acceptable to redirect a question to my accountant or lawyer. Most important, he emphasized that I was the CEO not only of my company, but also of my negotiating team. Keep that in mind at all times: It's your company, and the outcome should be your decision.

The Letter of Intent

The letter of intent (LOI) states the parties' plans to negotiate a transaction. (A sample letter of intent appears in the appendix, on page 257.) Although generally nonbinding, this letter summarizes the terms of a transaction and serves as an acknowledgment that the parties are "intent" on moving forward with a deal. The parties should identify those provisions of the LOI they deem to be binding, such as the confidentiality provision. A transaction does not necessarily take place simply because the LOI is signed; rather, it is a statement of intent to negotiate a definitive agreement. The common elements of a LOI are as follows:

- The type of transaction, such as a stock or asset sale, for which a definitive agreement will be negotiated
- The purchase or sale price and other price components
- A summary of assets or liabilities being acquired or disposed
- The term or time period during which the parties agree to negotiate and enter into the definitive agreement, with a start date and an end date so negotiations do not drag on indefinitely
- Confidentiality provisions that describe the use of confidential information and restrictions on its use
- Governing law

Other items may be included depending on the type of transaction negotiated. A buyer may write a "no-shop" provision into the letter of intent. This provision means your team of advisers cannot solicit or review any bids from other companies to buy your company. Courts tend to have unfavorable views of "no-shop" agreements because they can result in the company being sold below market value. Instead, some buyers write in a "breakup fee" clause. If the deal they are working on with you collapses because you get a higher offer and want to pursue it, the breakup fee clause says you'll reimburse the buyer for the time and expense they incurred in preparing the deal. Since the LOI's terms often repeat in a definitive agreement, parties may elect to go right from an NDA into a final purchase and sale agreement.

The Term Sheet

In some deals a term sheet is also prepared, outlining the key terms of the transaction. Unless otherwise stated, the provisions of the term sheet are usually nonbinding, with the exception of the confidentiality, nondisclosure, and payment terms. The term sheet includes a description of the parties, the time period in which negotiations will occur, and the guarantees that each party gives the other, known as "reps and warranties." Also featured are details of the due diligence process, through which the parties will get to know each other by reviewing documents such as noncompetes, employment agreements, liens, and client contracts. A sample term sheet appears in the appendix, on page 263.

Due Diligence

Due diligence is the complete investigation of your operation, a kind of "kicking the tires" from the inside out. If there are any discrepancies in your documents, or holes in your company's performance, expect that the buyer's team of advisers will find the problems and use them to negotiate a lower price. Due diligence covers several broad categories: corporate records; financing documents; a list of company assets, such as property, equipment, and inventory; financial statements; tax returns; personnel records; environmental and regulatory compliance filings; and litigation papers. A sample due diligence checklist appears in the appendix, on page 269.

At first glance a due diligence checklist can overwhelm you; there may be items on the list you've never even heard of. Don't be intimidated. When I was negotiating to sell my company, the buyer handed me and my team a long due diligence list. One glance at it and I knew it would never get done unless everyone on our team agreed to review it together and then divvy up the tasks. I was quite happy when I realized that some categories of due diligence simply weren't applicable to my company, such as "provide copies of SEC filings" (we were a private company) or "provide copies of lawsuits and outcomes of each" (we had no litigation issues).

Once you knock out what does not apply to your business, the task seems easier. My accountant took responsibility for assembling the financials, but all of us agreed that we would meet and review key documents first, to catch any glitches. I pulled together the employee manual, personnel records, and client contracts. I asked my office manager to give me the binders that contained all of our leasing and rental agreements. Fortunately, because we were entering the fourth quarter, she assumed I was simply doing my annual review of terms, for possible renegotiating purposes. Working together, we were able to present the buyer with all of the relevant documents, and the negotiations continued.

After you have handed over your stack of documents, the buyer's advisory team consults with your legal and accounting team, reviewing the papers you've assembled and combing at random through job files, receivables, payables, bank statements, inventory, and whatever else they deem important. The due diligence process can take between several days and several weeks, depending on how detailed and comprehensive your financial and job files are and whether your client contracts, business leases, and employee records are in order (see table 20). If these documents aren't in place, you and your advisers may end up spending a frantic couple of weeks getting your paperwork ready for the buyer's due diligence review. Be advised, though, that this type of delay may be a red flag to some buyers.

Table 20: Manage the Due Diligence Process

Create a climate of trust. Give the buyer access to your financial records, and other data they need to review, and then give them a quiet place to review your files without your continuous supervision.

Show the buyer your "red flags." If your earnings stumbled one year within the last five, point it out to them and provide the explanation; don't wait for them to ask you.

Be aware of tax exposures. Many smaller companies fail to manage use and sales tax properly. Tax laws vary from state to state, and whether or not you have an office in another state where you conduct business *can* affect your sales and use tax. Review the issue of sales and use tax with your lawyer and accountant carefully.

Make sure your internal financial controls are in order. The Sarbanes-Oxley Act of 2002 put some stringent financial reporting procedures in place. Make sure you know how your internal financial systems will measure up, and ultimately fit in, if a publicly traded company is acquiring yours.

Understand why the buyer is interested in acquiring your company. Knowing what the buyer is looking for—entry into a specific market, your growth potential, your cash flow—can help you meet the buyer's expectations smoothly.

Buyers want to protect their potential investment, so they take every reasonable step to ensure that they know what they are buying, what it is really worth, and what issues, if any, may exist. Any flaws get reported back and are used to negotiate your sale price lower. As the seller, you need to know where your company's weak spots are and plan how to address them at the negotiating table so your purchase price doesn't get whittled down.

To minimize the disruption to your business due diligence may cause, arrange for the teams to meet together in one large, off-site conference room. Your lawyer or investment banker should be able to host this gathering or find a location for it. When I sold my company, my accountant and I removed financial files and historical job files from my offices after business hours to keep my sales plans confidential. My company's financials were in good order, and I knew the gross revenues and earnings over the previous five years by heart. My company also had an up-to-date organizational chart, a well-written employee manual, client contracts, excellent cash flow, no lawsuits, and no debt. In such a case, due diligence proceeds quickly because there aren't any surprises for the buyer, and there aren't any significant issues such as a lawsuit to resolve. For others, the due diligence process is more frantic, and not every pursuit ends with a deal. When Rose Saia and her team negotiated with one group for a few months before calling the deal off, "it wasn't fun," she recalls. "Your buttons get pushed, and on top of that people get stuck on issues that you can't imagine even exist. I danced with them and walked on hot coals for over three months, but in the end we had to pull out."

Selling your company is an exciting idea, but the run-up is more taxing that anyone can imagine. "The process is inordinately, exponentially more stressful than running your business day to day," Rose Saia says, "because you have to take at least six months out of your life to prepare your company for sale and sell it; you have to keep your business running very well while you're engaged in the selling process, and it's also a full-time job to drive the sale process."

I was also initially excited at the unexpected prospect of selling my company for substantial money, but as the negotiating and due diligence process wore on into the busy third and fourth quarters, I found the evening meetings after long days in the office draining. Day and night ran together like they never had before. At times I felt like I was leading a secret life because no one but my investment adviser, lawyer, and accountant knew what I was up to. At one point I became so frustrated with the calls for more documents to fulfill due diligence requests that I nearly called the deal off from sheer exhaustion. But in the end it was worth it to see the transaction through.

What You Negotiate

Everything is on the table in a transaction negotiation (see table 21). You'll spend several weeks scheduling meeting after meeting to hammer out the details. The major points of your transaction are generally outlined in the term sheet. Then the fine-point negotiating begins. Any meeting that involves setting the total valuation for your deal or how you will be paid, including discussions addressing the specifics of your personal employment agreement, is one you should attend personally. As the process gets more intense, deal frenzy will set in. Your emotions will run from excitement to disbelief, exhilaration to feelings of loss, and sheer, relieving joy. Every negotiating setting, every set of players, and every deal is different; how your transaction turns out is ultimately up to you.

Table 21: Negotiating Tips

- **Be aggressive on the sale price.** For example, if you win an important client during the due diligence process, note it and bump up your purchase price.
- **Know your company's worth.** You know this number better than anyone. Professional advisers are invaluable at the negotiating table, but only you really know how far your company can go. Ask for what you want, and direct your team to get it for you. I pushed for more at the eleventh hour, and I got it.
- **Negotiate for as large a cash component as you can in your purchase structure.** You can't predict whether the company's stock

will plummet or the buyer will default on its promissory note to
you. Get as much cash as you can at the beginning.

- **Understand your earn-out, and allow for contingencies.** Many
  earn-outs are written such that if you don't hit a specific target, you
  get nothing. Instead, push for a sliding scale earn-out, based on
  your results raising your unit's performance in specific metrics
  such as gross revenues.
- **Secure your payments.** Ask your lawyer to be as appropriately aggressive as possible to ensure that payouts are guaranteed.
- **Be clear on your role after the sale.** Who is your boss? If that individual leaves the company, who will you report to? How many corporate meetings a year will you be required to attend, and where
  will they be held? My buyer held four annual meetings in different
  locations each year. Since I already did so much business travel, we
  worked it into the agreement that one of my three senior sales directors could attend a meeting on my behalf, and I was required to
  go only once a year.
- **Be clear on your location.** I had written into every employment
  agreement I got that I could not be transferred out of Manhattan
  for any reason. Make sure you know where your office will be for
  the duration of your new employment.
- **Negotiate your quality-of-life issues now.** Entrepreneurs are used
  to coming and going as they please, even if they always take work
  with them on a holiday. But in a more formal, bureaucratic structure this system may not fly. Get it in writing that you can work
  from home if this is important to you.
- **Write in a parachute clause.** Parachute clauses cover your severance payments, acceleration of vesting of stock options, health
  benefits, whether you will have office space for a specified period
  of time, and more. Be sure to discuss the tax implications of your
  parachute clause with your attorney and accountant. And be sure
  your lawyer addresses this before you close the deal.

As the buyer's due diligence turns up a flaw or two in your firm, you and
your team should be busy looking into their business, noting the ways in
which your company is adding value to theirs. As negotiating continues,
pay careful attention to your payment package (cash, stock, a promissory
note, and an earn-out plan per page 223) and your employment contract.
Remember, the sale of your company may be your last professional stop,
so make it a good one.

Payouts. Buyers generally like to structure a deal using a combination of payouts: cash, stock, and a promissory note. For example, if you both agree that the total valuation for your company is $10 million, the buyer might propose something like $1.5 to $2 million in cash at closing, perhaps $3 million in stock, and the remaining $5 million to be paid out over a three-year period, based on the length of time you will be working for the company. Under this plan you would be paid $1,666,666 every year on the same date for three consecutive years, for a total valuation of $10 million. You will want to start by negotiating for more cash up front, which lowers the risk to you if the buyer cannot make the payment, regardless of how well your company performs under its new owners. The time value (receiving more cash up front) also makes the deal more valuable to you, even if the buyer pays the notes on schedule. Similarly, if the buyer defaults on a bank loan, the company may then be restricted from making a promissory note payment to you. Check to see if this arrangement is written into your purchase and sale agreement and think carefully about its possible effect on your payout. Be sure you understand exactly what the risks are before you accept a large payment in stock or in the form of a note. Get a thorough financial picture of the company that's buying yours and its ability to meet its payments to you.

The earn-out. This step is often the trickiest part of negotiating your compensation package. Just as you want the money in cash at the beginning, the buyer wants to keep you working enthusiastically for the new company as long as possible while you wait to earn the rest of your sale price. Earn-outs are usually based on growing your company's revenues. You get more money if you meet certain goals set by the buyer. Typically, these goals are determined in the negotiating process and become part of the purchase and sale agreement. Ideally, ask for a sliding scale of some kind. For example, if the buyer wants you to increase gross revenues by 25 percent annually, ask what happens if you hit 21 percent. Negotiate for a range, a target of gross revenue increases between 18 percent and 25 percent, for instance. Ask for a bonus if you exceed the earn-out target. Next, be sure your earn-out covers contingencies such as national emergencies, major economic slumps, or problems at the buyer's company unrelated to your own unit.

The employment agreement. Their lawyers will draft it and your lawyers will read it carefully. This agreement will include a stiff noncompete clause; be sure you can live with it. (A strict noncompete will prevent you from starting another company to compete, or joining a firm that competes with them.) Check that your agreement spells out your responsibilities in detail and lists tasks for which you will not be responsible. To whom will you report? If you get that far, ask if you can meet a supervisor in the department, and try to talk to employees who work there. Where will your office be located? If you don't want to be moved out of the city where you currently work, write it in. In addition, ask how many corporate meetings you will have to attend, and where the meetings are held. Finally, ask about vacation and work-at-home policies. You need this spelled out in your employment contract as well so their expectations of you are clear to you from the beginning (see table 21).

The purchase and sale agreement. Drafted initially by the buyer's lawyers, this agreement spells out the purchase price for your company and details when and how you will be paid. The document also includes the assets and liabilities of your firm and its up-to-date financial statements. Both sides' lawyers will add representations and warranties as well as letters from each law firm stating that you are getting a fair price. In addition, the agreement includes the conditions necessary to close the deal and those that take effect after the closing, your employment agreement, an indemnification clause, and copies of the documents gathered for the due diligence process.

Every woman who told me about the sale of her company says that, like me, she was exhausted by this point. But a final rally is in order. Read your purchase and sale agreement as if it's the most important business document you've ever read. This stage is your last window of opportunity to clarify any questions about the deal before you go forward for good. When your lawyer and the buyer's lawyer agree that every item is in place, the teams retreat to review the document, checking for errors or last-minute questions. Sometimes, another meeting is called to resolve any lingering issues.

The closing and post-closing documents. All the top players on both teams attend the closing meeting. If last-minute changes pop up, the selling team steps out of the room to discuss a point or two, then everyone regroups. If some wording in the document has to change, everyone involved initials the pages where the changes are made and the closing continues. Feel free to bring a bottle of good champagne to celebrate with a toast. The following day your new professional life begins—as an employee.

Sometimes, the closing agreement calls for "post-closing" documents. For a variety of reasons, including tax considerations, both buyer and seller may determine that it is advantageous to close the deal on a particular date. Post-closing documents could include such details as an updated employee manual or a new client contract for an important account.

Post-closing activities. Unless your sale agreement doesn't call for you to work for the new company, don't leave town to celebrate just yet. The day after the ink is dry on the closing agreement, your work as head of a division in a larger company begins. You'll probably meet with people from the buyer's side to implement transition procedures, including:

- Informing your employees
- Informing your clients, with a press release or individual letters
- Informing your subcontractors
- Notifying your bank, your landlord, and your utilities of billing changes
- Setting a fast-track timetable to develop a new company brochure, or integrating your materials into the parent company's brochure
- Ordering new stationery and business cards
- Setting up your accounting system to conform to the new owner's system
- Scheduling visits to key customers to ensure a smooth transition

You've done it. Your company is sold, or you've seen it through to an initial public offering. How does it feel, and what happens next? To find out, see what the women who've done it have to say about their experiences—and lives—after their deals of a lifetime were completed.

SUCCESS

Marlene Canter negotiated the sale of her company, Canter & Associates, to Sylvan Learning Centers in 1998 for a valuation in excess of $65 million. Marlene and her key employees remained with Sylvan through the duration of her three-year employment contract. She and her team met their earn-out targets every year and received the full value of the earn-out. After fulfilling her contract, Marlene left Sylvan in good standing. Her suc-

continued

cessful contract negotiation when she sold her company gave her terms that motivated her to continue growing her group within Sylvan's organization.

REGRETS

Isabel Valdes founded Hispanic Market Connections, Inc., (HMC) in Los Altos, California, in 1985. The company provides Hispanic-specific qualitative and quantitative market research to Fortune 500 companies targeting the Hispanic population in the United States. Isabel wanted to grow her company faster so she "put her antennae up," as she says, to identify opportunities. As she mulled over a few ideas, a small, publicly traded company approached her. Before she knew it she was negotiating hard and eventually walked away with a $5.5 million valuation deal, including $1.5 million in cash and the remainder in the form of a promissory note and an earn-out of cash and stock.

But the thrill of the sale wore off fast. Isabel missed her first-year earn-out; shortly thereafter the parent company went into default. Realizing she was a lame duck, she left the company amicably. "I realize now that I should have taken more time and done more research," she says. The buyer's idea to buy a group of small companies and bundle their services together to sell to Fortune 500 corporations didn't pan out. "I would have been much better off," she says "selling to a much larger company that is in the same line of work as HMC, or selling to a similar business." Instead, the bulk of Isabel's deal value went up in smoke.

CHAPTER 10

Done Deals: Sold Companies and IPOs

Plenty of entrepreneurial businesswomen end up millionaires. We started out in ordinary careers, and then chose to launch our own businesses; not one of the women I interviewed who completed financially rewarding deals has an M.B.A.

What so few hard-working women entrepreneurs still don't appreciate is this: The biggest risk is behind you, now that you've started your company. The rest is making a consistent and continuous effort to implement the seven steps that can lead you to a rewarding exit transaction. All of us share three things in common:

- We learned how to play in the business game from entry to exit
- We learned how to talk about money—big money—comfortably
- We learned the seven steps to building a successful business and then put them in place

Here's what happened to us after that.

SOLD!

The four most exciting words for an entrepreneur to say are: "I sold my company!" Selling marks the successful end of the business game: You've won. But few entrepreneurs think about what lies ahead.

Deal outcomes fall into several different categories; some business owners stay with the firm that bought their company for years, others remain for the length of their contract only, while still others depart before they've fulfilled their obligation, either by choice or because they are forced out. Occasionally, an entrepreneur buys her own company back. Once the deal is finished, many entrepreneurs find themselves looking for something else to do. The women who sold their companies and shared their stories with me have outcomes as diverse as the deals themselves. The range of their experiences will give you a realistic idea of what's possible.

The Vacuum Cleaner Acquisition

Myriam Chen's family came from China and settled on the West Coast. Myriam moved to Oregon for a while, then returned to the San Francisco Bay Area about the time that Saigon fell, in 1975, and thousands of refugees began pouring into her area. Myriam applied for the director's job in a program established to assist the refugees in finding work and integrating them into the community. It was there, in the nonprofit sector, that Myriam learned about having to work long hours, raising money, and doing presentation after presentation. After several years she left to work for a small tech consulting company. Five years later she and a colleague, Tom McGinley, started their own consulting firm, Chen & McGinley. The company provided blue chip clients such as Bank of America, IBM, and Pacific Gas & Electric with consultants on projects ranging from systems integration to Internet development opportunities. "It was very, very difficult in the early years because our financial resources were so limited," Myriam says, but the pair was aggressive in pursuing clients and winning substantial pieces of business.

By 1999, Chen & McGinley had upwards of $30 million in annual revenues, making the firm one of the ten fastest-growing companies in the Bay Area. A global IT services company based in Pittsburgh, iGate, offered to buy the consulting firm, and the partners sold for $25 million. To ensure that their employees remained with the new parent company, Myriam and Tom created an incentive program and used 20 percent of their payment to fund it over a two-year period. This decision proved to be a mistake. "Looking back, I think we should have been a little less generous to [our] employees, because it's human nature that people will start to take something for granted," Myriam says. "Instead of knocking themselves out to earn it, they know the money's there and they just back off a bit, so I learned a lesson from it."

The pair was also surprised at how thoroughly their company was swallowed up within the bigger firm. At first, Myriam was very excited about the sale, which she found "thrilling." But after the acquisition, iGate sent a cadre of East Coast managers to California, where they set about remaking Chen & McGinley's business model and operations in iGate's image. The results disappointed Myriam: "It took us fifteen years to build our company and brand recognition disappeared in just ten months." It was tough for Myriam to accept that it wasn't her company anymore, but she knew she had to go along. "I told myself it's like any relationship; if you've had a few, you get numb to the loss. There will be another relationship on the horizon, and I have another one right now," she says. "There's no advantage to looking back; I always look ahead."

Myriam fulfilled her two-year employment contract with iGate and left as soon as her obligation ended. In 2001 she cofounded her second venture, a music production company, with Benjamin Sun, a passionate musician and composer.

Myriam's Advice: "Women tend to be gun-shy and insecure about who they are. That's the truth. At Chen & McGinley, half the employees were women; anytime you confronted one of them, they got very, very defensive because they didn't want to be wrong, to make a mistake. Working women still aren't as confident as men, because they've got years on us. I'd advise women to get the best advice they can, move forward, and don't be afraid if it doesn't work out. There's always opportunity."

The Boomerang Entrepreneur

Judee von Seldeneck began her career in Washington, D.C., as a secretary for then-Senator Walter Mondale. After years of living as a single, pressure from her mother finally got to Judee, and she and her boyfriend got engaged and moved to Philadelphia. There Judee met two women who had started a small business helping women job-share. She joined forces with them and bought them out nine months later, when they tired of the work.

As the company's sole owner, Judee changed the focus from job-sharing placement to finding full-time professional employment for women, a new idea in the staffing industry. The federal government was introducing hiring requirements for women and minorities, a market niche Judee decided to fill. She called on banks, the telephone company, and corporations around Philadelphia, letting them know she could fulfill their hiring objectives by providing a qualified woman or a minority to do the job. Not long after she started her firm, Diversified Search, *The New York Times* wrote an article on the company. "I got so energized by that," she says. "It felt so good, and it was exciting making this thing work." By the mid-1990's Diversified was humming, and in 1998 a publicly traded company, Jacksonville, Florida–based MPS Group, bought Judee's firm in an all-cash transaction.

After fulfilling her three-year employment contract, Judee stayed on as the company's CEO because she liked the business so much. But by 2004, MPS was losing money and refocusing on its staffing businesses. The CEO of MPS approached Judee about buying her company back, and she and some key employees reacquired it for substantially less than MPS had paid for it. The negotiating process took about three months. "We are thrilled to have it back," she says. "Business is booming, we've hired lots of new people, and we are in the process of finalizing an acquisition of a U.S. firm that will make Diversified the U.S. partner of the fourth-largest global partnership in the world." Judee is focused on continued growth and bringing in the next generation of leadership, some of whom she hopes will become equity owners.

Judee's Advice: "Figure out ways to keep your key people. I was challenged by one of my major revenue producers when it was time for me to ask them to sign noncompetes, so managing your revenue producers is vital. Also, get the best financial adviser you can find. I learned so much going through my transaction, but that's a difficult time to start learning. It's exciting but very distracting while you're trying to run a business."

Timing Is Everything

Rose Saia and her partners sold their company, Concord, Massachusetts–based Trilogy, Inc., seven years after they started it, for $4 million. Rose and her team were focused on sticking to their business plan, but in hindsight Rose feels they may have missed a window or two of greater opportunity to sell the company. Even after a successful transaction was completed, Rose says she "felt like I just didn't do as well as I could have, for the team, for my partners. . . . Could I have gotten $6 million or more if I'd just hung in there? I don't know." Rose spent considerable time working on one deal that collapsed, and, she says, she learned that "buyers and sellers may say they're on the same page, but they're not." In the summer of 2001 Rose was out with her children at an ice cream stand and while they slurped sundaes, she was locked in a heated discussion with the CEO of a potential buyer, arguing over the debt assumption on the term sheet. Shortly thereafter they called the deal off. Then September 11 happened, and the pace of deal making in her industry slowed dramatically, hurting Rose's ability to sell her company. Trilogy was finally sold in December 2001 to Funk Software.

Rose's Advice: "I encourage women to spend time planning and looking outside their company on a regular basis. You've got to measure your market tempo. Whatever you do, don't get a fixed idea in your head that either you don't have the revenues you really want, or the customers, or you don't feel ready [to sell]. Had we been smart about it, we would have exited in 1998 or 1999, because that's when things were gangbusters in our industry and we missed it. People were writing term sheets on the backs of paper napkins. It was a phenomenal, crazy time. The window to sell was wide open; companies with no earnings were getting $40 million, but we didn't feel ready, so we hunkered down and stayed on our business plan track. Had we marketed the company then, we would have received a lot more money. Ultimately, the company we sold to had the same window, and it closed for them too. Later, they were interested in being acquired and there weren't any buyers; their value was down 50 percent from where it had been. So if you're thinking about exit possibilities, especially a sale, my advice is: Pay attention to what and where your real opportunities are. It may not be the time to sell that is right for you, but it may be the only time."

Cash Is King

Harriette Waldron and Judy Kelly sold their company, Kelly/Waldron and Company, to publicly traded McKesson, Inc., in an all-stock deal valued at $100 million (the full story is on page 216 in chapter 9), but serious accounting problems shortly thereafter led to a massive devaluation of the stock payout they had received. Still, the four partners agreed to stick out their employment contracts. Both Harriette and Judy had solid relationships with their clients, and they didn't want to let them down. When the contracts were fulfilled, Harriette, Judy, and one other partner left McKesson and started a new consulting venture, KWS. McKesson is now one of their clients.

Harriette's Advice: "During the transaction process I thought I would never have to work again. No one prepared us for the possibility that even a solid blue chip NYSE company can develop serious problems. My advice is: Be sure you understand the long-term ramifications of your deal. If your fortune is tied to their stock, you'll suffer too if they lose market share."

Judy's Advice: "Selling was too emotional. The first year was horrible; I became a recluse and cried a lot. It took to the third year for me to adjust; then I was okay, because I just knew and accepted that I couldn't make any changes. But I'm quite happy now because I am a consultant; I've gone over the 'let-go' bridge and now we're on our own again."

Motivation to Sell

Not long after returning to Kansas City in 1978, Nancy Lauterbach went to work for Dick Gardner, the owner of National Association of Sales Education, a company that organized and managed motivational speakers and sales training events. Three years after Nancy started at the firm, Dick was killed in a car accident. Nancy felt she had to continue to run the company for Dick's widow and three young children while looking for a buyer for the firm. She succeeded in selling the company, remained on for a transition year, then left to join another firm. In 1988, she decided to go out on her own and launched Five Star Speakers and Trainers LLC. Her husband subsequently sold his real estate company and joined her. Five Star found success managing a small group of motivational, training, and entertainment speakers, which they provide to corporate clients such as Hallmark, Sprint, Yellow Freight, and Applebee's.

In February 2005, Nancy sold Five Star to a privately held company for a price that made her happy, with 75 percent cash upfront. The buyer was Steve Gardner, Dick's son, and his business partner. Steve had worked as a real estate salesperson for Nancy's husband's company, but after a year there he switched over to join Nancy's Five Star Group. He left for three years and returned, and a few years later decided to buy Nancy out.

Nancy's Advice: "My deal felt very good, from beginning to end. I wasn't out looking to sell my company, and in many ways [it was] hard to give up my baby. But it felt right. I knew it was the right time, the right person. I think most of us know when we are on the right path; when you go against what you feel is right, you know it in your heart, and that's when you'll have trouble. I still love what I do and my guess is I'll continue doing it. I have four years left in my employment contract, and then I may work fewer hours. Be sure you know what you want when you sell."

Serving Sales

Geralyn Kasmer worked full-time as a nurse while her partner ran the coffee shop they created, Belle and Maxwell's, in West Palm Beach, Florida. But once their coffee business had a following, the partners expanded into other uses for their space. When the shop was closed on Sundays, they hosted tea parties for small children, as well as bridal and baby showers. By this time Belle and Maxwell's also carried prepared vegetarian foods (Geralyn's partner opposed meat products) and baked goods. In addition, the store sold local artists' works, including furniture, wall hangings, and jewelry.

After six years, the partnership ran into trouble, and Geralyn bought out her partner. This move allowed her to begin serving meat on the menu, and she launched a catering business, which did well. But three years later, Geralyn was burned out and eager to travel. She approached a Realtor who specialized in selling specialty shops. The Realtor wasn't able to find her a deal, and, soured on the experience, she waited out her lease instead. At that point a local resident called her to inquire about buying the business. Geralyn sold Belle and Maxwell's for just shy of $100,000.

Geralyn's Advice: "I didn't have any business experience per se, but I love to cook, and I wasn't ready to simply step out of nursing. I met my partner through my mother; our mothers are very good friends. We had the same philosophy about food, but I actually did not know her well. I'm a bit more laid back and she is very controlling. Our personalities clashed. We had trouble in our partnership almost immediately. You've got to be very careful before you enter into partnership agreements. We had a lot of stress we could have avoided had we been more sophisticated and informed about business partnerships. But I loved every minute of having my own business, despite the partnership. I compromised on the sale price because I was ready to move on; I didn't want to stay on for any length of time, so I had to back off a bit on my asking price. In the end I stayed just two weeks. I didn't want to stay any longer."

The Internet IPO

Rosalind Resnick and Ryan Scott started their web design firm, Net-Creations, from Rosalind's house in 1995. Rosalind, a journalist, says Ryan, a software designer, was "the guy who could make anything and I was the girl who could sell anything." The company's breakthrough idea was a method for customers to opt in or out of e-mail marketing messages, giving NetCreations permission to send them targeted pitches about products and services on their interest lists. Response rates soared, and by the fall of 1998, with the Internet boom at its peak, online stores such as Amazon.com were lining up to rent NetCreations' list of e-mail addresses.

Trouble came in the form of DoubleClick, an upstart competitor that managed to raise $9 million in venture capital quickly, becoming NetCreations' biggest rival. NetCreations, which by 1999 had $20 million in revenue, did the rounds of venture capital firms and investment banks, but found no one willing to invest. Undeterred, Rosalind, the CEO, went on the road and raised $43 million in three weeks. This money allowed the partners to work full-time on their IPO, and the company went public later that year. By the end of the first trading day, the stock was worth $300 million and Rosalind's 51 percent stake had made her an instant multimillionaire. Within three months NetCreations had a market capitalization of $1 billion.

But the partners' fortunes were still tied up in the stock, which was subject to the whims of the market. When the market crashed in March 2000, many of NetCreations' customers went down with it. The company's sales began sinking. In fewer than two quarters, Rosalind and her partner knew they would miss their earnings estimates. What followed, Rosalind says, "was a blur." The announcement that NetCreations would miss its numbers cut the stock price in half. Frantically, Rosalind and Ryan put together a deal for DoubleClick, their archrival, to acquire NetCreations for $191 million, stock for stock. But the following week, DoubleClick announced that it too would miss its numbers, and its stock tumbled, dragging with it the value of the NetCreations deal. It finally settled out at a value of $50 million. Because the deal was rapidly devaluing, disgruntled shareholders then filed a class action lawsuit accusing Rosalind and her partner of self-dealing and other questionable actions. Then DoubleClick announced that once they had taken over NetCreations, they would replace Rosalind as CEO.

As the DoubleClick deal struggled forward, Rosalind and Ryan found a savior in SEAT Pagine Gialle, an Italian publishing and marketing conglomerate, which put forth an unsolicited offer to buy NetCreations for all cash. The SEAT deal closed in February 2001, with the company selling for $111 million. Rosalind and Ryan, who still owned 75 percent of the company, walked away with $40 million each, and Rosalind remained CEO until the end of the year.

Unlike many Internet darlings, NetCreations is still in business. Rosalind, meanwhile, has started another company, Axxess Business Centers, Inc., a storefront consulting firm for start-ups and small businesses.

Rosalind's Advice: "Upon reflection, I would not have managed anything differently. We made the right move at the right time, and even though I ended up leaving the company I loved, I'd do it all over again if I had the chance. From a financial point of view, it probably makes more sense to sell your company and pocket the money now than to try to take it public and take the risk that you won't be able to cash out. On the other hand, I can't blame any woman who wants to follow in my footsteps and climb to the top of the mountain."

From CEO to Philanthropist

Lois Silverman and her partner sold 49 percent of their firm, CRA Managed Care, Inc., for $51 million to a venture capital firm in April 1994. (Her full story appears in the "Success" box in chapter 8 on page 196.) Lois knew it was only a matter of time before she was out of the company completely. In May 1995 CRA went public, and she stayed on board for two more years.

By early 1996, Lois was ready to chart a new course. She says she "missed herself," and began to realize that "learning how to play was going to be harder than learning how to run a company." In particular, Lois says, "I wanted the opportunity to be a woman and to be with other women. I wanted to take the time now to build those relationships." Although she was still chairwoman of CRA, she was spending more time on outside charitable activities and less time at the company. By the summer of 1997, Lois had gathered ten top businesswomen in the Boston area who shared her views on giving back to the community. Lois started The Commonwealth Institute (TCI), a nonprofit organization that provides a range of services to Boston-area senior executives and CEO businesswomen, including peer-to-peer mentorship for women entrepreneurs. TCI opened a second program for businesswomen in the south Florida area in 2003. Lois's goal is to create more Commonwealth Institutes in other cities. In addition, Lois is chairman of the board of Beth Israel Deaconess Medical

Center, a top Boston hospital that also has a partnership with the Red Sox. When Lois became chairman, she decided to meet with John Henry, the owner of the Red Sox, and the team's management representatives. Lois says she simply told them that "we're on the same team," but that she wouldn't be organizing golf foursomes or going out for drinks "with the boys." Lois also is a former chair of the board of Community Servings, a program providing meals to individuals with AIDS.

Lois's Advice: "By the early nineties I knew I didn't want to be tied to the business for the rest of my life, and I kept pondering: How will I find peace for the rest of my life? I knew what I had to do. So my advice always is: Trust your gut. You know intrinsically where things are headed; act on that."

From Businesswoman to Politician

Hinda Miller and her partner Lisa created a dynamic business, JBI, Inc., and sold it to Playtex in 1990, twelve years after founding the company. (The full story is in chapter 2, on page 38.) A year later, Playtex became a division of the conglomerate Sara Lee Corp. "We had a lot of different management teams in the first two to three years," Hinda says, "but I stayed through the transition, and was president of my division of Sara Lee until 1997." A few years later Hinda ran for, and won, a seat in Vermont's state senate.

Hinda's Advice: "In my state, Vermont, 95 percent of jobs come from entrepreneurial companies, and more women than men today are starting companies here. I think women are well prepared to be entrepreneurs, but I'd still recommend that any woman starting a business learn about local organizations willing to support and help entrepreneurs. We have various professional groups as well as the banks, of course; a good local group of entrepreneurs can lead you to excellent accountants and lawyers, and act as a support group for you."

Nursing a Company to Profit

Cathleen Naughton left her job as a public health nurse in Rhode Island to raise four children. When they were all in school full-time, Cathleen went back to work, ultimately landing a job in a national for-profit home care company, where she became the director of nurses. Working there taught her about advertising and opening new offices. When she left the firm, she honored her one-year noncompete agreement before opening Cathleen Naughton & Associates in a one-room office in Providence in 1978. The new company provided physical therapists, X-ray technicians, medical secretaries, and medical transcriptionists. Cathleen produced her own promotional brochures and handled payroll too. As the company grew, Cathleen added a visiting nurse service and hired a scheduler and a nursing director. She also opened two new offices.

Not long after she started the company, her daughter, Carolyn, who was in college in Rhode Island, began working for Cathleen part-time. Carolyn and Cathleen worked together for years while Carolyn got married, had two children, and returned to school for her master's in health services. Cathleen officially retired three years ago and is less involved with the firm today. Although Cathleen still has control of the stock, she is in the process of transferring stock to Carolyn, now president and CEO, and other family members. Numerous buyout offers have come in, but Cathleen and Carolyn are determined to keep the company in the family.

Cathleen's Advice: "As you take steps to diversify, don't lose sight of your original mission. Be careful when you start to branch out. Also, stay aware of costs, and take what steps you can to keep costs down while you maintain a high level of service. This is really important as your company grows."

From Mother to Daughter

After years of successfully running her direct-sales company in Chicago, Madolyn Johnson plans to anoint her daughter Cari, a top manager at the firm, the next CEO. In the meantime, Madolyn has in place an experienced management team of professional executives, including an executive vice president of marketing and sales, who formerly worked for a $700 million direct-sales firm and a CFO who was a bank president after heading the finance operations of a $100 million manufacturing company. Although Madolyn frequently gets calls asking her to sell the company, she plans to maintain the ownership structure within the family for the next generation. She and Cari also work with a charity called Rebuilding To-gether, an organization that provides for the elderly and disabled by outfit-ting their homes so they can stay in them.

Madolyn's Advice: "You have to have balance between your passion and profitability. And if you don't get things set up properly—your legal status, accounting, and operations—rest assured your passion will not carry your company all the way."

From Mother to Son

Judy Warchol began working when she was fourteen. Divorced and remar-ried, with three children, she took a job working for a woman who subcon-tracted people to type envelopes at home. When Allstate Insurance, her largest client, discovered their mailings weren't going out as scheduled, Judy went alone to a district sales meeting, explained her boss couldn't do the job, and took over the assignment herself. Her new business did the typing, stuffing, metering, and mailing for Allstate's direct-mail pieces, as well as typing term papers and doing secretarial work for other customers. Today Judy's Mailing & Secretarial Services focuses on mail fulfillment, such as sending out reminder letters and postcards for magazine subscrip-tion renewals. The firm has grown in earnings almost every year over the last two decades.

Ten years ago, Judy's niece, who had been working for her, gave notice to leave. Judy called her son in Texas and gave him a choice: He could re-turn to Chicago to work in the business or she would sell it. He decided to come home, and is now running the company with his mother. At seventy-six, Judy still goes to the office every day but has positioned her son to take the reins.

Judy's Advice: "Adaptability is key. When I started working typing en-velopes, we didn't even have self-correcting typewriters or Xerox ma-chines. As new developments occurred, I had to stay up-to-date and learn to use new technologies. As the new equipment brought about changes in how people worked, I also had to see and adapt to what services clients re-ally needed. I got up early, went back to work after dinner, slowly but surely reduced secretarial services because it wasn't profitable and shifted to fulfillment. Our annual revenues are a few million a year now, a long way from when I was typing envelopes."

A Housewife Home Run

Shortly after Dolly Peters joined Investment Equity, a real estate broker-age, she and three partners bought the Florida company, assuming its debt. At the time, the company's fifteen agents operated out of a 2,000-square-foot office with a leaky roof. The new ownership team, including Dolly, two other "housewives," as they called themselves, and a male part-ner, quickly turned the company around. Shortly thereafter, the house-wives bought the male partner out. Within fifteen years the business had 145 Realtors and several office locations. The first Realtors in the area to use voice mail, they also had a website well ahead of many competitors.

The company's success attracted the attention of Prudential Real Es-tate, which flew the three women to California to convince them to buy a Prudential franchise and become a Prudential branch. They agreed, and became the first Prudential franchise in northern Palm Beach County. But the arrangement didn't work out, and six months later the trio bought out the rest of their franchisee contract, losing $250,000 in the process. In-stead, they became an affiliate of Christie's Real Estate.

Then Dolly had to have major surgery. She asked her son, Michael, to consider leaving his teaching job to join her in the firm. He decided to make the move, and after her recovery remained with the company. Sev-eral years ago Dolly and her partners sold the firm to Illustrated Properties. "Now," says Dolly, sixty-five, "my housewife partners retired, and I'm free to concentrate on just selling real estate." She and Michael recently had the second-highest home sale in Florida, when a sale closed for $27 million.

Dolly's Advice: "So many business partners have difficulty but I was very fortunate. My two women partners and I knew what we wanted and we knew what we were doing. We built a solid infrastructure too, which is a must. After going through several managers, we hired a top lady; she was excellent and kept our real estate offices at the forefront, introducing voice mail and a state-of-the-art computerized system ahead of competitors. Our bookkeepers and accountant were also first class. Without this superior in-frastructure, we might not have fared as well."

What Happened to the Rest of Us?

Lane Nemeth, founder of Discovery Toys, sold her company to Avon Prod-ucts in 1997. Lane knew Avon's chairman and felt things would go well.

She would run the U.S. business and focus on sales and marketing, and Avon would provide the infrastructure and the funds. The deal was completed in three months. A year later, Avon sold Discovery to a private investment firm. Lane exercised the "parachute clause" in her contract that allowed her to leave the company if such a sale occurred. She wanted to pursue other ventures. In 2004 Lane started PetLane, a company that sells pet-care products and pet toys through home parties. Her daughter, Tara, works with her. Her new business, Lane says, is a "sheer joy."

Marlene Canter received millions by fulfilling her three-year earn-out with Sylvan Learning Centers after the company bought her teacher-training firm, Canter & Associates. The period after the sale but before her final exit was stressful for her, however. "There was a change in the company culture," she says. One employee who had been with Marlene for two decades left the company. But Marlene and other senior executives stayed, and Marlene eventually departed on good terms. Marlene had never thought much about what she would do after selling out. She rented a house in the south of France for a summer and mulled over her next entry point, considering all avenues, even thinking about becoming a rabbi. When she returned to Los Angeles, Marlene decided to run for the Los Angeles County Board of Education and financed her own campaign.

I sold my second company, AM Medica Communications, twelve years after I started it, to a small publicly traded company in October 1998. In addition to receiving millions in cash at closing, I also took a promissory note for several million dollars, to be paid out in three installments annually, beginning in October 1999. But when the first payout date came, the company was in default. The fine print in my purchase and sale agreement stated that if the company went into default, the bank loans had to be brought current before a promissory note payment could be made. No one on my advisory team thought a default was likely, but it happened. One adviser thought I should resign immediately; after all, he argued, if they can't pay you, why stay? And, he told me, they'll have a tough time holding you to a noncompete. But I wasn't interested in that kind of fight, and I could not imagine competing against my colleagues. I remained in place, talking with the CEO and CFO to see what could be done. I also knew that if my unit did not keep producing there wasn't any chance I would get paid, so I had to stay on track and keep my team working hard. I had a clause in my employment contract that allowed me to resign in March 2000, and I exercised it. A gamble, I predicted that my quitting abruptly would get their attention. The tactic worked. My lawyer and I quickly renegotiated a deal releasing me from my responsibilities as president of AM Medica and from all responsibilities for running the company. Instead, I signed on as a retained consultant, for a solid monthly fee and the ability to work from home. I agreed to accept payment on the promissory note in substantial monthly installments at 12 percent interest. In June 2003 the company accelerated a lump-sum payment to me, and my relationship with the company ended. During this time I was able to maintain a good rapport with my clients and nearly all of my employees, some of whom I still count as friends today. And I collected an additional substantial amount in interest payments on the note. Since then, I've joined The Commonwealth Institute, a nonprofit organization that mentors women executives and entrepreneurs, and I serve on the advisory board of its south Florida organization. I am also exploring investment opportunities in start-up companies, and I took up writing again, my first love, beginning with *There's a Business in Every Woman*.

Information and Networking

Women's Business Enterprise National Council (WBENC)
1120 Connecticut Ave., N.W., Suite 1000
Washington, DC 20036
Phone: 202-872-5515, ext. 10
Fax: 202-872-5505
E-mail: admin@wbenc.org
www.wbenc.org

West Coast Operations of WBENC
Contact: Regional Director, West Coast
3579 East Foothill Blvd., Suite 188
Pasadena, CA 91107-3119
Phone: 626-836-9288
Fax: 626-836-5709

WBENC offers various programs around the country. Go to:
http://www.wbenc.org/programs/accelerator/index.html

Center for Women's Business Research
1411 K St. N.W., Suite 1350
Washington, DC 20005-3407
Phone: 202-638-3060
Fax: 202-638-3064
www.nfwbo.org
The Center provides research, consulting, and education services. The research is supported by and carried out for various corporations. The Center also provides seminars, speeches, and executive roundtables for women-owned firms.

The Commonwealth Institute
www.commonwealthinstitute.org
TCI, with chapters in Boston and south Florida, is a dynamic organization that supports women entrepreneurs and executives by helping them succeed in growing their businesses.

The Center for Women & Enterprise
www.cweonline.org
CWE was created to empower women to become economically self-sufficient and prosperous through entrepreneurship. The group has locations in Boston, Worcester, Massachusetts, and Providence.

Entrepreneur.com
http://www.entrepreneur.com
Information for small business owners, with a special section for women in business.

Women-21.gov
http://www.women-21.gov/
Women-21 is an initiative of the Department of Labor and the Small Business Administration. This government entity recognizes the importance of women-run businesses in our economy and hopes to assist them through networking opportunities and a bevy of web-based resources.

Women in Business Resources
http://h2obeta.law.harvard.edu/57892
A site provided by Harvard that offers a listing of the latest articles for women in business, covering subjects from venture capital to networking to blogs.

Women's Institute
http://www.womensinst.org/
The Women's Institute is a nonprofit organization that seeks to establish equality for women in business leadership positions. It aims to achieve this goal through enhancing the entrepreneurial spirit of businesswomen via seminars and other support mechanisms found through the website.

WomanOwned: Business Networks for Women
http://www.womanowned.com/
WomanOwned is a for-profit corporation formed in 1998. It provides an extensive resource of articles relating to issues women business owners con-

*front. The catalog is updated frequently. Additionally, networking opportu-
nities, tools, and other resources are featured on the website.*

Women's Leadership Exchange (WLE)

www.womensleadershipexchange.com
*WLE offers all-day educational and networking conferences in cities
throughout the country for established business owners. It also has an e-
newsletter and other services.*

National Association of Women Business Owners

www.nawbo.org
*Founded in 1975, this national organization has chapters throughout the
United States and welcomes sole proprietors as well as women running large
companies. NAWBO members can access a wide range of services and products to help grow their firms.*

Women Presidents' Organization

www.womenpresidentsorg.com
*This group is active in more than twenty states and Canada, and multi-
ple chapters in several states. To join, women must have an ownership interest in their business and meet annual revenue criteria. Annual dues
apply.*

Small Business Administration

    409 Third St., S.W.
    Washington, DC 20416
    Phone: 1-800-U-ASK-SBA, or 202-205-6533

*SBA has an office in every state and Puerto Rico. Larger states, such as New
York, have more than one office. (New York has six.)*

SBA's Women's Network for Entrepreneurial Training (WNET)

    National WNET Roundtables Coordinator
    San Francisco, CA 94127
    Phone: 415-566-1975
    WNET does not have a headquarters; their events are arranged through
    local SBA offices.
http://www.wnet.bz

Service Corps of Retired Executives (SCORE)
SCORE Chapter 1, District of Columbia
   1110 Vermont Ave. N.W., 9th Floor
   Washington, DC 20005
   Phone: 202-606-4000, ext. 287
   Fax: 202-293-0930
   1-800-634-0245
   SCORE has 389 chapters throughout the country.
http://www.score.org

Useful Websites:

Women's Small Business Research
http://www.sba.gov/advo/research/women.html

Office of Entrepreneurial Development
http://www.sba.gov/ed/wbo/index.html

Women Entrepreneurship in the 21st Century
http://www.women-21.gov/

Gateway for Women-owned Businesses Selling to the Government
http://www.womenbiz.gov/

Online Women's Business Center
http://www.onlinewbc.gov/

Funding and Lending

Amber Grants
http://www.womensnet.net/ambergrants/
Amber Grants is a foundation formed in 1998 that provides grants to women-owned businesses. The grants are usually small ($500 to $1,000) and are intended to be used to upgrade outdated business equipment. An application is required.

Bank of America Women's Entrepreneur Connection
http://www.bankofamerica.com/smallbusiness/resourcecenter/women_business/
Bank of America lists several organizations it has formed alliances with in order to help women achieve their goals in business. This site provides women with information pertaining to each organization. The site also provides information about the banking services they provide for women business owners.

Bank One (JPMorganChase) "Women-owned Businesses"
http://www.bankone.com/answers/BolAnswersSeg.aspx?top=biz&segment=SMB&topic=BusinessServices.WomenOwnedBusinesses&item=
This site outlines the bank's line of services for women business owners, including advisory and lending services.

Capital Across America
http://www.capitalacrossamerica.com/
Capital Across America has three SBICs that seek to assist women in gaining financing for their businesses. It is a mezzanine lender (mezzanine financing falls between traditional secured bank loans and venture capital) with $75 million in available investment capital. The founder, Whitney Johns Martin, is the chairman of the Nashville Branch of the Federal Reserve Bank of Atlanta, and is a past president of the National Association of Women Business Owners.

Citigroup's Women & Co.
http://www.womenandco.com
This membership program from Citigroup brokerage house Smith Barney offers women investors financial educational and planning services for an annual fee of $125.

Count Me In for Women's Economic Independence
http://www.count-me-in.org
Provides loans ranging from $500 to $10,000 to women in business. Many applicants who receive loans have been turned down by other banks. The site also offers resources for women in business.

IBM's "Women Entrepreneurs"
http://www-1.ibm.com/businesscenter/smb/us/en/women
This highly informative site offers a panel of experts that will answer ques-

tions from women business owners. There is also a special section on how women can obtain venture capital funding. The site provides substantial venture capital advice and support.

Key Bank's Key4Women
http://www.key.com/html/I-5.html
Includes links to Key's lending, banking, and payroll services, as well as networking events and information on obtaining WBE certification.

McColl Garella
http://www.mccollgarella.com
This financial firm specializes in mergers and acquisitions, access to capital, and strategic advice. The firm shares its investment banking skills, as well as a wealth of contacts, with women business owners, presidents, CEOs, and CFOs.

OPEN from American Express
Open.americanexpress.com
OPEN is a division of American Express that provides numerous services to small business owners, including credit cards and access to capital. For information, call 1-800-NOW-OPEN.

Springboard Enterprises' "Women-Capital-Connections"
http://www.springboardenterprises.org/
Springboard is a nationwide nonprofit organization that helps women business owners gain access to equity markets. The group does not have local chapters but it does travel across the country holding forums and workshops.

Wachovia's Women Business Owners
http://www.wachovia.com/small_biz/page/0,,447_624,00.html
This bank offers credit services, human resources help, and personal financial planning for executives.

Wells Fargo Women's Business Services
http://www.wellsfargo.com/biz/intentions/women_bus_svcs.jhtml
Wells Fargo has a team that assists women business owners exclusively. The team helps the business owner obtain the best possible loans, institute the easiest method of bookkeeping, and even offers assistance in the investment of profits.

ESOP Sources

These sites provide information on employee stock option plans that can be used to buy out the business owner.

http://www.esop.org/info/esop-howto.html

http://www.cpateam.com/tax-esop.htm

http://www.the-esop-emplowner.org/

Venture Capital for Women-Owned Businesses

Axxon Capital
http://www.axxoncapital.com/
Axxon is a venture capital firm devoted to women and minorities. It typically invests between $500,000 and $3.5 million in women-owned businesses that are in technology-related, high-growth industries.

Boldcap Ventures LLC
http://www.boldcap.com/pages/1/index.htm
Boldcap is a venture capital firm that provides funding to women-owned businesses in the technology or health care arenas. It usually invests from $5 million to $15 million. The investor base is almost entirely from New York and is composed of "highly professional women."

Capital Across America
http://www.capitalacrossamerica.com/
Capital Across America provides what it terms "dequity." Essentially, this is funding that is provided as debt but acts as equity since it is "patient money." Three years or more of operating activity, a growth rate of more than 15 percent, profitability, and reputable management are recommended prior to applying for funds.

Fund Isabella
http://www.fundisabella.com/IT.html
A venture capital firm that seeks relationships with women-owned businesses. Founded by an executive who worked for Procter & Gamble for seventeen years, the fund targets companies with more than 25 percent annual growth and looks for CEOs with a strong vision and a history of leadership.

Inroads Capital Partners
http://www.inroadsvc.com/
A small venture capital firm with a total of $50 million under management, Inroads specializes in minority- and women-owned businesses. Investments range from $1 million to $4 million.

LFE Capital
http://www.lfecapital.com/
LFE Capital is a private investment firm, based in Minneapolis, with a "special focus" on the woman's market and in the business services, consumer, and health sectors.

Milepost Ventures
http://www.milepostventures.com/
A venture capital firm that invests in companies founded or cofounded by women, or in businesses that target women as customers.

Small Business Administration loan programs
Venture Capital
http://www.sba.gov/womeninbusiness/wventurecapital.html
Basic 7(a) Loan Program
http://sba.gov/financing/sbaloan/7a.html
Prequalification Program
http://sba.gov/financing/sbaloan/prequalification.html
Micro Loans
http://sba.gov/financing/sbaloan/microloans.html
CAPLines Loan Program
http://sba.gov/financing/loanprog/caplines.html

Seraph Capital
http://www.seraphcapital.com/
Seraph Capital Forum is an organization of women angel investors in the state of Washington's Puget Sound area, funding and providing advice to early-stage companies.

FundingPost
http://www.fundingpost.com/glossary/venture-glossary.asp?refer=
This informational site offers a glossary of venture-financing terms. Useful for the entrepreneur considering seeking venture capital.

Going Global

Small Business Administration's International Trade Loans
http://www.sba.gov/financing/loanprog/tradeloans.html
This page of the SBA site explains who qualifies for and how to obtain a loan for international trade.

GlobeTrade
http://www.globetrade.com
This consulting and marketing firm sells advisory services to small businesses that want to expand internationally.

GlobeWomen
http://www.globewomen.com
An online businesswomen's resource for international trade and related activities, this site offers information, networking, and the Global Summit of Women, a conference the group likens to the Davos forum (a world economic forum of top political and business leaders).

Businesswomen in Trade
http://www.infoexport.gc.ca/businesswomen/menu-e.asp
Hosted by the Canadian government's trade office, this site offers information for businesswomen on doing business in Canada.

Organization of Women in International Trade
http://www.owit.org/
This 2,000-member nonprofit group promotes international trade by offering education and networking venues.

Minority Business Owner Resources

Department of Commerce's Minority Business Development Agency
www.mbda.gov
This agency funds Business Development Centers around the country that work with minority-owned entrepreneurial businesses. The site offers information on how to apply for programs and grants.

National Bankers Association
www.nationalbankers.org
This Washington, D.C.–based trade group represents minority-owned banks that target their lending to minority-owned businesses.

Minority and Women's Pre-Qualification Pilot Loan Program
http://www.sba.gov/business_finances/prequal
This program provides loans up to $250,000 to companies 51 percent or more owned by a woman or a person who is an ethic or racial minority.

Sample Business Documents

A company's income statement charts its sales and expenses. By reading the income statement, it is possible to tell how much the company sold in a given reporting period, usually a year or a quarter, and how much it spent. The difference between the two is profit, or net income.

SAMPLE INCOME STATEMENT

Company A
For the Year Ended December 31, 200_

Sales Revenue
    Sales
    Less: Sales discounts
        Sales returns
    Net sales revenue

Cost of Goods Sold (COGS)
    Merchandise inventory, Jan. 1, 200_
    Purchases
    Less purchase discounts
    Net purchases
    Freight and transportation in
    Total merchandise available for sale
    Less merchandise inventory, Dec. 31, 200_
        COGS
    Gross profit on sales

Operating Expenses
    Selling expenses
        Sales salaries and commissions
        Sales office salaries
        Travel and entertainment
        Advertising expenses

Freight and transportation out
Shipping supplies and expense
Postage and stationery
Depreciation of sales equipment
Telephone and telegraph
Administrative expenses
Officers' salaries
Office salaries
Legal and professional services
Utilities expense
Insurance expense
Depreciation of building
Depreciation of office equipment
Stationery, supplies, and postage
Miscellaneous office expenses

Income from Operations

Other Revenues and Gains
Dividend revenue
Rental revenue

Other Expenses and Losses
Interest on bonds and notes
Income before taxes
Income taxes
Net income for the year

THE BALANCE SHEET

Businesspeople see a balance sheet as a snapshot, recording a company's assets and liabilities at a given moment in time. Think of it as a bank statement that shows all the money available to a company, how much its assets are worth, what debts it owes, and the leftover equity that represents the owner's stake in the company.

SAMPLE BALANCE SHEET

Company A
December 31, 200_
Assets

Current Assets:
    Cash
    Accounts receivable
      Less: Doubtful accounts
    Merchandise inventory
    Prepaid expenses
    Notes receivable
    Inventories
    Supplies on hand
      Total current assets:

Fixed Assets:
    Vehicles
      Less: Accumulated depreciation
    Furniture and Fixtures
      Less: Accumulated depreciation
    Equipment
      Less: Accumulated depreciation
    Buildings
      Less: Accumulated depreciation
    Land
      Total fixed assets:

Other Assets:
    Goodwill
      Total other assets:

Total Assets:

Liabilities

Current Liabilities:
    Notes payable to banks
    Accounts payable
    Accrued interest on notes payable
    Income taxes payable
    Accrued salaries, wages, and other liabilities

    Total current liabilities:
    Long-term debt (e.g., debentures)

    Total liabilities:
    [Stockholder's equity, if any]

    [Total stockholders' equity, if any]

TOTAL LIABILITIES [AND STOCKHOLDERS' EQUITY]:

The cash flow statement documents where a company's cash goes. The statement shows exactly what cash comes in and what goes out. Because companies' accounting records include expenses and revenues that don't translate to cash right away, the cash flow statement is the best way to see how much cash is available in a company and to review where the money is actually going.

SAMPLE CASH FLOW STATEMENT

Company A

Cash Flow from Operating Activities
    Net income
    Adjustments to reconcile net income to net cash provided by operating activities
      Depreciation expense
      Amortization of intangibles
      Gain on sale of assets
      Increase in accounts receivable (net)
      Decrease in inventory
      Decrease in accounts payable
    Net cash provided by operating activities:

Cash Flow from Investing Activities
Sales of assets
Purchase of equipment
Purchase of land
Net cash used by investing activities:

Cash Flow from Financing Activities
Payment of cash dividend
Issuance of common stock
Redemption of bonds
Net cash provided by financing activities:

Net Increase in Cash
Cash at beginning of year:
Cash at year's end:

When a company prepares for a sale, it will sign a letter of intent with its acquirer or merger partner. This legal document is a formal notice that the two companies intend to go through with a transaction. It sets out the terms of the sale and states what needs to be done before the deal can close. Despite a signed letter, however, many deals do eventually fall through.

SAMPLE LETTER OF INTENT

[Date]

[Seller's Address]

Re: Letter of Intent

[Dear Buyer]:

This letter of intent (this "LOI") confirms our discussions and understanding to date regarding the possible sale by Company A ("Seller") to Company B ("Buyer") of certain assets related to Seller's **[insert type]** store, (the "Operations") conducted at Seller's facilities located at **[insert address]** (the "Facility"), and commercial transactions related to that sale, all of which are described below (collectively, the "Transaction").

Upon execution by the parties, this LOI will constitute an expression of our mutual intent to pursue the consummation of the Transaction on the terms set forth below, but, except for Paragraphs 6, 9, and 10 below, this letter shall not constitute a binding agreement and does not create any rights or obligations in either party. The Transaction and the matters set forth in this LOI are subject to satisfactory completion of negotiations and due diligence, [**approval by the parties' boards of directors,**] receipt of any necessary third-party consents, and the execution and delivery of a definitive purchase agreement and other definitive agreements contemplated thereby (collectively, the "Definitive Agreements"). The rights and obligations of the parties shall be only as set forth in the Definitive Agreements, and each party reserves the right not to enter into any such agreement. In addition to the terms set forth below, the Definitive Agreements shall contain covenants, conditions to closing, representations and warranties of the parties, indemnifications, and such other terms and conditions, all as are reasonably satisfactory to the parties.

1.   *Basic Transaction.* The Transaction shall consist of the following elements:

(a) *Sale of Assets.* Seller shall sell, transfer, and convey to Buyer all of Seller's rights, title, and interests in and to the operating facilities, property, equipment, products, and associated intellectual property located at the Facility (the "Assets") for the price set forth in Paragraph 2 below (the "Purchase Price"), with the Assets to be delivered to Buyer upon the closing free and clear of all liens, mortgages, pledges, encumbrances, and security interests of any kind. The Assets include, without limitation, the following:

(i)   (A) The Facility: Seller holds the tenant's interest under a lease agreement (the "Lease Agreement") at the Facility, which Lease Agreement includes a purchase option (the "Purchase Option"). Accordingly, it is understood by the parties that on the date this LOI is signed by Seller (the "Signing Date"), Seller is the tenant under the Lease Agreement and does not own the Facility but, on the First Closing Date of the Transaction (as provided in Section 1(b) below) Seller will convey, transfer, and assign to Buyer all of Seller's right, title, and interest in and to the Lease Agreement.

(ii)   equipment located at the Facility, including packaging and labeling equipment for the sale of various products, equipment for various utilities except the assets set forth on Exhibit B attached hereto;

(iii) documents related to the Assets, including all technical, regulatory, supplier and customer lists, equipment drawings, relevant regulatory authority documents, and all other documentation necessary for or related to the Operations, all in print and, where available, in electronic form, except the documents set forth on Exhibit B;

(iv) intellectual property necessary for or used in the Operations, including trade secrets and know-how except the intellectual property set forth on Exhibit B; and

(v) all of Seller's rights to assignable registrations, licenses, permits, and approvals used in or relating to the Assets or the Operations; and all of Seller's rights to the products and related intellectual property specified on Exhibit A attached hereto (the "Products"), including but not limited to all related technology, data, regulatory filings and approvals, and records.

The Assets and the Operations shall be more fully described and documented in the Definitive Agreements.

(b) *Closing Procedure.* Upon execution of the Definitive Agreements (the "First Closing Date"), Seller will convey, transfer, and assign to Buyer and Buyer will purchase and acquire from Seller, all of Seller's right, title, and interest in and the Lease Agreement all other Assets associated therewith. Seller shall have vacated the Facility prior to the First Closing Date. Not later than ten (10) days following Seller's receipt of shareholder approval to sell to Buyer the remaining Assets (as provided in Section 3(c) below) (the "Second Closing Date"), Seller will convey to Buyer and Buyer will purchase from Seller Seller's right, title, and interest to the remaining Assets.

(c) *Assumption of Liabilities and Accounts Receivable.* Buyer shall not assume any liabilities of Seller and Buyer shall not assume any accounts receivable of Seller.

(d) *Hiring of Employees.* Buyer may, but shall not be obligated to, interview and/or offer employment to any employee of Seller who is an employee of Seller at the Facilities whom Buyer desires to employ.

2. *Purchase Price; Taxes*

(a) The total Purchase Price shall be [$] payable in two equal installments of [$], each in U.S. Dollars, on the respective closing dates.

(b) All taxes imposed on the Transaction (not including any taxes based upon the income of the parties), including, without limitation, any sales, use, and transfer taxes imposed in connection with the sale of the Assets from Seller to Buyer, shall be borne as set forth in the Definitive Agreements.

3. *Other Terms*

(a) The Definitive Agreements will contain representations and warranties of Seller typical in a transaction of this type, including but not limited to representations and warranties as to ownership and title to the Assets, due authorization to complete the transaction and environmental matters, if any, provided that the operating condition of the Assets will be "as is." Buyer and Seller will provide indemnities for the other party typical in a transaction of this type. Seller's indemnity obligation shall not exceed [$], except that the limitation shall not apply to indemnities in connection with tax, title, or environmental matters or liabilities not assumed by Buyer.

(b) The consummation of that portion of the Transaction to be completed at the First Closing Date would be subject to the following conditions and other customary conditions:

(i)   the receipt of all consents required of third persons, including governmental entities; and

(ii)   the execution of a sublease or other use and occupancy agreement between the parties providing for Buyer's permitted use, occupation, and operation of the Assets and the Facilities pending the Second Closing Date.

4. *Nonsolicitation.* For a period of one (1) year after the consummation of the Transaction, Seller shall not directly or indirectly solicit, divert, or take away any employees of Buyer, notwithstanding that such employees may have been originally obtained or recruited through the efforts of Seller.

5. *Due Diligence.* Seller will afford Buyer and Buyer's authorized representatives ("Representatives") reasonable access to the Facilities and Seller's personnel, properties, contracts, and books and records related to the Operations and the Assets for purposes of conducting reasonable due diligence related to the Transaction. Buyer and its Representatives will conduct the due diligence in a reasonable manner, at times reasonably acceptable to Seller, and shall complete their due diligence before the First Closing Date.

6. *Confidentiality.* The Nondisclosure Agreement entered into by and between Buyer and Seller dated [   ] shall remain in full force and effect and shall apply to all information provided by a party to the other party in connection with Buyer's due diligence hereunder and any negotiation of the Definitive Agreements.

7. *Schedule for Consummation of Transactions.* Subject to Section 11 hereof, parties shall use commercially reasonable efforts to cooperate with one another and seek to:

(a) Arrive at and execute mutually agreeable Definitive Agreements and complete that portion of the Transaction to be completed on the First Closing Date on or before [   ]; and

(b) Satisfy all conditions to the closing of that portion of the Transaction to be completed on the Second Closing Date on or before [   ].

8. *Conduct of Business.* During the period from the date hereof until the termination of this LOI as provided in Section 11 below, Seller will operate the Facility and Operations in the ordinary course consistent with its practices as of the date hereof. Buyer is aware that Seller is implementing a restructuring of its operations at the Facility, which involved, among other things, a substantial reduction of operations.

9. *Expenses.* Except for Section 2(b), each party shall be solely responsible for all expenses incurred by it in connection with pursuing or consummating the Transaction, including without limitation finder's or broker's fees, expenses of due diligence, and legal, accounting, and consulting expenses. Closing costs will be borne as set forth in the Definitive Agreements.

10. *Disclosure.* Except as required by law, without the prior written consent of the other party, neither Buyer nor Seller will, and each will direct its

Representatives not to make, directly or indirectly, any public comment, statement, or communication with respect to, or otherwise publicly disclose, the existence of discussions regarding a possible transaction between the public parties or any of the terms, conditions, or other aspects of the transaction proposed in this LOI. If a party is required by law or the rules of the principal stock exchange on which the stock of a party is traded to make any such disclosure, the parties shall consult with each other and seek to agree upon appropriate language for such disclosure. Nothing herein shall be deemed to prohibit or limit a party's confidential consultation with other parties in deciding whether to proceed to signing the Definitive Agreements.

11. *Termination.* This LOI may be terminated by either party on the earlier of (i) the provision of written notice to the other advising as to such termination, effective on the date of delivery of such notice, or (ii) in the event the Definitive Agreements shall have not been executed on or prior to [   ]. Notwithstanding any such termination, the terms of Sections 6, 9, and 10 shall remain binding and in full force and effect. Notwithstanding anything to the contrary contained herein, neither Buyer, any its affiliates, nor any of its officers, directors, or agents shall be prohibited from discussing and negotiating with third parties relating to the sale of the Facility and the Assets during the term of this LOI. Additionally, the execution of this LOI shall not impose on any party a good faith duty to negotiate with respect to the matters contemplated hereby.

12. *Ability to Negotiate With Others.* Buyer and Seller acknowledge that in view of Section 11, Seller may continue to accept offers and decide to sell to a third party the Assets and Operations contemplated for purchase in the Transaction at any time prior to entering into a definitive binding agreement with Buyer.

13. *Governing Law.* This Agreement shall be governed by and construed in accordance with the internal laws of the State of [   ], without application of its conflicts of law rules. If you are in agreement with the foregoing, please sign and return one copy of this LOI, which thereupon will constitute our agreement with respect to its subject matter.

Very truly yours,

Company A
By: _____

Name: _____

Title: _____

Acknowledged and Agreed:

Company B

By: _____

Name: _____

Title: _____

When a company acquires another firm, the terms of the transaction are set out in a formal term sheet that both parties sign. This legal form spells out in detail what the buyer will pay, how the deal is structured, and any conditions necessary for the deal to happen.

SAMPLE TERM SHEET FOR ACQUISITION

This Term Sheet ("Term Sheet") summarizes the principal terms and conditions of the proposed transaction between Company A, a [**insert state**] corporation with its principal offices at [**insert address**] ("Buyer"), and Company B, a [**insert state**] company with its principal offices at [**insert address**] ("Seller"), as contemplated by the parties on this day, _____, 2005.

WHEREAS, Buyer and Seller desire to [**insert purpose**]

Now, therefore, the two parties agree as follows:

1.	Buyer	Company A, with its principal offices at _____.
2.	Seller	Company B, with its principal offices at _____.
3.	Shareholders[1]	[**Names of shareholders, if any**].
4.	Option Holders[2]	[**Names of option holders, if any**].
5.	Transaction	Buyer acquires [**insert description of what is being purchased**]

[1] To be included if Company A has issued shares.
[2] To be included if Company A has issued options.

6.	Shares[3]	The total outstanding shares of the Company consist of _____ shares of common stock, plus [_____] shares of common stock reserved for the issuance of options and warrants.
7.	Closing	The parties intend that the definitive terms of the Transaction will be agreed upon on or before _____, and the closing of the Transaction would occur on or before _____.
8.	Purchase Price	Based on the information known to Buyer on the date hereof, the consideration shall be: $_____.
9.	Purchase Price Adjustment[4]	The purchase price shall be adjusted [**upward/downward**] $_____ in the event of [**insert reason**].
10.	Due Diligence	Customary investigation into the prospect, business, assets, contracts, rights, liabilities, and obligations of the Seller, including financial, marketing, employee, legal, regulatory, and environmental matters.
11.	Definitive Agreements	Buyer will provide Definitive Agreements promptly following the parties' agreement on the basic terms of the transaction. The parties will work together diligently to seek to negotiate the Definitive Agreements and present the Transaction to their respective boards of directors for approval.

[3] To be included if Company A has issued shares.
[4] To be included if certain contingencies may affect Company B's value.

12.	Conditions Precedent	Except for the Binding Provisions (defined below), this Term Sheet is not intended as a legally binding commitment by Buyer, and the Transaction is expressly subject to the following:
		(a) Receipt of all necessary consents and approvals of governmental authorities, lenders, lessors, and other third parties;
		(b) Completion of due diligence to the satisfaction of Buyer;
		(c) The assignment of Seller's contracts to the Buyer, including consents of third parties, where necessary;
		(d) Satisfactory resolution of the ongoing management issues of Seller;
		(e) Preparation, negotiation, execution, and delivery of Definitive Agreements in form and substance satisfactory to Buyer and its counsel;
		(f) Opinion of counsel of Seller rendered to Buyer in form and substance satisfactory to Buyer and its counsel.
13.	Closing Conditions	Customary for transactions of similar nature.
14.	Representation and Warranties and Covenants	Customary for transaction of similar nature.
15.	NonCompete	Seller shall enter into NonCompete Agreements, at Closing, in form and substance satisfactory to Buyer, with all stockholders, founders, key employees, and consultants determined specifically by Buyer during its due diligence review, to provide for each such person's agreement not to compete with the Buyer for ____ years after Closing.

16.	Confidential Information and Invention Assignment Agreement	Each officer, director, and key employee of Seller shall enter into a Confidential Information at Closing, in form and substance satisfactory to Buyer.
17.	Access	Seller shall provide Buyer complete access to the Seller's facilities, books, and records (including, without limitation, all financial statements as of ____, all financial projections, all financial commitments, all corporate documents, contracts, and other documents that may affect the rights or obligations of Seller) and shall cause its directors, employees, accountants, and other agents and representatives (collectively, the "Representatives") to cooperate fully with Buyer and Buyer's Representatives in connection with Buyer's due diligence investigation.
18.	Exclusivity	In consideration of the time, expense, and effort, which has been and will be incurred by Buyer in considering the Transaction, and until termination of this Term Sheet, as provided below, the shareholders shall not and shall cause the Seller not to, directly or indirectly, through any Representatives or otherwise, solicit or entertain offers from, negotiate with, or in any manner encourage, discuss, accept, or consider any proposal of any other person relating to the acquisition of ____ of the Seller, its assets, or business, in whole or in part, whether through direct purchase, merger, consolidation, or other business combination.
19.	Conduct of Business	Until the Definitive Agreements have been duly executed and delivered by all the par-

		ties, or the Binding Provisions have been terminated as provided below, Seller shall conduct its business only in the ordinary course and not engage in extraordinary transactions without the consent of Buyer.
20.	Nondisclosure	Except (i) as required by applicable law or for the purpose of responding to any judicial, governmental, or regulatory authority or to requests or demands in any judicial or administrative proceeding; or (ii) for purposes of obtaining legal advice, the parties shall and shall direct their representatives not to, directly or indirectly, make any public comment, statement, or communication with respect to, or otherwise disclose or permit the disclosure or existence of discussions regarding, a prospective transaction between the parties or any of the terms, conditions, or other aspects of the Transaction unless mutually agreed upon by the parties.
21.	Confidentiality	Except (i) as required by applicable law or for the purpose of responding to any judicial, governmental, or regulatory authority or to requests or demands in any judicial or administrative proceeding; or (ii) for purposes of obtaining legal advice, Buyer shall not disclose or use, and shall cause its Representatives not to disclose or use any Confidential Information (defined below) provided by the Seller or its Representative to Buyer and its Representative for the purpose of evaluating the Transaction. Confidential Information for purposes of this provision means any information about the Seller stamped "confidential" or identified in writing as such to Buyer by the

		Seller, provided that it does not include information which Buyer can demonstrate (i) is generally available or known to the public other than as a result of improper disclosure by Buyer or (ii) is obtained by Buyer from a source other than the Seller, provided that such source was not bound by a duty of confidentiality to the Buyer or another party with respect to such information.
22.	Legal Fees and Costs	Buyer and Seller shall be responsible for their respective legal fees and other expenses incurred in connection with the Transaction.
23.	Binding Provisions	Provisions 18–25 are the Binding Provisions.
24.	Termination	The Binding Provisions may be terminated (i) by mutual consent of the Buyer and the Seller; or (ii) upon five (5) days written notice by any party to the other party if Definitive Agreements have not been executed by _____; provided, however, that the termination of the Binding Provisions shall not affect the liability of the parties for breach of any of the Binding Provisions prior to termination. Upon termination of the Binding Provisions, the parties shall have no further obligations hereunder, except as set forth in provisions 21–23.

The undersigned hereby agree to the terms set forth in this Term Sheet effective as of the date first written above.

Buyer: **Seller:**

By: _____   By: _____

Name: _____   Name: _____

Title: _____   Title: _____

Before a sale, the buyer investigates the company it plans to acquire to make certain there are no unresolved financial, operational, or legal issues. This extensive checklist includes documents that a buyer might request as it performs its due diligence survey of the target company. Not all items will apply to every company.

SAMPLE DUE DILIGENCE CHECKLIST

1. *Corporate Records and Organization:*

1.1. Organizational and ownership charts or other information relating to the Company and its subsidiaries.

1.2. The Company's charter documents, and the charter documents of any significant subsidiary, all as amended to date.

1.3. The bylaws of the Company and any significant subsidiary, as currently in effect, and amendments thereto since January 1, [____].

1.4. Minutes of all meetings of the board of directors, any committees of the board of directors, and shareholders of the Company and any significant subsidiary since January 1, [____].

1.5. All documentation relating to the incorporation and initial organization of the Company and any significant subsidiary, including assignments and assumptions.

1.6. Schedule of shares issued and outstanding for the Company and its subsidiaries.

1.7. All quarterly and annual reports and any other communications to shareholders of the Company and any significant subsidiary since January 1, [____].

1.8. All available good standing and tax certificates.

1.9. History of business activities, including acquisitions, restructurings, reorganizations, dispositions, and repurchases.

1.10. A list of jurisdictions in which the Company and any significant subsidiary is qualified to do business or is otherwise operating.

2. *Financing:*

2.1. Schedule of all short-term and long-term debt (including capitalized leases, guarantees, and other contingent obligations).

2.2. All documents and agreements evidencing borrowings or available borrowings in excess of $[**insert figure**], whether secured or unsecured, by the Company or its subsidiaries, including indentures, loan and credit agreements, promissory notes, and other evidence of indebtedness and guarantees.

2.3. All documents and agreements evidencing other material financing arrangements, including sale and lease-back arrangements, installment purchases, etc.

2.4. Correspondence with and reports to lenders since January 1, [_____], including all compliance reports submitted by the Company or its subsidiaries or its independent public accountants.

2.5. Recent compliance certificates concerning satisfaction of covenants contained in the Company's obligations for money borrowed or other debt and any other debt covenant compliance calculations, if applicable.

3. Assets:

3.1. List of real property owned (whether or not currently owned) by the company and its past or present subsidiaries, together with (a) location and brief description, (b) description of all encumbrances, and (c) appraisal reports, if any.

3.2. List of real property leased (whether or not currently leased) by the company and its past or present subsidiaries, together with (a) location and brief description, and (b) if available, a summary of date, term and termination rights, renewal rights, and rent.

3.3. List of material personal property owned, together with any security interests or encumbrances thereon.

3.4. List of material personal property leased, together with, if available, a summary of date, term and termination rights, renewal rights, and rent.

3.5. Results of all lien searches.

4. Other Material Agreements:

4.1. All joint ventures and partnership agreements to which the Company or any of its subsidiaries is a party.

4.2. All agreements encumbering real or personal property owned by the Company or any of its subsidiaries, including mortgages, deeds of trust, and security agreements.

4.3. All leases of real property and all leases of any substantial amount of personal property to which the Company or any of its subsidiaries is a party, either as lessor or lessee.

4.4. Forms of all material rental, warranty, and service agreements of the Company or any of its subsidiaries.

4.5. All material licensing agreements, franchises, and conditional sales contracts to which the Company or any of its subsidiaries is a party.

4.6. All material research and development agreements.

4.7. All material supply or requirements contracts to which the Company is a party.

[4.8. All contracts relating to the Company's securities to which the Company is party, including stock option plans, forms of stock option agreements, and agreements pursuant to which the Company has agreed to issue securities or to register securities under the Securities Act of 1933.][5]

4.9. All title insurance policies for properties owned or leased by the Company or any of its subsidiaries.

4.10. All collective bargaining agreements, employment agreements, and material consulting agreements to which the Company or any of its subsidiaries is a party.

4.11. All significant documents, including indemnity agreements, relating to any material acquisitions or dispositions by the Company or any of its subsidiaries.

[4.12. All contracts or agreements with or pertaining to the Company or any of its subsidiaries and to which directors, officers, or owners of more than 5 percent of the stock of the Company are parties.

4.13. All documents relating to any other transactions between the Company or any of its subsidiaries and any director, officer, or owner of more than 5 percent of the stock of the Company.

4.14. All documents pertaining to any receivables from or payables to directors, officers, or owners of more than 5 percent of the stock of the company.][6]

4.15. A list of all customers who, since January 1, [_____], have accounted for or will account for in excess of [_____] of the Company's or its subsidiaries' revenues in any six-month period.

4.16. All forms of contracts typically entered into between the Company or any subsidiary and its customers or suppliers in the ordinary course.

4.17. Intangibles:

    a. A schedule for all patents, trademarks, copyrights, service marks, and applications therefor used in the business or which relate to the Company's business or name, indicating those owned, subject to adverse claims, and jurisdictions in which registered.

    b. List of patents, trademarks, copyrights, service marks, and appli-

---

[5] To be identified if the company being purchased is publicly listed.
[6] To be identified if the company being purchased is publicly listed.

cations therefor used in the business or which relate to the Company's business or name that are not owned (and any related claims or litigation). Identify owner of such information and provide license or other royalty agreements.

    c. Description of material nonpatented proprietary information.

    d. Technology sharing, use, and disclosure agreements.

    e. Confidentiality and nondisclosure agreements.

    f. Description of any interference, infringement, or unfair competition matters, whether current or potential.

4.18. All contracts or agreements which obligate the Company to indemnify a third party where the potential obligation of the Company is not insignificant.

4.19. All engagement letters or contracts entered into with any financial adviser, investment banker, or finder for which there might be any obligations in a proposed transaction; list of all advisers retained, fees payable to them, and claims for payment; copies of all related indemnification agreements.

4.20. All contracts or agreements involving an amount in excess of $[**insert figure**] for the future purchase of, or payment for, supplies, products, or services.

4.21. All contracts or agreements involving an amount in excess of $[**insert figure**] to sell or supply products or to perform services.

4.22. All contracts or agreements (current or proposed) limiting or restraining the Company or any subsidiary from engaging in or competing in any lines of business, or locations, with any person, firm, corporation, or other entity.

5. *Financial Data:*

5.1. Annual and quarterly financial statements for the past five years and the latest interim financial information available for the Company and its subsidiaries.

5.2. Internal budgets and projections for the Company and its subsidiaries, including the assumptions used in preparation thereof.

5.3. Inventory and accounts receivable review.

5.4. Breakdown by operating division and corporate.

5.5. Sales, operating income, and assets by location (e.g., state, territory, country).

5.6. Detail of sales, cost of goods, sales detail, marketing, and R&D by product.

5.7. Detail of capital expenditures.

5.8. Detail of pro forma balance sheet line items and contingent liabilities.

5.9. Detail of foreign currency adjustments.

5.10. Detail of reserves.

5.11. Reviews of major operational and accounting changes over the past five years.

6. *Environmental and Related Matters*:

6.1. All internal Company reports, or reports prepared by third parties and furnished to the Company, concerning environmental matters relating to current or former Company properties or current or former properties of any of the Company's current or former subsidiaries.

6.2. Copies of any statements or reports given by the Company or any of its subsidiaries to the federal Environmental Protection Agency or any state department of environmental regulation or any similar state or local regulatory body, authority, or agency.

6.3. All notices, complaints, suits, or similar documents sent to, received by, or served upon the Company or any of its subsidiaries by the federal Environmental Protection Agency or any state department of environmental regulation or any similar state or local regulatory body, authority, or agency.

6.4. All Company or outside reports concerning compliance with waste disposal regulations (hazardous or otherwise).

6.5. A list of all "hazardous materials," "hazardous substances," or "hazardous wastes" used or generated at any of the Company's (or any subsidiary's) facilities.

7. *Personnel*:

7.1. Organizational charts and biographies of key employees of the Company and its subsidiaries; list of current officers and directors.

7.2. Documents representing any bonus, retirement, profit sharing, incentive compensation, pension, and other employee benefit plans or agreements of the Company or its subsidiaries, and any material correspondence relating thereto with beneficiaries thereof or any regulators.

7.3. Schedule of all restricted stock/options.[7]

7.4. Documents representing or relating to workers compensation or disability policies, and any material claims with respect thereto.

---

[7] To be identified if company is publicly listed.

7.5. All liability insurance policies for directors and officers of the Company or its subsidiaries.

7.6. Actuarial reports and IRS Form 5500s for pension plans and welfare plans.

8. *Tax Matters:*

8.1. All federal, state, and local (including foreign) tax returns filed by the Company and any significant subsidiaries for the latest five years and copies of any IRS determination letters; list of all open years (federal, state, and local), and applicable waivers.

8.2. All audit and revenue agents reports for the last five years, closing agreements, and ruling requests for all open years.

8.3. All documents pertaining to the Company's and its subsidiaries' compliance with material tax laws and regulations.

8.4. Schedule of all pending tax liabilities.

8.5. Tax basis in assets.

9. *Litigation, Government, and Regulatory Issues:*

9.1. A schedule of all material suits, actions, litigations, claims, administrative proceedings, or other governmental investigations or inquiries, pending or threatened, affecting the businesses or operations of the Company or its subsidiaries.

9.2. All consent decrees, judgments, other decrees or orders, settlement agreements, and other agreements, to which the Company or any of its subsidiaries is a party or is bound, requiring or prohibiting any future activities.

9.3. All correspondence with, reports of or to, filings with, or other material information with respect to any other regulatory bodies which regulate a material portion of the Company's business.

9.4. All reports, notices, or correspondence relating to any alleged violation or infringement by the Company or its subsidiaries of, or otherwise relating to, the status of the Company's or its subsidiaries' compliance with, any local, state, or federal law of governmental regulations, orders, or permits including: (a) equal employment opportunity; (b) OSHA; (c) antitrust; (d) intellectual property; and (e) **[add any additional regulatory matters or agency reports that might apply to the Company, especially in light of the industry within which it operates]**.

9.5. All material governmental permits, licenses, etc., of the Company.

9.6. A schedule detailing the number of customer complaints for each of the last five years, including an analysis of such complaints and the appropriate resolution, including annual costs relating thereto.

10. Auditors:

10.1. All letters from the Company's or any subsidiary's attorneys to the Company's or any subsidiary's independent public accountants since January 1, [_____].

10.2. All letters from the Company or any subsidiary to the Company's or any subsidiary's independent public accountants since January 1, [_____], regarding certain representations requested by the Company's or any subsidiary's independent public accountants in connection with their audit of the Company.

10.3. All reports from the Company's auditors to the Company since January 1, [_____].

11. Regulations and Filings:

11.1. All SEC filings (with exhibits) made by the Company since January 1, [_____].

11.2. All of the Company's proxy materials since January 1, [_____].

11.3. All applications for permits filed with agencies having blue-sky jurisdiction over the issuance of securities of the Company, and all permits and qualifications in respect thereof.

11.4. All filings relating any acquisition or dispositions since January 1, [_____], and any filings related to material acquisitions prior to that date.

[11.5. The company's latest filing under the Hart-Scott-Rodino Antitrust Improvements Act of 1976, as amended.

11.6. All 144A offering circulars, private-placement memoranda, and syndication memoranda prepared and/or used by the Company since January 1, [_____].

11.7. All Schedules 13D or 13G filed with respect to the Company since January 1, [_____] (including any prior filings for which amendments have been filed after such date).][8]

12. Miscellaneous:

12.1. Recent analyses of the Company or its industries prepared by investment bankers, engineers, management consultants, accountants, or others, including marketing studies, credit reports, and other types of reports, financial or otherwise.

---

[8] To be identified if company is publicly traded.

12.2. A schedule of all insurance policies and self-insurance programs, including detail on premiums and claims recoveries/payouts in the last five years; copies of existing insurance policies (including property damage, third party liability, D&O, and key employee), including liability retention limits, self-insurance, and intergroup premium reimbursement agreements.

12.3. Insurance analyses or reports prepared internally or by consultants.

12.4. All significant recent management, marketing, sales, or similar reports relating to broad aspects of the business, operations, or products of the Company or its subsidiaries.

12.5. All press releases issued by the Company or any significant subsidiary since January 1, [_____].

12.6. All recent articles or brochures relating to the Company or its subsidiaries or any of their products, services, or material events.

12.7. Analyst reports and internal studies of the business or industry.

12.8. Any other documents or information which, in your judgment, are significant with respect to any portion of the business of the Company or which should be considered and reviewed in making disclosures regarding the business and financial condition of the Company to prospective investors.

Non-Disclosure Agreement

The non-disclosure agreement ("NDA"), also known as a confidential disclosure agreement ("CDA"), is a preliminary but crucial agreement in the deal-making process. The NDA serves to protect the confidential information of one or both parties to a transaction. Generally, an NDA may be two-way (i.e. free flow of information being disclosed and received by both parties) or one-way (i.e. one party discloses information to the other party).

The NDA identifies the type of confidential information that will be disclosed, to whom, and under what conditions. The key provisions of an NDA are: (1) the proper identification of the parties to the agreement; (2) the subject or type of NDA (e.g. evaluation purposes or a particular transaction); (3) definition of confidential information (which should include both written and oral disclosures); (4) how confidential information will be protected; (5) how confidential information will be used; (6) who can use confidential information; (7) the term of the NDA; (8) governing law; (9) exceptions to confidential treatment; and (10) remedies for breach of the NDA.

In the buy/sell context, the NDA will be used to evaluate the business opportunity presented (e.g. the financial picture of both parties; the product being sold; the structure of the business entities; and any other information pertinent to the evaluation process). Essentially, the NDA is a tool that allows the parties to share information freely for the purpose of deciding whether to enter into a particular transaction. If the parties ultimately decide to engage each other in a subsequent business transaction, the terms of the NDA may be superceded by the confidentiality provision of the final purchase agreement, or incorporated by reference to the extent that the provisions are applicable and offer sufficient protections.

SAMPLE MUTUAL CONFIDENTIAL DISCLOSURE AGREEMENT

THIS AGREEMENT is made as of the date signed by the last party to sign below (the "<u>Effective Date</u>"), by and between [**INSERT 1st PARTY NAME**] ("_____"), and [**INSERT 2nd PARTY NAME**] having a place of business at [_____] ("_____") (each, individually, a "<u>Party</u>" and collectively, the "<u>Parties</u>").

WHEREAS, [**INSERT 1st PARTY NAME**] and [**INSERT 2nd PARTY NAME**] are interested in considering and evaluating a potential venture, transaction or relationship with each other and each of [**INSERT 1st PARTY NAME**] and [**INSERT 2nd PARTY NAME**] own certain Confidential Information (as defined below) that such Party is interested in allowing the other Party to receive and/or observe, and each Party is interested in receiving and/or observing the Confidential Information that the other Party discloses hereunder, all upon the terms and conditions, and solely for the purpose, set forth herein.

NOW, THEREFORE, in consideration of the mutual promises of the Parties hereunder and other good and valuable consideration and intending to be legally bound, the Parties hereby agree as follows:

1.   Definitions.

   (a) *"Confidential Information"* shall mean all written or other tangible form, visual, graphic, oral and electronic data and information, both technical and non-technical, relating to the Disclosing Party's business, products, processes, techniques, research, development, inventions, testing procedures and marketing that are disclosed to the Receiving Party by the

Disclosing Party under this Agreement. Confidential Information shall include, without limitation, know-how, data and results, methods and related information, processes and techniques, formulae, flow sheets, technical plans, operational details, historical production data, patent applications, technical specifications, volume data, quality assurance documents, research and development plans, business plans, product and market descriptions, sales, cost and promotional expenditure data, plans and projections, as well as any other technical, financial, and business information of whatever nature. In order to be eligible for confidential treatment hereunder, Confidential Information disclosed in writing or electronically must be prominently designated as "Confidential," "Proprietary," etc. at time of disclosure, and Confidential Information disclosed visually or orally must be stated to be such at the time of disclosure and shall be confirmed in a written summary describing same in reasonable detail that the Disclosing Party shall provide to the Receiving Party within 30 days after such disclosure; *provided, however,* the failure to do so shall not destroy the confidential nature of the information, whereas identifying the information as confidential shall be conclusive evidence that the Parties consider the information to be confidential.

(b) *"Disclosing Party"* shall mean a Party that discloses Confidential Information to the other Party under this Agreement.

(c) *"Receiving Party"* shall mean a Party that receives Confidential Information from the other Party under this Agreement.

(d) *"Subject Matter"* shall mean [**insert the purpose**].

2.   *Disclosure.* Following the execution of this Agreement each Disclosing Party shall disclose Confidential Information relating to the Subject Matter to each Receiving Party. Thereafter each Disclosing Party may disclose such other Confidential Information relating to the Subject Matter as such Disclosing Party deems necessary and desirable. Nothing in this Agreement, however, requires the Parties to disclose any particular Confidential Information. Each Receiving Party may disclose the Disclosing Party's Confidential Information to any of its Affiliates which (i) need to know such Confidential Information for the purpose of evaluating or entering into a possible business relationship, (ii) are advised of the contents of this Agreement, and (iii) agree to be bound by the terms of this Agreement, *provided, however,* that only an Affiliate to which such Confidential Information is actually disclosed and received will be bound by the terms of this Agreement. For purposes of this Agreement, "Affiliate" means any person, corporation, firm, partnership or other entity which directly or indirectly controls, is controlled by or is under common control with ei-

ther Party. For purposes of this Agreement, "<u>control</u>" shall mean the ownership of at least fifty percent (50%) of the voting share capital of such entity or any other comparable equity or ownership interest.

3.   *Exceptions.* This Agreement shall apply to all of the Confidential Information that the Disclosing Party discloses to the Receiving Party hereunder, except to the extent that the Receiving Party can prove, by competent proof, that any such Confidential Information:

(a) is in the public domain at the time of disclosure by the Disclosing Party;

(b) becomes part of the public domain by publication or otherwise after disclosure by the Disclosing Party, other than by breach of this Agreement by the Receiving Party;

(c) was lawfully in the Receiving Party's or any of its affiliates' possession, without restriction as to confidentiality or use, at the time of disclosure by the Disclosing Party; or

(d) is provided to the Receiving Party or any of its affiliates, without restriction as to confidentiality or use, by a third party lawfully entitled to possession of such Confidential Information and who does not violate any contractual, legal or fiduciary obligation to the Disclosing Party by providing such Confidential Information to the Receiving Party; or

(e) was or is independently developed by or for the Receiving Party without reference to the Confidential Information either directly or indirectly, as evidenced by the Receiving Party's written records.

In addition, Section 4 shall not apply to any Confidential Information of the Disclosing Party that the Receiving Party is required to disclose under applicable laws or regulations or an order by a court or other regulatory body having competent jurisdiction; *provided, however,* that except where impracticable, the Receiving Party shall give the Disclosing Party reasonable advance notice of such disclosure requirement (which shall include a copy of any applicable subpoena or order) and shall afford the Disclosing Party an opportunity to oppose, limit or secure confidential treatment for such required disclosure. In the event of any such required disclosure, the Receiving Party shall disclose only that portion of the Confidential Information of the Disclosing Party that the Receiving Party is legally required to disclose. Further, specific Confidential Information disclosed to the Receiving Party by the Disclosing Party shall not be deemed to be publicly known, or in the Receiving Party's prior possession, merely because such Confidential Information is embraced by more general information which is publicly known or in the Receiving Party's prior possession. Likewise, specific Confidential Information disclosed to the Receiving Party by the Disclosing Party shall not be deemed to be publicly known merely because other Confidential Information contained in the same document or embodiment becomes publicly known.

4.   *Use of Confidential Information.* The Receiving Party shall use the Confidential Information of the Disclosing Party solely for the purpose of evaluating a potential business relationship between the Parties with respect to the Subject Matter. The Disclosing Party shall not have any liability for any evaluations or investigations carried out by the Receiving Party relating to the Confidential Information of the Disclosing Party. The Receiving Party's right to use the Confidential Information of the Disclosing Party shall terminate upon the completion of such evaluation. Any further use of the Confidential Information of the Disclosing Party by the Receiving Party, if any, shall be governed by a separate written agreement between the Parties. The Receiving Party shall protect the Confidential Information of the Disclosing Party against disclosure to or use by third parties, shall use the same standard of care that the Receiving Party applies to protect its own confidential information of like character (but which in any event shall be not less than a reasonable standard of care), and shall not use the Confidential Information of the Disclosing Party except for the evaluation specified above. The Receiving Party shall not disclose the Confidential Information of the Disclosing Party to any person other than employees and scientific consultants of the Receiving Party who have a direct need to know such same for the performance of their employment duties in connection with the evaluation specified above. The Receiving Party shall not disclose any Confidential Information of the Disclosing Party to any other person without the express written permission of the Disclosing Party. Furthermore, the Receiving Party shall obligate all such employees, agents and consultants, both during and after their relationships with the Receiving Party, to use and hold in confidence the Confidential Information of the Disclosing Party in a manner consistent with the obligations of the Receiving Party under this Agreement and shall take all necessary and reasonable actions to assure such compliance. The Receiving Party shall assume full responsibility and liability to the Disclosing Party for any unauthorized use or disclosure of any Confidential Information of the Disclosing Party by any of the Receiving Party's employees, agents, consultants or Affiliates.

5.   *Return of Confidential Information.* Within [**30 days**] after completion of the evaluation specified in Section 4 (unless such period is extended by the Disclosing Party) or upon the sooner written request of the

Disclosing Party, the Receiving Party shall return to the Disclosing Party all written materials and documents, software and other things made available or supplied by the Disclosing Party to the Receiving Party that contain Confidential Information of the Disclosing Party, and all copies thereof, as well as all copies of all notes (including notes generated on Confidential Information given orally), summaries, analyses and reports made by the Receiving Party's employees, agents and consultants containing same; provided, however, that subject to the terms and conditions of the Agreement, the Receiving Party shall be entitled to retain one archival copy thereof for purposes of determining its obligations under this Agreement.

6.   *Representations or Warranties.* The Receiving Party acknowledges that the Disclosing Party makes no representations or warranties, express or implied, as to the accuracy or completeness of the Confidential Information and the Receiving Party agrees that the Disclosing Party will have no liability to the Receiving Party for any errors therein or omissions therefrom.

7.   *Term.* The Receiving Party's obligations under this Agreement shall expire on the [5,7,10] anniversary of the Effective Date, except that the Receiving Party's obligations under Section 8 shall survive indefinitely.

8.   *No Further Rights, Obligations.* Nothing in this Agreement shall create or imply any license or grant of rights to the Receiving Party under, or act as a waiver of any rights that the Disclosing Party may have to prevent infringement or misappropriation of, any patents, patent applications, trademarks, copyrights, trade secrets, know-how or other intellectual property rights owned or controlled by the Disclosing Party or any of its Affiliates. Furthermore, the Receiving Party shall not have any right, title or interest in or to any of the Confidential Information of the Disclosing Party. The Receiving Party shall not seek, because of or based upon any Confidential Information of the Disclosing Party, patent or any other form of intellectual property protection with respect to or related to the Subject Matter or use the Confidential Information of the Disclosing Party to obtain, or seek to obtain, a commercial advantage over the Disclosing Party. Nothing in this Agreement is intended to create or imply any obligation on the part of either Party to negotiate, discuss or enter into any other transaction or agreement with the other Party.

9.   Remedies.
     (a) The Receiving Party acknowledges that its breach of any of its obligations under this Agreement shall cause the Disclosing Party irreparable harm, for which monetary damages will be an inadequate remedy.

Therefore, in the event of any such breach, the Disclosing Party shall be entitled, in addition to any other remedy available under this Agreement, at law or in equity, to injunctive relief, including an accounting for profits, specific performance of the terms hereof and other equitable relief for such breach or the material anticipatory breach of this Agreement, without the posting of bond or other security.

(b) If Confidential Information of the Disclosing Party enters the public domain after it is disclosed to the Receiving Party, as provided in Section 3(b), such entry shall not affect the Disclosing Party's right to obtain damages or other remedies for any unauthorized use or disclosure of same prior to the date it entered the public domain.

10.   *No Public Disclosure.* Unless otherwise required by law, neither Party shall disclose the existence of, any of the terms and conditions of, or the results of any evaluation performed under, this Agreement without the prior written consent of the other Party. The Parties acknowledge and agree that any and all Confidential Information disclosed pursuant to this Section 10 shall not lose its confidential status through such use, and the Receiving Party shall take all reasonable and necessary steps to protect its confidentiality during such use, to the extent possible.

11.   *Waiver.* No failure on the part of either Party to exercise, and no delay in exercising, any right or remedy hereunder shall operate as a waiver hereof, nor shall any single or partial exercise of any right or remedy hereunder preclude any other or a future exercise thereof or the exercise of any other right or remedy granted hereby or by any related document or by law.

12.   *Governing Law.* This Agreement shall be governed by, construed and interpreted in accordance with the internal laws of the [**Insert State**] applicable to agreements made and to be performed within such jurisdiction, without giving effect to principles of conflicts of laws.

13.   *Assignment.* Neither Party may assign its rights or obligations hereunder without the express written consent of the other Party.

14.   *Notice.* Any notice required or permitted hereunder shall be in writing and shall be deemed effectively given upon actual receipt.

15.   *Existence of Agreement.* The Parties agree that they shall not disclose the existence of this Agreement, any of the activities which may take place pursuant to this Agreement, the relationship formed, if any, under this Agreement or the Party's interest in the Subject Matter to which this Agreement relates, to anyone except those persons within the Disclosing Party

and the Receiving Party and their necessary employees, officers, directors or other authorized representatives, consultants or agents with a need to know.

16. *Subsequent Agreement.* Should the Parties decide to pursue a venture, transaction or relationship, it is anticipated that the Parties will negotiate and enter into a definitive agreement for the purpose of setting forth their respective obligations under such venture, transaction or relationship. Such definitive agreement may incorporate the terms and conditions of this Agreement by reference, may supplement or modify the terms and conditions of this Agreement or may supersede and replace the terms and conditions of this Agreement.

17. *Miscellaneous.* This Agreement sets forth the entire agreement and understanding between the Parties as to the Subject Matter and merges all prior discussions, agreements, and negotiations between them as to the Subject Matter. No change or supplement to this Agreement shall be valid or effective unless made in writing and signed by a duly authorized officer of each Party. This Agreement shall be binding upon and accrue to the benefit of the successors and permitted assigns of the Parties. The descriptive headings of this Agreement are for convenience only, and shall be of no force or effect in construing or interpreting any of the provisions of this Agreement. This Agreement shall not be strictly construed against either Party. This Agreement may be executed simultaneously in any number of counterparts, any one of which need not contain the signature of more than one Party, but all such counterparts taken together shall constitute one and the same agreement. If any provision of this Agreement shall be held to be invalid or unenforceable by a court of competent jurisdiction, no other provision of this Agreement shall be affected thereby.

IN WITNESS WHEREOF, the Parties have caused their duly authorized representatives to execute this Confidential Disclosure Agreement as of the date(s) set forth below.

[INSERT 1st PARTY NAME]   **[INSERT 2nd PARTY NAME]**

By: _____   By: _____

Name: _____   Name: _____

Title: _____   Title: _____

Date: _____   Date: _____

To illustrate some financial concepts, we present a hypothetical catering company's financial statements and refer to them throughout the glossary.

CATHY'S CATERERS

FINANCIAL STATEMENTS

Income Statement

Sales	$100,000
Cost of Goods Sold	$40,000
Gross Profit	$60,000
SG&A	$25,000
Depreciation	$5,000
Income Taxes	$10,000
Net Income	**$20,000**

Assets		*Liabilities and Equity*	
Cash	$10,000	Current Liabilities	$10,000
Accounts Receivable	$20,000	Long-Term Liabilities	$30,000
Fixed Assets	$50,000	Total Liabilities	$40,000
Total Assets	**$80,000**		
		Capital Stock	$10,000
		Retained Earnings	$30,000
		Shares Outstanding:	1,000
		Total Equity	$40,000
		Total Liabilities + Equity	**$80,000**

8K—Periodic filings with the SEC when a major corporate event occurs, such as the hiring or firing of a top executive.

10K—Annual filings of audited financial statements required for all publicly traded companies.

10Q—Quarterly unaudited financial statements filed with the SEC.

Accelerated depreciation—Used to recognize the declining value of fixed assets such as machinery, this accounting method allows you to take a higher deduction in the first few years of the asset's life.

Accrual accounting—Using this method, income is recognized as soon as it is earned, whether or not your company has been paid (accrued revenue). Expenses are recognized when they are incurred (accrued expense).

AMEX—American Stock Exchange

Amortization—Similar to depreciation, an accounting process that recognizes an asset's declining value over time. Used only for intangible assets such as patents or intellectual property.

Angel investor—An individual who invests money early in a start-up company. Angel investors differ from venture capitalists because angel investors use their own money and typically do not take an equity stake greater than 30 percent.

Annual report—Issued once a year, a written report detailing how the company is doing. It includes the company's audited financial statements. The report is required by the SEC for public companies. Some private companies also distribute annual reports to their shareholders.

Asset sale—One method of selling a company. A buyer of assets owns only those assets, not the whole company.

Assets, tangible—Physical assets, for instance, equipment, buildings, or vehicles.

Assets, intangible—Nonphysical assets, including loans, patents, and goodwill.

Audited financials—Financial statements audited by an independent certified public accountant.

Balance sheet—The financial statement that shows the monetary position of a company, it summarizes assets, liabilities, and owners' equity on a specified date.

Book value—The balance-sheet value of the business, determined by subtracting liabilities and depreciation from assets. Cathy's assets are $80,000 and her liabilities are $40,000, so her book value is $80,000 minus $40,000 equals $40,000.

Cash flow—The net cash that comes in and out of the business during a specific period.

Cash method of accounting (also called **cash basis**)—Income is counted when payment is made, and expenses are counted when they are paid.

C Corporation—A corporation organized under the tax code's Subchapter C. These larger corporations can have many shareholders who are legally shielded from liability, but profits are taxed at the corporate level and again at a personal level when they are distributed.

COGS (cost of goods sold)—Direct costs of products sold. Total revenue minus cost of goods sold equals operating profit.

Corporation—A legal entity, chartered by a state, with ownership divided into transferable shares of stock.

Debt-to-equity ratio—Total liabilities divided by total assets, indicating the percentage of assets financed through borrowing.

Deferred charges—An expenditure that benefits the company over several accounting periods is capitalized and written off during the periods benefited. Costs are shown as an asset on the balance sheet.

Deferred income taxes—Timing differences between tax and accounting methods of calculating financial statements could result in either an asset or a liability on the balance sheet.

Deferred revenue—When a business gets paid for services before they are performed, the deferred revenue is shown on the balance sheet as a liability and recognized as revenue when the services are performed.

Dividend—Distribution of earnings in cash by a corporation to shareholders. The board of directors decides whether to declare dividends based on the cash needs of the corporation and its long-term goals.

Dividend yield—The amount a company pays out to shareholders as a dividend, expressed as a percentage of the share price.

Due Diligence—The thorough audit of a selling company by a company looking to acquire it.

Earnings per share (EPS)—Net income of a company for a period of twelve months divided by the average number of shares. Cathy has net income of $20,000 and 1,000 shares outstanding, so her EPS is $20,000 divided by 1,000 equals $20.

EBIT (earnings before interest and taxes)—Cathy has $30,000 in EBIT: $60,000 in gross profit minus $25,000 in SG&A and $5,000 in depreciation equals $30,000.

EBITDA—(earnings before interest, taxes, depreciation, and amortization)—Cathy has $35,000 in EBITDA: $60,000 in gross profit minus $25,000 in SG&A equals $35,000.

EDGAR—The SEC's online system, found at www.sec.gov, containing companies' public financial statements.

ESOP (employee stock ownership plan)—A program that sells part or all of a company to its employees.

Fair market value—Price at which a seller will sell and a buyer will buy a company.

GAAP—Generally accepted accounting principles: the accounting rules that govern financial statements.

Goodwill—Extra money paid to acquire a business or an asset, above its market value. Goodwill is considered an asset and sits on the balance sheet of the acquiring company until it is considered impaired, when the company determines that the acquired asset no longer holds that extra value.

Gross profit—Revenue from sales minus any cost of goods sold.

Gross revenues—Revenue from sales.

Income statement—The financial report used to evaluate the performance of a business through revenue and expenses for a specific period.

Indemnification—An agreement in a sale contract that the seller will take responsibility for certain liabilities that arise from the business after it is bought.

Inventory turnover—Ratio showing how many times inventory is sold and replaced during a specific period. A higher number indicates a company is using its assets efficiently.

Investment banker—A financial consultant who leads the company through the financing steps, including venture capital, bridge financing, and eventually the IPO. Can also advise on mergers and acquisitions.

IPO (initial public offering)—Selling stock in a company to the public for the first time.

Letter of intent—A nonbinding agreement detailing terms of a sale.

Liquidity—A company's ability to meet financial obligations with cash or other assets that can be sold for cash.

Lockup period—Usually a 180-day period after an initial public offering when company insiders cannot legally sell their shares.

NASDAQ—National Association of Securities Dealers Automated Quotation system, a computerized stock exchange that specializes in high-tech companies. There is no physical Nasdaq.

Net profit—Profit after expenses are deducted from gross profit; also called net income.

Nondisclosure agreement (NDA)—An agreement not to disclose confidential information to outsiders.

NYSE—New York Stock Exchange.

OTC (over-the-counter)—Stocks with small market capitalizations are traded on the OTC Bulletin Board.

P/E (price/earnings) ratio—The market price per share divided by earnings per share. It indicates whether the price of the stock is in line with earnings. Often this ratio is compared with a benchmark for the industry to see whether the stock is expensive or cheap.

Point of sale—The location of a sale. For instance, the checkout counter in a store is a point of sale.

Prepaid expenses—Money paid in advance for expenses such as insurance or rent.

Profit margin—The percentage of profit a company generates.

Promissory note—A formal written promise to repay at a later date an amount borrowed plus interest.

Prospectus—Disclosure document for a public securities offering registered with the SEC.

Proxy—A legal form allowing a shareholder to designate someone else to vote her shares in a company.

Representations and warranties—Promises made by the seller to the buyer of a company.

Return on assets—The amount of profit business owners get for every dollar of assets. Expressed by dividing net income by total assets.

Return on equity—The amount of profit business owners get for every dollar of equity in the business. Expressed by dividing net income by equity.

Return on investment (ROI)—A test of management's efficiency in using available resources expressed as a percentage. The figure is obtained by dividing the income from the investment by the amount of the investment.

Return on sales—The amount of profit business owners get for every dollar of sales. Expressed by dividing net income (before interest and taxes) by sales.

Reverse merger—When a larger company is acquired by a smaller company, with the smaller company becoming the surviving firm.

Road show—The series of presentations a company's management makes to potential investors prior to an IPO.

S corporation—A small corporation organized under Subchapter S of the tax code, it is taxed as if it were a partnership. All income can be distributed to shareholders without paying corporate taxes. Shareholders pay taxes at their own personal tax rates.

SEC (Securities and Exchange Commission)—The government agency that reviews financial statements of a corporation if it has publicly traded stock or bonds, and is responsible for administering all securities laws in the U.S. Their mission is to ensure efficient markets and protect investor interests.

SG&A—Sales, general, and administrative expenses. Commonly known as overhead.

Shareholder (or **Stockholder**)—An individual or company that owns one or more shares of a firm.

Sole proprietorship—Business owned and operated by one person, for instance, a one-woman accounting practice. Legally, the owner is personally liable for the firm's debts.

Stock sale—Sale of a company's stock to outside investors.

Stock (or Share)—One unit of ownership in a company.

Stock option—An option to buy stock at a specified price. Start-up companies often use stock options to compensate employees when they don't have the cash to pay them enough at the beginning.

Straight-line depreciation—With this accounting method, which recognizes the drop in an asset's value over time, deductions are made in equal amounts over the life of the asset.

Strategic fit—One company acquires another and fills a void in its own capacities, for example by adding a product to its line.

Synergy—Two companies merge and benefit from the relationship, for instance, by consolidating back-office functions.

Term sheet—A document outlining the terms of a proposed sale.

Underwriters—The investment banking firm that handles the sale of a corporation's stock to the public.

Valuation—The process of estimating the value of a business.

Venture capital—Start-up money used to finance a new business, usually invested by venture capital firms.

Work in Progress (WIP)—Inventory that has added value due to processing or labor at a specific stop point.

Working capital—Current assets minus current liabilities. Cathy has $20,000 in working capital: $10,000 in cash plus $20,000 in accounts receivable equals $30,000 in current assets. When $10,000 in current liabilities is subtracted, the remaining $20,000 is her working capital.

NOTES

PART I
A 7-STEP GUIDE TO DISCOVERING, STARTING, AND BUILDING
THE BUSINESS OF YOUR DREAMS

1. "Completing the Picture: Equally-Owned Firms in 2002," Center for Women's Business Research, Washington, D.C., underwritten by PitneyBowes, Inc., Wells-Fargo, NAWBO Philadelphia Chapter, April 2003.

2. Whiteley, S., Elliott, K., and Duckworth, C. *The Old Girls' Network*. New York: Basic Books, 2003, p. 47.

3. Frankel, Lois P. *Nice Girls Don't Get the Corner Office: 101 Unconscious Mistakes Women Make That Sabotage Their Careers*. New York: Warner Business Books, 2004, p. 20.

4. Perle, Liz. *Money, A Memoir: Women, Emotions, and Cash*. New York: Henry Holt & Co., 2006.

5. "Entrepreneurial Vision in Action: Exploring Growth Among Women- and Men-Owned Firms," Center for Women's Business Research, Washington, D.C., February 2001, p. 13.

6. Ibid.

Chapter 3
1. Ibid., p. 13.

Chapter 4
1. Ibid., p. 20.

Chapter 8
1. Ibid., p. 13.

2. Stein, Mark. "Selling a Family Enterprise: Tough to Decide and to Do," *The New York Times*, February 19, 2004, Section C, p. 6. Late Edition, East Coast, C7.

ACKNOWLEDGMENTS

So many women helped me create this book, beginning with all of the women who graciously agreed to share their entrepreneurial stories with me, that, thanks to them, any woman dreaming of the day she'll start her own business, as well as all of those women who already have their companies up and running, should benefit from the thoughtful advice these entrepreneurs provide. For this book I interviewed more than one hundred women from around the country who started or are running their own companies. They range in age from twenty-three to seventy-six and represent a wide range of ethnicities. The industries they are working in are similarly varied: staffing, special events and meeting planning, interior design, software solutions, waste management consulting, graphic and industrial design, and manufacturing, with products ranging from chocolates to pale-gold rubber bands and gun-cleaning kits. I spoke to women who created their own real estate firms, started successful restaurants and catering firms, and founded companies to sell products they designed themselves, from custom-made party invitations to jewelry, children's books, costumes, and clothes. I also talked with women who are running their own electrical and general contracting businesses, among others, about the challenges and rewards of being your own boss, especially in a man's field. In addition, I interviewed three women who generously spent time discussing their entrepreneurship stories with me, but who did not, in the end, make it into the book. They are Cathleen Dougherty, Melinda K. Partin, and Denise Slavitt.

Several of the women who told me their stories of entrepreneurship are former employees of mine, and a few are professional acquaintances. Many others were referred to me by friends and colleagues, and without those referrals this book would lack dimension. In particular I wish to thank Tricia Wasserman, who was the editorial director at the second company I started, AM Medica Communications. Tricia has always been there to lend a helping hand on any project I dream up. Barbara Monaghan, Kelly Tiernan Morgan, Ginny Holmes Carroll, Erica Holmes, Beth DiLuglio, Emily Bloomfield, Anne Cunningham O'Neil, Mary Jane MacLean, Michael McMahon, Dr. Joe Chazan, Dr. Chris Sullivan, Lydia Parker, Liam Donohue, and David J. Ryan all led me to inspiring women entrepreneurs who contributed their time and cooperation to making this book as useful as possible for any woman who is thinking about starting her own company or has already done so. Liam

Donohue, general partner in Top Line Capital Management, LP, a venture capital firm in Boston that invests in early-stage technology companies, and Dave Ryan, managing partner in Mission Ventures, a venture capital firm in San Diego, both gave generously of their time, identifying women to interview and sharing their business expertise.

In other instances, women whom I interviewed then passed along leads and made introductions to facilitate the interview process. A special thanks to Susie Clendenen and Jill Gaynor, both of whom not only agreed to lengthy interviews, but also put time and thought into referrals, which helped me make this book better for all. The rest of the women whom I interviewed came from a list of the top 500 woman-owned businesses in the United States (ranked by gross revenues). The list is available at www.diversity.com. Thanks to Rinda Meunier for calling many of the companies listed, obtaining fax numbers, and sending and following up on my requests for interviews. I also want to thank Lori Buehler and Barbara Drillings, assistants to Himanshu Bhatia and Sharon Lobel, respectively, who quickly orchestrated their bosses' schedules and mine so we could do an interview.

Two professional women's organizations also provided me with assistance, making introductions for me. Jodi Cross, director of operations, south Florida, of The Commonwealth Institute, a nonprofit organization that provides peer-to-peer mentoring for women entrepreneurs, women senior executives, and women CEOs came up in a day with a list of women for me to contact. The Institute was founded in Boston by Chairwoman Lois Silverman, who also agreed to share her story of taking her company public the moment I asked her to. Carol Malysz, director of The Center for Women & Enterprise in Providence and Stacey D. Carter, president of SDC Resources in Barrington, Rhode Island, which provides training and development services for employers and nonprofits, and feasibility planning and strategy for women entrepreneurs, also provided valuable leads.

Toria Fordham, executive director of the Miami-Dade County MicroBusiness USA Program, a private, nonprofit intermediary lender for the Small Business Administration, also suggested women to interview and responded to my requests for information.

Several professional colleagues and friends also gave me considerable time, and their efforts on my behalf are most appreciated. These include So-June Donohue, who worked very hard to help me assemble a list of women who had started and sold their companies successfully, and my accountant, Irvin P. Schmutter of Levine & Schmutter LLP, New York, who responded to numerous questions, reviewed chapter 4 for technical accuracy, and worked with me to develop box 2 in chapter 8, Valuation Methods: An Overview. Finally, Mr. Schmutter also worked on the glossary for me with his associate Debbie Penna. Bill Griffith, a lawyer and friend, also responded to numerous technical questions and referred me to a colleague within his firm, ReedSmith LLP, who worked diligently to ensure that this book included samples of standard business documents. The documents in the appendix are provided courtesy of

ReedSmith LLP and were reviewed by Christopher Ayala. Mr. Ayala also reviewed the stock exchange information in chapter 8, box 6.

A very special and heartfelt thanks to Devin Fargnoli, a law student at Case Western Reserve University in Cleveland, who worked with me to assemble and check the Resource Guide, and then graciously agreed to update it as the book approached production. In addition, Mr. Fargnoli prepared the stock exchange information that Mr. Ayala reviewed.

Without the fast and accurate work of word processors Teresa Miller, Tequesta, Florida; A Squared in Florida, Inc., owned and run so efficiently by Ann Edison, Jupiter, Florida; and Liz Groden, New York, I wouldn't have a manuscript. The graphics were created by Mike Sahagian, Everlasting Designs, Inc., Wood River Junction, Rhode Island. David Vernaglia, president of Everlasting Designs, supervised the design process.

My agent at International Creative Management in New York, Jennifer Joel, guided me effortlessly through the proposal-to-publication maze, and made brilliant suggestions and contributions throughout the development of this book, including introducing me to Chana Schoenberger, who also worked tirelessly on my behalf helping me edit and streamline the manuscript. Finally, a special thanks to Ben Loehnen, my editor at Random House, who made important recommendations throughout and put the finishing editorial touches on the book.

I hope that every woman entrepreneur today, as well as every aspiring woman entrepreneur, enjoys reading this book and gets as much from it as I did from writing it.

ABOUT THE AUTHOR

A successful entrepreneur for more than twenty years, ANN M. HOLMES was a cofounder of TransMedica, Inc., which created MD/TV, the first medical education network broadcast on open-channel television. In 1984, she and her partner sold TransMedica, Inc., to CBS. Holmes then started AM Medica Communications, LLC, and subsequently cofounded AMM-Adelphi, LLC, and MultiMedia in Medicine, LLC. A member or supporter of several professional organizations that support women in business and women entrepreneurs, she is on the South Florida Advisory Board of the Commonwealth Institute, an organization that provides peer-to-peer mentoring for women entrepreneurs, women CEOs, and senior executives. She has also served as a mentor at the Center for Women & Enterprise in Providence, Rhode Island. Visit the author's website at www.ann-holmes.com.